P9-DGT-764

FRANCE IN THE TWENTIETH CENTURY

PHILIP OUSTON

PRAEGER PUBLISHERS
New York · Washington

BOOKS THAT MATTER

Published in the United States of America in 1972
by Praeger Publishers, Inc., 111 Fourth Avenue,
New York, N.Y. 10003

Library of Congress Catalog Card Number: 72–76972

Printed in Great Britain

FOR ELIZABETH

Contents

List of Maps and Diagrams

Maps

Diagrams

List of Plates

Acknowledgements

Many colleagues and friends helped me to write this book. I thank them all, and should like in particular to record here my deep gratitude to Bill Cooper, Jonathan Dale and Philip Thody, who read the entire first draft, and who made many invaluable suggestions for its improvement, and to Xavier Beauchamps, Christopher Blake, Harry Brumfitt, John Coombes, Ian Higgins, Kay MacIver and Philippe and Elizabeth Servan-Schreiber, who devoted much time, unbounded kindness and an abundance of special skills and knowledge to the elaboration of individual chapters. I am also most grateful to Harry Bawden for the patience and discernment he has brought to the task of seeing this book through the press. The errors are mine.

PHILIP OUSTON

St Andrews
August 1971

The author and publishers wish to thank the following, who have kindly given permission for the use of copyright material: George Allen & Unwin Ltd for the extract from *Economic Planning in France* by J. and A. M. Hackett; Jonathan Cape Ltd for the extract from *The Sovereigns (325,000 francs)* by Roger Vailland, translated by P. Wiles; André Deutsch Ltd and Rosica Colin Ltd for the extract from *Memoirs of a Dutiful Daughter* by Simone de Beauvoir, translated by James Kirkup; Victor Gollancz Ltd and Curtis Brown Ltd for the extract from *France: Change and Tradition* by Professor Laurence Wylie; Hodder & Stoughton Ltd for the extract from *The Generous Earth* by Philip Oyler; Pitman Publishing for the extract from *The Dominici Affair* by Jean Giono, translated by P. de Mendelssohn; Weidenfeld

& Nicolson Ltd and Hill & Wang Inc. for the extract from *A Modern French Republic* by Pierre Mendès-France.

Map 1 is based on *Statistiques et Indicateurs des Régions Françaises* (Institut National de la Statistique et des Études Économiques, 1967), with additional information from *Atlas of Western Europe* (John Murray, 1963). Maps 2–4 have been specially drawn by Dr K. M. MacIver: of these, 3 and 4 are based on the Larousse *Atlas Moderne*. Other maps are reproduced by kind permission of the following: Macdonald & Evans Ltd (Map 5, from J. J. Branigan, *Europe excluding the British Isles and the U.S.S.R.*, 1965); John Bartholomew & Son Ltd (Map 6, from *The Statesman's Year-Book 1968–69*); Butterworth & Co. Ltd (the superimposed east–west boundary, from I. B. Thompson, *Modern France: A Social and Economic Geography*, 1970); Presses Universitaires de France (Map 7, from Pierre George, *La France*, 1967); Les Éditions Ouvrières (Map 8, from R. Livet, *L'Avenir des Régions Agricoles*); Délégation à l'Aménagement du Territoire et à l'Action Régionale (Maps 9 and 10); Map 12 was originally drawn by M. le Chanoine Boulard; Librairie Protestante (Map 13, from S. Mours, *Les Églises Reformées en France*). Figure 2 is based on data published in A. Cobban, *A History of Modern France*, 1965; G. and E. Bonnefous, *Histoire politique de la Troisième République*, 1960–8; and Philip Williams, *Crisis and Compromise: Politics in the Fourth Republic*, 1964, and *French Politicians and Elections 1951–1969*, 1970.

The author and publishers also wish to thank the photographers and organisations whose names appear in the list of plates, and in particular M. Pierre Bringé of the French Ministry of Agriculture; the staff of Documentation Française, which in many cases was the primary source; and the publishers of *Paris-Match*, for their help in identifying pictures which had appeared in their columns.

The publishers have made every effort to trace the copyright-holders, but if they have inadvertently overlooked any, they will be pleased to make the necessary arrangement at the first opportunity.

Part One: The Nation

1 The Land and the People

THE CRUCIBLE

The French inhabit 213,000 square miles of land astride the main cape of Western Europe: a nation of fifty-one million people occupying territory more than twice as extensive as either of its most powerful neighbours, Great Britain and Federal Germany, but with less than half their density of population (see Map 1).[1] Its geographical setting, at once Atlantic, Mediterranean and continental, is comprehensively European, and its ethnic origins are correspondingly diverse. Continuously from prehistoric times, the land that is now France has been a racial and cultural melting-pot. The French nation was formed by the combined energies, characters and skills of Ligurians, Iberians, Celts, Greeks, Romans, Franks, Scandinavians, Jews, Spaniards, Italians, Russians, Poles, Portuguese, Algerians – coming in wave after wave, as hunters, warriors, farmers, traders, craftsmen, administrators, manual workers, refugees and teachers – just as surely as the French state was built, century after century, by the stubborn defence, against rival dynastic and national ambitions, of its patiently extended and consolidated frontiers.

The area in which such complex and prolonged genetic and cultural mixing has taken place is itself made up of an exceptionally wide and well-balanced range of the land-forms, soils and climates of temperate Europe. French geography books re-echo with praise for the diversity of skills and the continuity of labour by which generations of farmers and builders have made a civilised landscape from the raw materials of Nature's open-handed bounty in France.[2] Historians for their part point to what the civilisation in turn owes to the mixed origins of the nation, the varied resources of the land, and the conscious, patiently applied arts of assimilation and refinement at which the French excel. The French possess a deep sense of the specially privileged, slowly matured

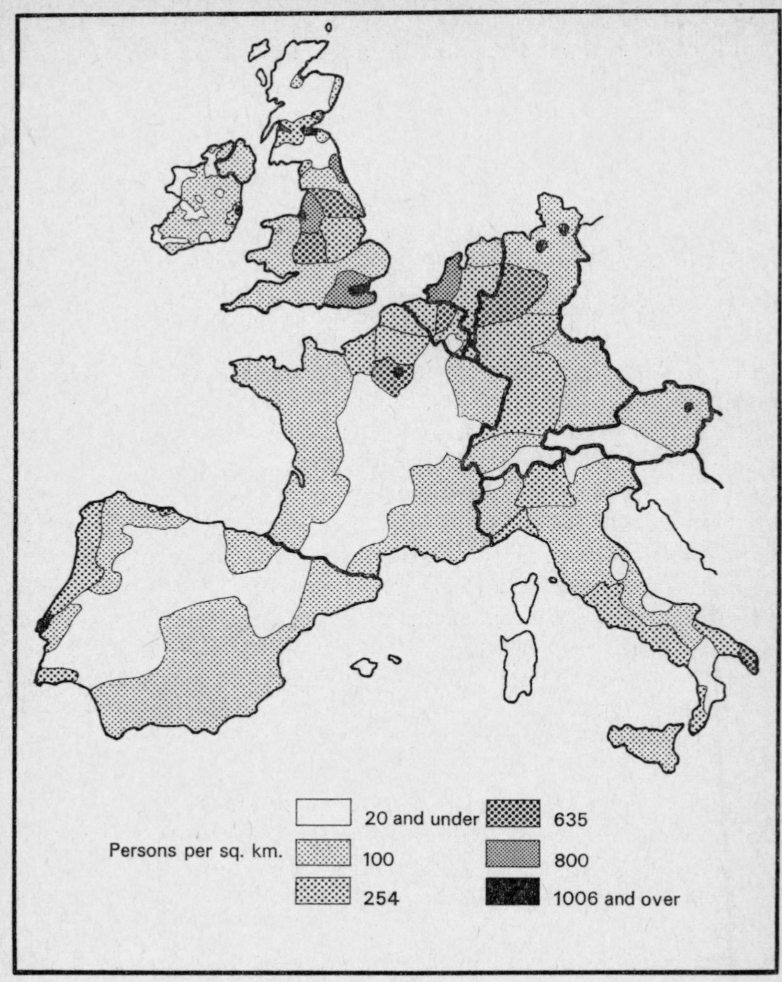

Map 1. Density of population in Western Europe

completeness of their culture, and if they have a particular vanity it is to assume that it epitomises the best of European civilisation, and indeed that it provides mankind as a whole with a universal pattern of humane values, taste and behaviour.[3]

For obvious reasons the French are disinclined to take any simple racial theory of nationhood at all seriously. The idea of France's 'natural frontiers' has had more success. Strictly speaking, of course, the frontiers of the country are no more natural than the racial constitution of the people is pure. But as three of its borders are sea-coasts, and two are, for the most part, mountainous, the so-called French 'hexagon' that they enclose does constitute a geographical area that has a measure of unity, and into which the historically evolved, man-made French nation may be said to fit more or less naturally. Only along its sixth, north-eastern edge is the extent of French territory not physically defined, and it is there that its integrity has proved most vulnerable to dispute and assault. For centuries the European powers fought to possess the strategic features of the eastern, continental, portion of this blood-stained frontier: Belfort Gap (between the Jura and the Vosges mountains), Saverne Gate (between Alsace and Lorraine), the banks of the Rhine and the Meuse rivers; while its almost featureless western, maritime, sector, in the Plain of Flanders, between the Ardennes (pivot of highland, Hercynian Europe) and the English Channel, lay wide open to the seemingly endless tides of armed men marching and counter-marching in the 'cockpit of Europe'.

'The Frenchman is married to France,' wrote the nineteenth-century historian Jules Michelet:

> The English, not having roots in the soil like us, emigrate where profit beckons. . . . With us men and land are one, and will not be parted. They are joined in true wedlock, till death parts them.

France remained a predominantly peasant country until the First World War; later, that is, than her peers and neighbours, Germany and Britain; later than the United States. Michelet's patriotism of the soil reflects this peasant mentality consciously, but not this alone. The broad and boldly drawn

French hexagon stands in a Frenchman's imagination for something more than earthy stability and possessiveness. It also symbolises the ideal of balanced human completeness that is the noblest, the least material form of his patriotism. This is nowhere more evident than in Michelet's own *Tableau de la France,* written nearly a century and a half ago, but still, through its impact on successive generations of writers, schoolteachers and schoolchildren, an active influence on the way the French consider their inheritance. For Michelet, France is first of all a language; secondly, a land, 'delineated by its mountains and rivers', and anatomised for ninety pages as a dozen vigorously diverse frontier and near-frontier provinces; thirdly, in a five-page climax, it is the powerful centralising force by which a long dynasty of French kings, and their revolutionary successors, all operating from Paris, in mid Île-de-France – the 'centre of the centre' – forged the unity of the nation-state from the manifold genius of its constituent regions, a living unity of the highest kind: 'England is an empire, Germany a country, a race; France is a person.'

There is much romantic exaggeration and distortion in Michelet's portrait of France. But in the overriding importance he attaches to locality and to language, in his pointed omission of racial vanity, in his sense of what his country owes both to its many and varied provinces and neighbours (in war and peace, through conflict as well as through collaboration), and to the assimilative, moderating genius of the ruling centre, he is close to every Frenchman's France.

Half of French territory is a wide plain, varying in height from sea-level to 600 ft., lying mostly within the cool temperate climatic zone, and sweeping westwards and southwards from the Ardennes Highlands across the well-watered basins of the Seine, the Loire and the Garonne, to the long wall of the Pyrenees, beyond Atlantic Aquitaine and Mediterranean Languedoc. This is a magnificently endowed stretch of open country, settled and farmed from prehistoric times, where, long before the medieval clearings, it was comparatively easy to move, across naturally forest-free limestone, from the northern seaboard, through the Gates of Poitou and Carcassonne, to the Mediterranean south, and thence up the Rhône and Saône valleys, through the Gate of Burgundy, to the Rhine valley, or back to the basin of the Seine and the

Channel coast. This was where French civilisation grew up in the Middle Ages, from well-favoured country, easy communications, trade fairs, market towns, cities, castles, abbeys and universities (see Map 2).[4] And here also the most famous farmlands of France still flourish: Norman apple-orchards and dairy-meadows, the Charolais beef-cattle ranges of Burgundy, the great wheatfields of Île-de-France, Picardy, Champagne and Beauce, the truffles, walnuts and fat geese of Périgord, the vines of Bordeaux and Burgundy, and of the Charente, Loire, Rhône, Meuse and Moselle river valleys, and in Champagne (where technique and patience triumph over poor soil and weak sunlight, at the northern limit of viticulture), and on the southern lowlands of Languedoc (at its southern limit in France, where coarse wine is made quickly, in over-abundance, and where modern irrigation has also brought high yields from orchards and rice-fields).

French highland terrain, and the comparatively modest resources of France's mineral subsoil, occupy a smaller proportion of the national territory, concentrated, for the most part, along the southern, eastern and north-eastern edges of the country, and in its so-called Massif Central (see Map 5).

BORDERLANDS

The eastern borderland of France, from Strasbourg to the Mediterranean Sea, is, for most of its length, an upland one, behind a 'natural', mountainous frontier. This consists of three ranges, with crestlines running, and rising, north to south, from the Vosges (1,200–4,700 ft.) to the Jura (up to 5,700 ft.) and the Alps (6,000–16,000 ft.). The barrier is broken by a number of gaps, passes and river valleys, however, and the inhabitants of eastern France share with their South German, Swiss, Piedmontese and Ligurian neighbours, with whom they have often been in conflict or competition, and never out of touch, a marked talent for turning the resources of a beautiful but not easy environment to good account. The textile manufacturers and watchmakers, the dairy-farmers and hydro-electric engineers, the ski-slope, lakeside and seaside hoteliers of this part of France have earned their high reputation.

At one point, in the north, French territory overspills its

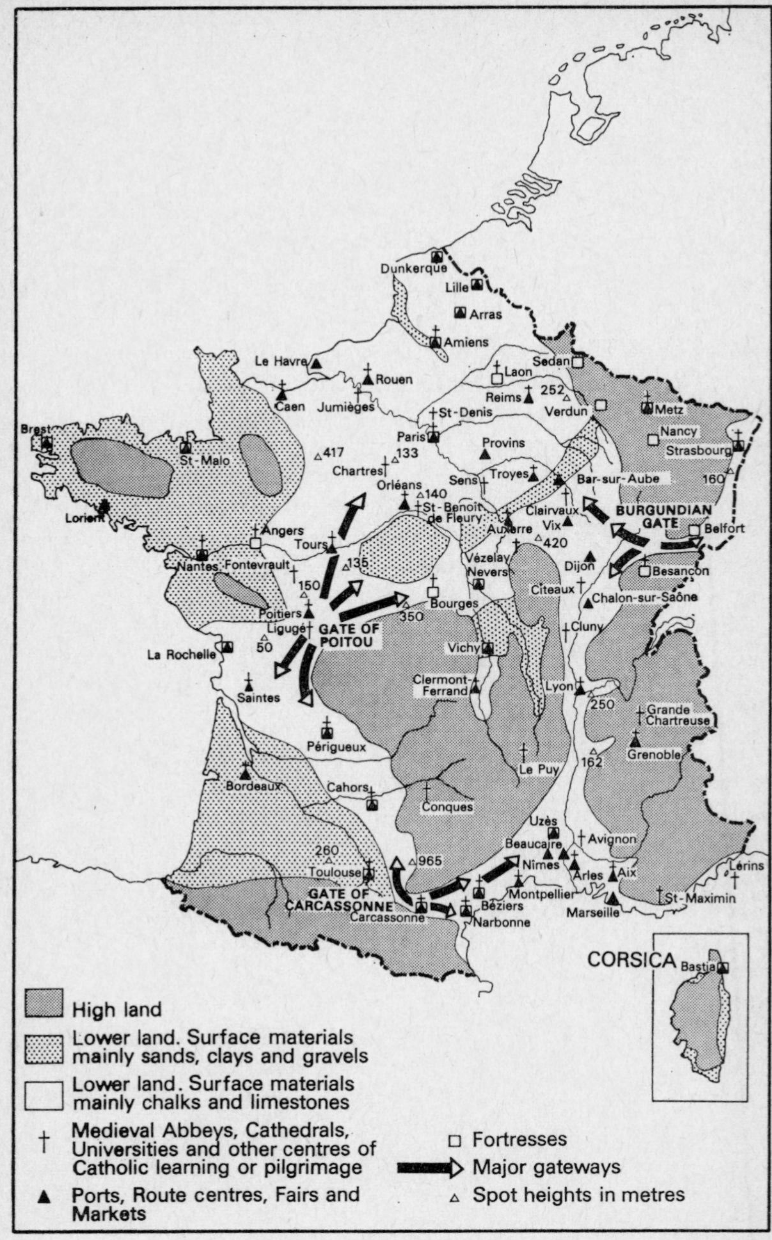

Map 2. Centres of culture and lines of movement

Map 3. Place-names and Provinces

eastern bastion of mountains, reaching out through the Vosges and across the fertile plain of Alsace, to the west bank of the Rhine. Acquired by the French kings of the seventeenth century, this natively German-speaking, but now generally French-orientated, province was annexed by Germany after her victory over France in 1870, together with part of eastern Lorraine. Both were returned to France in the Versailles Treaty of 1919, retaken by Hitler for the Third Reich in 1940, and recovered by France in 1945, a rich prize of fruitful acres and of industrious towns, whose people, having been forced by the laws of war, and without consultation, to change their national affiliation four times in seventy-five years, have naturally enough found some difficulty in adapting themselves completely to the French way of life, even within the comparatively liberal framework of the modern Republic. It is equally natural that peace between France and Germany should bring special relief and hope to this part of the country, as the post-war economic unification of Europe is already bringing a particular increase in activity and prosperity to its factories, offices and communications network, and to its capital, Strasbourg. Alsace today occupies a privileged situation at the industrial and linguistic centre of Western Europe.[5]

The Alps plunge into the Mediterranean a few miles east of Nice (which became French in 1792, was lost in 1815 and recovered in 1860), and from here the sea-coast runs for 320 miles in a reversed S-curve west-south-westwardly to the Pyrenees. The hot, rocky Côte d'Azur (between the Italian frontier and Marseille), the marshes of the lower Rhône delta, the sand-dunes and beaches between the Rhône and Spain, made up as harsh an environment as anywhere in France, until the invention of sunbathing around 1926, of holidays with pay ten years later and of electrically pumped irrigation channels in the 1950s. But the cultural history of the area, and its historic role as a gateway into France for men and women, crafts and creeds, systems and skills and tastes coming north out of Greece, Italy, Asia Minor and Africa, are deep in the foundations of French civilisation. Two contrasting sites epitomise the ancient destiny of the French Mediterranean south (*le Midi méditerranéen*): Marseille, the greatest port and the third city of modern France, founded by Greek colonists six hundred years before Christ, and Vix, near Châtillon-sur-Seine, at the northern exit from the Rhône–Saône 'corridor' (a tradeway of Phoenician merchants which seems likely to become a main axis of the twentieth-century European Common Market), where a magnificent Greek *cratera* of the sixth century B.C. was recently unearthed from the grave of a Gaulish princess.

Since the Crusades, but especially in modern times, traders, teachers, missionaries and colonisers have also gone out of France by this route, to sail for all parts of the Mediterranean and, after the piercing of the Suez Canal in 1869, beyond. France remains influential in the Levant, Egypt and western North Africa, even though her former political dominion over Syria, Lebanon, Tunisia, Algeria and most of Morocco has come to an end.

Marseille is an exceptionally cosmopolitan city. In the early 1930s nearly a quarter of its population was of non-French extraction. In most years since 1954 between 100,000 and 200,000 North Africans have disembarked there in search of work in the city and further north. Since the decolonisation of former French North Africa, some three-quarters of a million white settlers have landed, about 120,000 having subsequently settled in the city and its immediate hinterland.[6]

There are two parts to the French Mediterranean Midi, joined to France in 1271 and 1481 respectively: Languedoc, which lies westwards of the Rhône (its name being derived from the southern version *oc* of the Vulgar Latin affirmative particle *hoc ille*, which in the north became *oïl, oui*), and Provence (originally the Roman Provincia), which lies to the east.

Provence is more than a great cosmopolitan port and an equally international strip of seaside hotels and residences, though most of the population and wealth of the region is now concentrated in Marseille and along the coast. Inland, 'High', Provence has an ancient pastoral culture, which is in decline; but it also holds three trump cards for a twentieth-century economic revival, namely sunshine, snow-slopes and hydro-electric power. Taken as a whole, the area bounded by the Alpine crests, the Rhône river and the Mediterranean coast of Provence has in recent years attracted more new citizens than any other part of France except Paris, and from all points of the compass. Its annual rate of growth between 1962 and 1968 (2·7 per cent) was almost twice that of the Paris region (1·5 per cent). Some see it becoming Europe's California, at the gate of the future grand European waterway linking the Rhône and the Rhine, with a vast new industrial, oil-refining and port area reinforcing Marseille in the Gulf of Fos. Westwards the sand-dunes and lagoons of the as yet emptier coast of Languedoc, backed by nature reserves in the Camargue marshes and the Cévennes mountains, are also being developed fast, as overspill resorts for Provence's now overcrowded Côte d'Azur.

Languedoc extends from the Rhône as far as Toulouse. Its political independence, its heretical Cathar religion and its refined Troubadour culture were all crushed brutally by the northern French in the Albigensian Crusade (1208–29), but its individuality survives in strongly held attitudes of anti-governmental, anti-Parisian independence such as Protestantism (deeply rooted since the sixteenth century), Radical Republicanism (after 1870), Communism since the 1930s and anti-Gaullism in the 1960s. An even older, but less political, spirit of independence is to be found among the Basque people who live at the Atlantic end, and on both the Spanish and the French flanks, of the Pyrenees.

The Pyrenean range forms France's most obviously natural land frontier, presenting a high unbroken rampart all the way from the Basque country in the west to the Col du Perthus, some fifteen miles from the Mediterranean coast, in the east. The peoples of French Languedoc and Spanish Catalonia, separated only by this easy eastern pass, have much in common. The rest of Spain, though less accessible physically, has exercised considerable influence on the imagination of Frenchmen. Indeed, the fascination wrought on many generations of French readers and playgoers by the Spanish nobleman's austerity and pride, by the spectacular puritanism and the cruel symbols of Spanish religion, by the ritual of the bullring, by the fanatical ruthlessness of Spanish partisans and *conquistadores,* may well spring from the very remoteness of such things from the main traditions of *douce France.*[7] Actual confrontation has been sporadic, usually dramatic, and by turns hostile (the dynastic wars of the seventeenth century, Napoleon's campaign of 1808–13), uneasy (the general anguish and the conflicting loyalties aroused by Spain's Civil War of 1936–9), or simply acquisitive (today: cheap holidays in the sun, cheap domestic labour).

The western seaboard of France has given the French nation Atlantic and New World ambitions, though these have never been strong enough to pull effectively against the continental and Mediterranean destiny written along her other borders; which is the reason, perhaps, why Churchill's famous warning to de Gaulle during the Second World War, that Britain, faced with a similar dilemma, will always 'choose the open sea',[8] sounds so convincingly alien to French ears. France, like Britain, has felt the pull of *le grand large* none the less; mainly through her 'colonial' ports of Bordeaux, Nantes and Lorient, made prosperous in the eighteenth century by the sugar, spice, tobacco, cotton and slave trades of the West and East Indies, and in the nineteenth and early twentieth centuries by imports from French colonial territories in tropical Africa. Most of France's possessions in America and India were lost to Britain in the Seven Years and Napoleonic wars, or were absorbed by the United States, but she has left her mark on the New World, from the still French Caribbean islands of Martinique and Guadeloupe, northwards through Louisiana and the Mississippi Basin to Maine, and to Canada's Quebec Province, stirring somewhat restlessly in the arms of the British Commonwealth. Bordeaux, moreover, still does a fair volume of business with French-speaking West and Equatorial Africa, while its earliest export trade, in the great wines of the Bordelais hinterland, is maintained all over the world, and keeps a considerable foreign business colony in the city. This has particularly strong British connections, first forged in medieval times, when Bordeaux was the capital of the English kingdom in France.

The most westerly province of France is Brittany, where on the weathered rocks and difficult soils of Arcoet and the Armorican peninsula, jutting out into the Atlantic Ocean, one of the earliest cultures of Europe still preserves a distinct identity within and, for a small number of extreme Breton nationalists, against, the political unity of the 'one and indivisible' French Republic. The Romans conquered the mixed race of aboriginals and Celts living in what they called Britannia Minor in 56 B.C. After the fall of the Empire,

Brittany's Celtic language and customs were reinforced by settlements of refugees fleeing before the Anglo-Saxon invaders of the British Isles. It remained comparatively untouched by the Frankish and Norman invasions and was taken fairly late into the kingdom of France, between 1491 and 1532. Since then, the Breton's characteristic spirit of adventure, love of independence and sense of the supernatural have brought much to the development of French civilisation.

Dependent very largely for its prosperity on sea communications, Brittany was badly hit by interminable wars between France and the United Kingdom during the eighteenth and early nineteenth centuries, and has never since been able to provide enough work for a teeming population, in spite of the many hands needed on its small cereal and dairy farms, and in its fruit-orchards and market-gardens. Recent mechanisation has cut down these high labour requirements, and the effect of this is only partly offset by some improvement of marketing methods, by the tourist trade and by a measure of Paris-planned decentralisation of industry. So the Breton, besides being, by tradition, a seafarer, and the heart of the French Navy, is also frequently, perforce, like his brother Celts of Scotland and Ireland, an emigrant: to other parts of France, notably Paris, and to North America. From 1872 to 1962 Brittany normally had a higher net rate of emigration than any other French province. Those who remain behind are, typically, farmers or fishermen (sometimes both, changing their jobs with the seasons); more recently, employers or employees of the hotel and the canning industries. Traditionally, the Breton is a devout Christian, wary of the godless 'Frenchmen' to the east, who rent his scenery and services in the summertime but whose middlemen cut his profit on artichokes and cauliflowers (too often – through bad organisation and poor communications – a glut in the market, or stale and overpriced before they reach it), and whose state schools and examination systems are indifferent or inimical towards his Catholic religion and Celtic language.

Eastwards of Brittany, with a coastline facing southern England across the narrowing waters of the English Channel (La Manche), lie the fertile fields and famous cities and ports of Normandy, a country settled by the Northmen of Scandinavia in the tenth century and joined to the French crown in the thirteenth. Like Brittany, it is a province with a high birth rate and a vigorous native culture, and has contributed much to the fusion of races, customs and tongues by which the French nation, and also, of course, after the Conquest of 1066, the neighbouring English nation, were made.

As striking and as important as the proximity, here and on into Picardy and Flanders, of the French and the English coasts, is the comparatively short land and sea passage between the capital cities of France and of Great Britain. None of the ancient capitals of Europe lies so close to another as do Paris and London, and no two have influenced each other's history and culture for so long and in so many different fields and ways. Nor so continuously: nothing in the stormy history of Franco-British relations could interrupt the stimulating exchange of ideas and tastes by which the 'hereditary enemies' of medieval and modern Europe, allies now though rivals still, have for so many centuries grown rich, not without many misunderstandings and much mutual exasperation.

The frontier by which the territory of France is divided from Belgium, Luxembourg and Germany is a haunted line of fortresses, battlefields, war memorials and military cemeteries, smashed and rebuilt villages and towns, some of them without a building more than fifty years old, running from Calais and Dunkirk in the 'cockpit of Europe', past Loos, Arras, Rocroi, Sedan and Verdun, to the old middle kingdom of Europe: Lotharingia (Lorraine). Modern Lorraine is the remnant of Lotharingia (which stretched in the ninth century from the Rhine to the Rhône and at first included northern Italy) in much besides its etymological derivation. Hardly had the rich central share of Charlemagne's empire been carved out for Lothaire and his successors at the Treaty of Verdun in 843 than it became a bone of contention for the two stronger powers on either side, who set about winning and losing it by turns for the next millennium. Unlike Alsace, most of Lorraine is natively French-speaking and strongly French-thinking, having looked westwards from the mid-seventeenth century. German annexation of its eastern part after the victory over France in 1870, as a strategic glacis against the supposedly still explosive force of 'Jacobin' nationalism,[9] and, for its iron ore, as a valuable industrial prize, changed this very little. But it was one of the reasons why some 400,000 French and Germans died fighting each other in 1916, for possession of the old town of Verdun, where Christian Europe had been divided by treaty one thousand and seventy-three years before.

In modern times economic rivalry increased the historic tensions of the Franco–German border. The region in which France and Germany confronted each other in 1914, and again in 1939, is not only the most artificial and vulnerable of French frontiers but it contains some of the richest mineral deposits in Europe. Immediately behind it, within a triangle whose approximate vertices are Dunkirk, Strasbourg and Paris, France mines 75 per cent of her coal and over 90 per cent of her iron ore, while a high proportion of her textile and heavy industries are concentrated in the same area or near by. The French capital itself is only 112 miles from the Belgian and 249 miles from the German frontier posts.

Flanders and Lorraine, at each end of this border, are both located at important European crossroads, which frequent wars and impermanent peace treaties, from the fifteenth to the eighteenth centuries, and again in the last hundred years, have repeatedly blocked with conventional frontier lines representing nothing more than a temporary balance of military power. Flanders in particular has suffered from this form of frustration. In the early Middle Ages it was a busy thoroughfare for pilgrims and traders, and a densely populated and productive area of settlement and culture. With every subsequent interval of peace, its fields, factories and ports quickly recovered their prosperity. Wealth came to Lorraine much later, with the discovery by Thomas and Gilchrist of a way to smelt its enormous reserves of highly phosphorous iron ore. Both territories have much to gain from the unification of Europe, which will facilitate natural outlets to the north and east in Germany, Luxembourg and the Low Countries, and eventually, perhaps across (or under) the Channel, to a European Britain. The north-eastern marchlands of French territory embody the manifestly European destiny of France in one further respect: the industrial working population of Lorraine and Flanders (with adjacent Artois) has a very high proportion of immigrant Italians, Poles, Spaniards and North Africans, a phenomenon which antedates by several decades the present universal movement of labour into the 'golden triangle' of north-western Europe. In the steel town of Briey, for instance, just over half the population as long ago as 1914, and just under half in 1930, were foreigners, mostly Italians.[10] Alsace-Lorraine was also an important staging-post for Jews migrating westwards out of Central Europe during the nineteenth century: after 1870, thousands left the 'lost provinces' of Alsace-Lorraine for Lille, Lyon, Marseille and, especially, Paris, where the Jewish community, already well established and assimilated, having multiplied by the factor of eight since 1808, were prominent in the élites of the Third Republic (1870–1939).

French national expansion and political unification were complete by the end of the nineteenth century, with the exception of Alsace-Lorraine and French Algeria, whose political destinies hung on the changing balance of power in Europe and Africa until 1945 and 1962 respectively.[11] On the other hand, movements of population continued, and continue, into and within the six-sided crucible where French unity was forged, and these can tell us much about continuing processes of fusion and change in the living nation, processes resulting mainly from the industrial and transport revolutions of the last century and a half.

STATIC FRANCE AND DYNAMIC FRANCE

A short, steep climb from Pont-Saint-Esprit, on the Rhône north of Avignon, through the gorge to the source of the Ardèche, in high grasslands, leads up from the flood-plain of the Mediterranean Midi to the northern catchment area which drains the great bulk of French territory into the Atlantic Ocean and the English Channel. The rivers watering nearly every part of the country, except the Midi and the east, all have considerable headwaters, if not their actual named source, near by, in the 2,000–3,000-ft. granite plateau, broken by mountains of volcanic origin, which is known as the Massif Central, or Central Highlands of France. The Allier–Loire (which is the longest French river system, draining north and west into the Atlantic) rises within fourteen miles of the Ardèche. The Lot, flowing south-west to the Atlantic (after joining the Tarn, the Aveyron and the Pyrenean Garonne), rises seventeen miles from the same spot. The Dordogne, also draining westwards to the Atlantic, has its source less than a hundred miles away, to the north-west, in the Auvergne mountains, the loftiest part of the Massif (6,200 ft.). The Yonne rises in Morvan, which is the extreme northermost tip of the Central Highlands; and the springs of the Seine, the Aube, the Marne, the Aisne and the Meuse all rise on or near the Plateau de Langres, which is separated from the Massif only by the gap which carries the main road from the Paris Basin through Burgundy to the Rhône valley and the Mediterranean. Throughout this heartland of France the movements of men and of water have corresponded closely since industrialisation got under way a century and a half ago. Some concentrations of industrial labour occurred early at the edge of the Massif itself, near small coalfields, at Decazeville, Alais, Saint-Étienne and Le Creusot, and at Clermont-Ferrand, in the trough of the river Allier, which is also a very fertile agricultural district (La Limagne). But the great natural reservoir that geographers call *le château-d'eau de la France* (the water-tower of France) has sent most of its highlanders, with its streams, much further afield: to Lyon and the Rhône valley, to Toulouse and the Basin of Aquitaine, and northwards down the long dip-slopes to the Paris Basin, drained by the Seine, the Marne and the middle Loire.

The Massif Central, occupying approximately one-sixth of the total area of France, is the largest of its demographically negative zones, and has lost a quarter of its population since the middle of the last century.[12] Paris, its opposite extreme, lying approximately equidistant from the geographical centre of France, is historically France's strongest pole of attraction, concentrating nearly a sixth of the French people, over eight million, in a city and suburban area spanning some forty miles from east to west and pushing longer tentacles north and south, along suburban railway lines and the new Lille–Paris–Lyon–Marseille motorway.

The nucleus of the French capital is a small island called La Cité, forming an easy crossing-point of the Seine river, ninety miles from the sea, where the medieval cathedral of Notre-Dame stands near the emplacement of a Gallo-Roman temple, and the Palace of Justice of the French Republic occupies the site of former palaces for Roman governors and French kings. On the Left Bank of the Seine opposite La Cité

3. A nose for Armagnac

4. Laboratory work at Rennes Agricultural College

1. La Grande Motte, on the coast of Languedoc

2. Saint-Cirq-Lapopie, Lot

7. Vineyard workers in Burgundy

8. Greater Paris and the wheatfields of Brie meet at Créteil-sur-Marne

5. Wedding group in Savoie

6. Reception of a new 'Immortal' at the French Academy

is the Latin, or University Quarter, comprising not only the oldest and most famous French university (now subdivided and partly dispersed to peripheral sites), but also many of the leading secondary schools (*lycées*) and most of the top *grandes écoles,* such as *Polytechnique, Normale Supérieure, Chartes* and *Mines,* which give specialised tertiary instruction to an élite of engineering, science and arts students.[13] On the northern, Right Bank, crowded into the old East End districts of Saint-Martin, Saint-Antoine and Le Marais, in and among the crumbling, or recently restored, town houses of the sixteenth- and seventeenth-century aristocracy, lie thousands of small workshops, where the high reputation of Paris for the design and manufacture of clothes, jewellery, furnishings and furniture was made, and is maintained, side by side with an almost infinite variety of wholesale, retail, service and entertainment trades, the great newspaper presses, and, until 1969, Les Halles, the huge central food market, employing some 35,000 workers, which has now, at last, been removed to more accessible sites at the north-eastern and southern limits of the capital (La Villette and Rungis). The old fortifications of the city, 'bulwarks' long since turned into 'boulevards' lined with cafés and theatres, carry business traffic and pleasure-seeking crowds through the Paris of kings and emperors, whose magnificent palaces, squares and formal gardens the Republic has taken for its museums, picture galleries, ministries, embassies and promenades. The business and social centre merges westwards again into the spacious avenues and parks of the modern residential quarters: *les beaux quartiers* of L'Étoile, Chaillot, Passy, Auteuil and, on the Left Bank, Le Champ de Mars. Surrounding the city is a belt of manufacturing suburbs: Saint-Denis, Belleville, Aubervilliers, Clichy, Boulogne-sur-Seine, Billancourt, Ivry, where working-class dwellings rise side by side with factories employing nearly a quarter of France's industrial workers, producing more than a third, by value, of the nation's exports. More than half of those engaged, in the mid-1960s, in the French motor and aeronautical industries, the electrical and pharmaceutical trades, and in printing and publishing, lived and worked in the capital and its suburbs. Nearly half the population of Greater Paris is employed in industry.[14]

Within a radius of two miles from Notre-Dame are the six

terminal stations of the Paris-centred French railway network, which has brought so many new citizens to the capital during the last hundred years, from the French provinces and abroad. Between 1901 and 1936, during which period the total population of France increased by only 821,000, that of Greater Paris grew by nearly two million. More than half the present population was born in provincial France.[15] Beyond still rapidly expanding suburbs and 'satellite' new towns, the city dominates a large area bounded on the north by the industrial belt along the Belgian frontier, on the west by the Channel coasts of Picardy and Normandy, on the east by the headwaters of the Seine and its tributaries, and on the south by the valley of the middle Loire.

Historically the influence of Paris on its surrounding region has been a largely negative one: the draining of men and resources from an area containing in 1964 no town of more than 50,000 inhabitants within a radius of sixty miles from the capital.[16] Young agricultural and industrial workers from Picardy and Flanders continue to emigrate into Paris in large numbers. On the other hand, the challenge to farmers in the fertile Paris Basin of the competitively high wage-rates of the capital, as well as the opportunities of an incomparable mass market for their produce, have had the positive effect of encouraging the development of efficient, mechanised, low-labour-cost agriculture: wheat, sugar-beet and potatoes on the plains of Beauce, Vexin, Valois, Brie, Bray and Champagne; market-gardening on the drained river banks of the Somme, Marne and Oise; dairy-farming and cheese-making in the valleys of Bray and Brie (see Map 4).[17] Substantial middle-class investment in the purchase and conversion of country cottages and farmsteads as 'secondary residences', for weekends, holidays and retirement, doubled the price of property throughout the area between 1958 and 1964. In addition, recent spontaneous and government-inspired decentralisation of industry, offices and university education has given new vigour to the 'coronet' of historic towns encircling the capital just outside the medieval province of Île-de-France, notably Orléans, Troyes, Reims, Saint-Quentin, Amiens, Rouen, Évreux, Caen. One hundred and fifty miles downstream from La Cité lies the third largest river port of France – Rouen,[18] in the Seine valley down which 'Paris of the Year 2000' may be

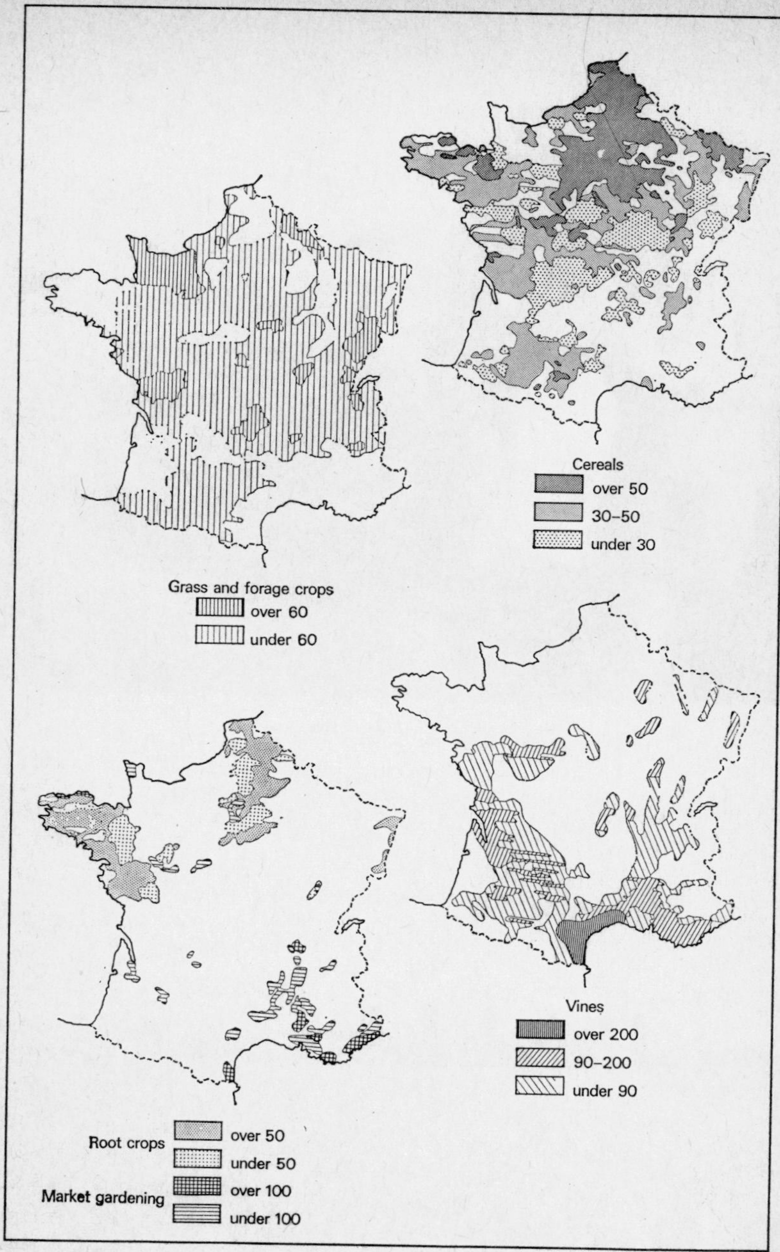

The coefficient of intensity (*after* J. Klatzmann) expresses the average yield per hectare in the various categories of land use. The basic unit of reference is the average yield of one hectare of grass. Thus: grass = 1·0; cereals = 1·5; fodder crops = 1·5; root crops = 4·0; vines = 5·0; market gardening = 10·0

Map 4. Agricultural land use – distribution of types of cultivation

B

expected to have grown most naturally, towards Le Havre, France's second largest seaport.

The contrasting demographic histories of the Massif Central and Paris exemplify the predominant type of population shift in twentieth-century France (and Europe): from highlands and heathlands to valleys, plains and industrial towns. But other 'negative areas' exist in France beside the Central Highlands and the Breton peninsula. In Brittany, unlike the Massif Central, an exceptionally buoyant birth rate has made up much of the loss caused by emigration. The southern French Alps, the High Jura, the upper Saône and Meuse valleys, on the other hand, were already severely and no doubt irreversibly depopulated thirty years ago. The population of Corsica, from which mainland France has recruited, besides its most famous little corporal, a significant proportion of its police forces, its excisemen and other government servants in the last two hundred years, fell by 35 per cent between 1880 and 1962, though the island is now, like the rest of Mediterranean France, attracting new residents.[19]

The first phase of the French rural 'exodus', which got under way later and developed more slowly than in Britain and Germany, had the effect of filling up the north and east of the country, including, especially, Paris and its suburbs, and emptying the centre, west and south-west, since not only the capital city of a state which had been centrally governed for more than two hundred years, but also nearly all the mineral deposits required for power and as raw materials in the first industrial revolution, the so-called palaeo-technic age of coal and iron, as well as most of the sites of its old-established steam-driven or water-powered textile industries (cotton, linen and wool in Normandy, Picardy, Flanders, Alsace and Lorraine, woollens in Champagne, silk at Lyon), lay north and east of a line joining the Seine estuary and the Rhône delta. A line may still be drawn to divide what is called, broadly speaking, 'static France' – the west and the south-west, predominantly rural, comparatively poor, with a backward, declining and, in most districts, ageing population – from the 'dynamic' north and east, with their generally more efficient modern factories and farms, their growing population, their rising standards of living, their higher proportion of young men and women, and their greater accessibility to

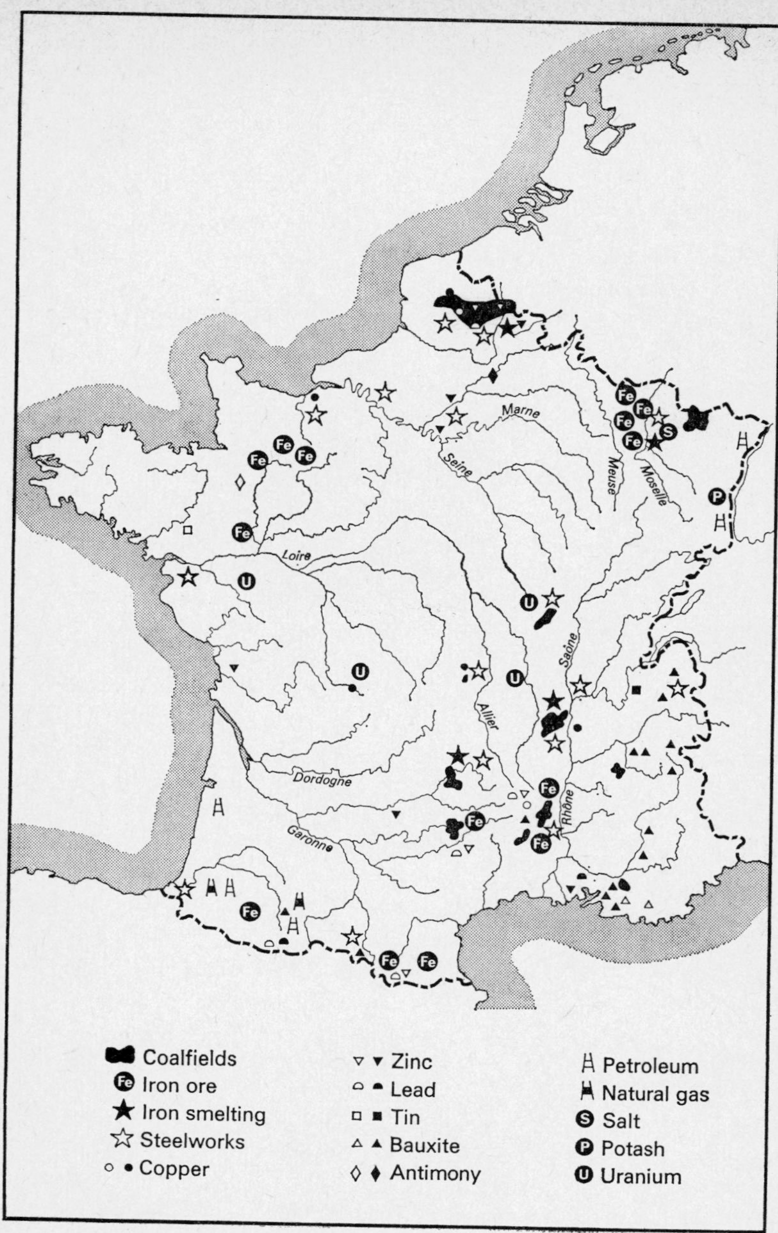

Open symbols for metals (other than iron ore and uranium) denote mining regions, solid symbols the sites of smelting or processing plants

Map 5. Mineral resources

new ideas. But the geographical division is not quite so clear-cut or stable as it was even twenty years ago. Since the Second World War, the palaeo-technic mining and textile industries of the north-east have drastically reduced their labour forces, causing unemployment and emigration out of once intensively active areas such as Lorraine and Flanders, while new industrial development has spread westwards from the Seine valley into Basse-Normandie and a strongly attractive centre of neo-technic growth, powered by electricity, has sprung up at the southern end of the 'line of economic imbalance' (see Maps 6 and 7).[20]

Many things have combined to turn Rhône–Alpes and Provence–Côte d'Azur into the two most dynamic of the new Economic Regions of mid-twentieth-century France: hydro-electric power and controlled irrigation available from an ambitious scheme of new dams and canals extending down from the High Alps to the lower Durance and Rhône; the good agricultural soils and the sunshine of the river-plain and delta; the port facilities of Marseille and the Gulf of Fos (handling oil and foreign iron ore); the tourist and residential amenities of mountain and coast; new centres for the production and advanced study of nuclear energy at Marcoule and Grenoble; the vigorous Science Faculty of the University at Grenoble, a city which, with its region, the broad Val d'Isère, has a comparatively long tradition of advanced technology applied to industry, and which has attracted to its laboratories, factories, municipal council chambers (and nearby ski-slopes, freshly equipped for the 1968 Winter Olympics) a particularly lively and self-confident élite of young technocrats to push and manage its exceptional rate and scale of advance. Some of this new vitality extends westwards of the Rhône (and so across the old line of imbalance). It has been stimulated by state aid for tourism, irrigation, hydro-electric and atomic power, the French aircraft industry (which has had a strong base at Toulouse since the First World War, for strategic reasons); by American investment in fruit-growing and the canning industry; by some enterprising French business leaders and local co-operatives; and by the arrival of tens of thousands of energetic expatriate *pieds noirs* (European settlers from former French North Africa) to the sleepy countryside of Languedoc, and to such congenially southern

Map 6. Distribution of manufacturing industry

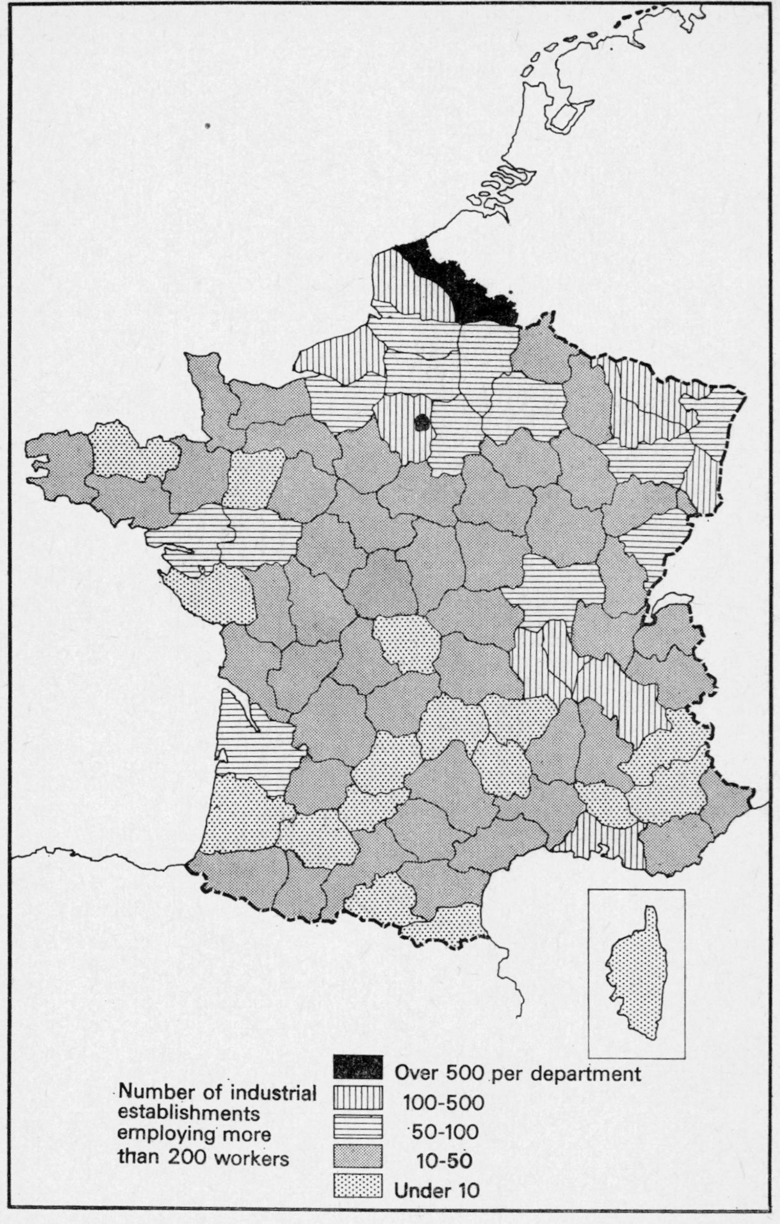

Map 7. Industrial establishments employing more than 200 workers

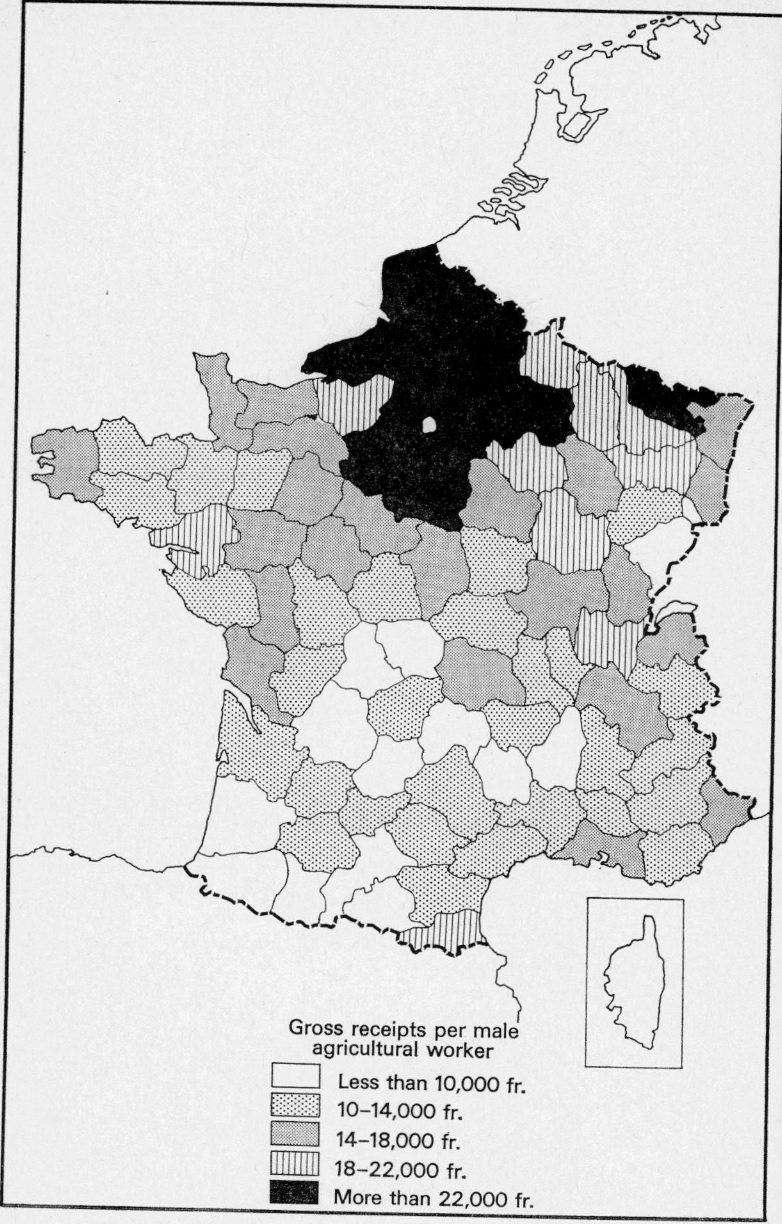

Map 8. The rewards of farming – gross receipts per male agricultural worker

towns as Toulouse and Montpellier (from 1962 to 1968 the fastest growing city in all France).[21] Despite these recent aids and arrivals, however, coming after several previous waves of immigrants (from Brittany, Vendée, Spain and Italy), the south-west, where the indigenous birth rate is low, remains generally speaking as thinly populated and as poorly developed as the Massif Central (which has more natural disadvantages), while in the north-west there are not enough jobs for an abundant and prolific population.

Since 1950, French governments have striven to get a better balance generally between the stagnant west and the progressive north and east, by planned regional development (*l'aménagement du territoire*). They have built new electric power stations and tapped the natural gas and oil of southern Aquitaine; subsidised several brand-new holiday resorts and yacht marinas on the formerly underdeveloped coasts of Languedoc and Aquitaine; encouraged or ordered a number of factories and research laboratories for the automobile, aerospace, atomic, electronic and telecommunications industries to move to the west; favoured western industry generally by differential tax allowances and investment subsidies (see Map 9). Three of the eight new 'counterweight' regional capitals (*métropoles d'équilibre*), Toulouse, Bordeaux and Nantes, are sited in the west (see Map 10). Moreover, French planners are aware that it is no good trying to decentralise industry in order to keep the western provinces populated and alive without providing local centres there of first-class education and culture also, so as to prevent the men of brains and drive from slipping off (or back) to Paris with their families at the first opportunity. University cities all over France are the ones in which growth has been proportionately greatest in recent decades. The central planners intend to exploit this trend. Besides the universities of the *métropoles d'équilibre*, there are particularly good ones (and active *Maisons de la Culture*[22]) at Caen in western Normandy and at Rennes, the Breton capital.[23] The planning authorities in Paris, and energetic provincial leaders such as Mayor Fréville of Rennes, and Jacques Chaban-Delmas, Mayor of Bordeaux (and Prime Minister of France since 1969), can justly claim a measure of success for their efforts. The west's share of the overall national population increase is rising, and in some parts of

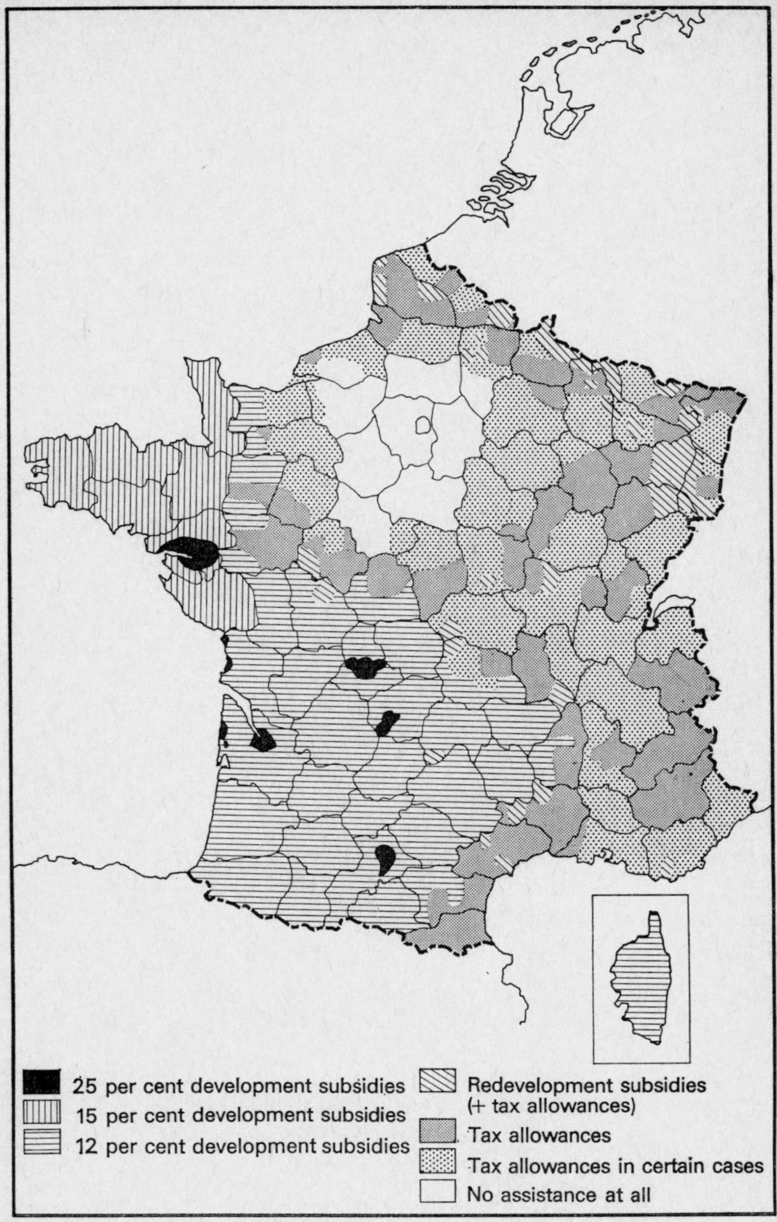

Map 9. Distribution of subsidies and tax abatements for the encouragement of industrial growth in underdeveloped areas

Map 10. *Départements* and *Régions*

Départements with their Post Office Code Numbers

Ain	01
Aisne	02
Allier	03
Alpes (-de-Haute-Provence)	04
Alpes (Hautes-)	05
Alpes-Maritimes	06
Ardèche	07
Ardennes	08
Ariège	09
Aube	10
Aude	11
Aveyron	12
Bouches-du-Rhône	13
Calvados	14
Cantal	15
Charente	16
Charente-Maritime	17
Cher	18
Corrèze	19
Corse	20
Côte-d'Or	21
Côtes-du-Nord	22
Creuse	23
Dordogne	24
Doubs	25
Drôme	26
Eure	27
Eure-et-Loir	28
Finistère	29
Gard	30
Garonne (Haute-)	31
Gers	32
Gironde	33
Hérault	34
Ille-et-Vilaine	35
Indre	36
Indre-et-Loire	37
Isère	38
Jura	39
Landes	40
Loir-et-Cher	41
Loire	42
Loire (Haute-)	43
Loire-Atlantique	44
Loiret	45
Lot	46
Lot-et-Garonne	47
Lozère	48
Maine-et-Loire	49
Manche	50
Marne	51
Marne (Haute-)	52
Mayenne	53
Meurthe-et-Moselle	54
Meuse	55
Morbihan	56
Moselle	57
Nièvre	58
Nord	59
Oise	60
Orne	61
Pas-de-Calais	62
Puy-de-Dôme	63
Pyrénées (-Atlantiques)	64
Pyrénées (Hautes-)	65
Pyrénées-Orientales	66
Rhin (Bas-)	67
Rhin (Haut-)	68
Rhône	69
Saône (Haute-)	70
Saône-et-Loire	71
Sarthe	72
Savoie	73
Savoie (Haute-)	74
Paris (Ville de)	75
Seine-Maritime	76
Seine-et-Marne	77
Yvelines	78
Sèvres (Deux-)	79
Somme	80
Tarn	81
Tarn-et-Garonne	82
Var	83
Vaucluse	84
Vendée	85
Vienne	86
Vienne (Haute-)	87
Vosges	88
Yonne	89
Belfort (Territoire de)	90
Essonne	91
Hauts-de-Seine	92
Seine-St-Denis	93
Val-de-Marne	94
Val-d'Oise	95

'static' France the historic trend of depopulation has been slowed down (Brittany, Basse-Normandie, Pays de la Loire, Poitou–Charentes) or reversed (Limousin, Auvergne).

France's entire urban population is now growing fast at the expense of her rural communities, though not at the expense of agricultural production (which rises in proportion to the contraction of small-scale manual farming), nor, any longer, so exclusively for the advance and increase of the north-east generally and Paris in particular. Compared with Britain, Germany and the United States, France still has few large cities. Beside Paris (8,200,000), only four French cities have more than half a million citizens: Lyon (1,100,000), Marseille (964,000), Lille–Roubaix–Tourcoing (881,000) and Bordeaux (555,000). A quarter of the French still live in a countryside fairly evenly settled with more than 30,000 small towns, villages and hamlets of fewer than two thousand inhabitants. The density of the rural population is highest in Brittany,

Flanders and Alsace. Paris still gets more new citizens every year than any other city (and has nearly a quarter of the nation's entire urban population), but since the Second World War, for the first time this century, many provincial towns have been growing faster than the capital. Between 1962 and 1968, twenty-one towns grew approximately twice as fast as Paris, of which Toulouse, Nîmes, Tours, Perpignan and Rennes are important western and south-western towns; and a further ten grew three or more times as fast, of which Pau (at an average annual rate of 4·3 per cent), Montpellier (5·6 per cent) and Caen (4·0 per cent) are also in the west.[24]

The French population as a whole has increased rapidly in the last quarter of a century, after a hundred years of stagnation. In 1800, with a population density similar to that of Germany and Italy, France had been the largest of the European powers, dominating the Continent by its mass as much as by its unity and genius. By the beginning of the Second World War, however, it had fallen behind to fourth place, having been overtaken by a united Germany in the third quarter of the nineteenth century, by Great Britain around 1895, and by Italy in the late 1930s (see Fig. 1). The birth rate had begun to decline in France (for reasons which remain obscure, but partly at least in response to the 'possessive individualism' of the morally emancipated, property-owning and competitive society engendered by the French Revolution) a good deal earlier than in the more traditionalistic nations round about her.[25] The rate of infant mortality was also reduced, but not very significantly until after the First World War, that is later than in Britain, Sweden, Switzerland and the United States, and not sufficiently to compensate for the terrible death toll of 1914–18: nearly 1,400,000 soldiers killed, and a further million civilian deaths from wartime or post-war hardships and epidemics, besides the shortfall due to long absence from home of some eight million mobilised men.[26] Twenty years later, as the reduced generation born in the Great War reached manhood, and drew near to another war, there was a short period when there were fewer births than deaths in France. The total population of the country (including Alsace-Lorraine) actually declined, between 1906 and 1946, from forty-one million to forty million and a half.

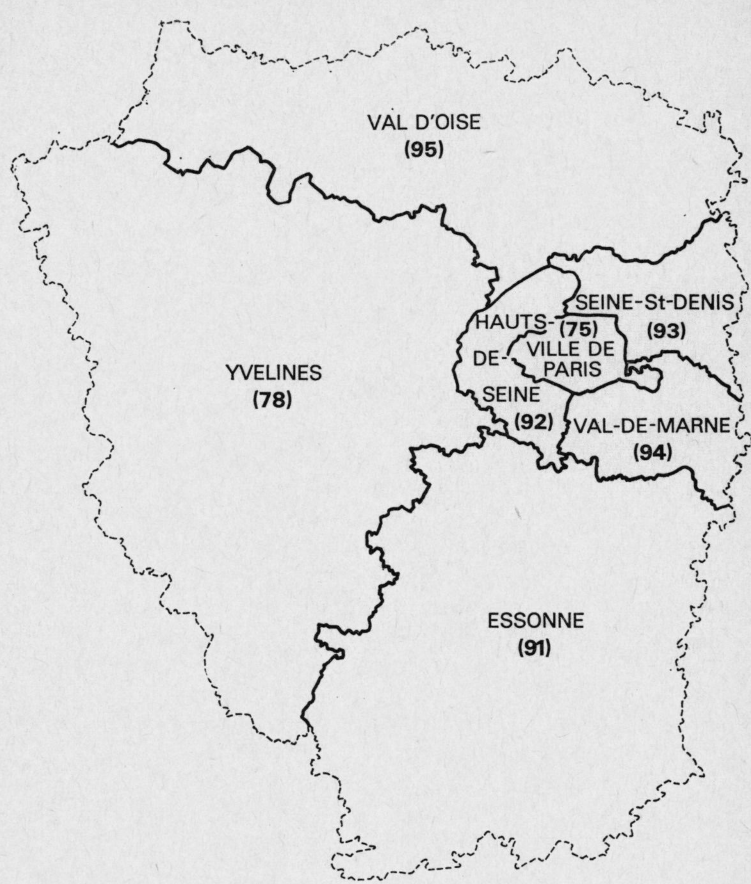

Map 11. The Paris Region

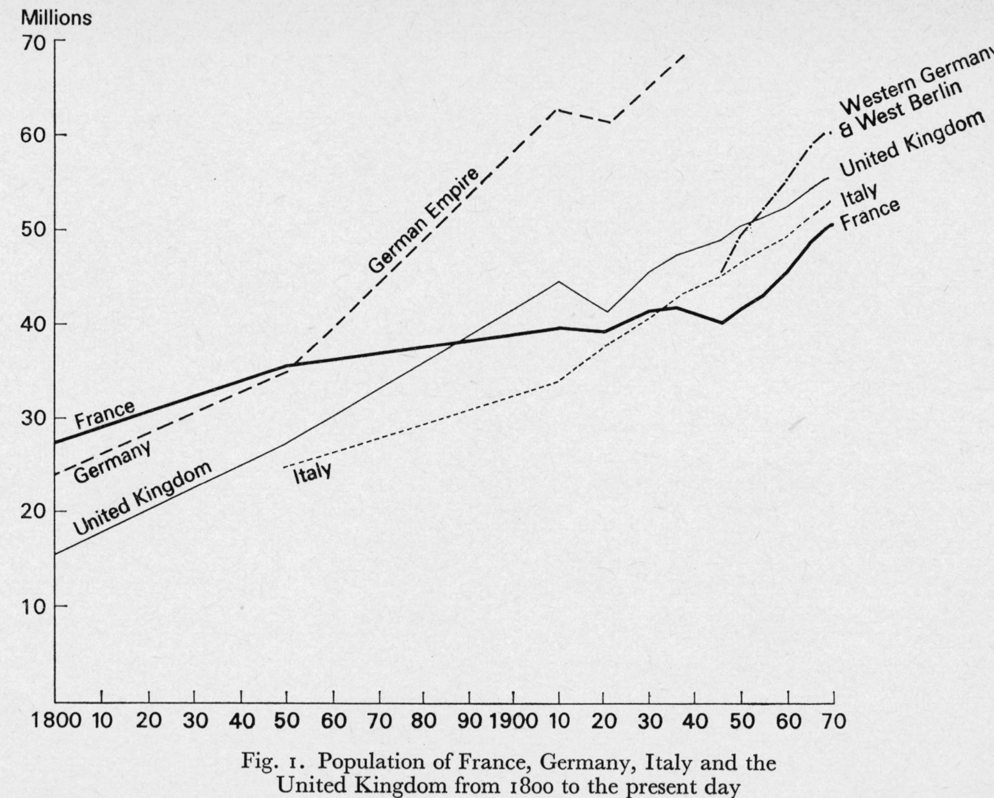

Fig. 1. Population of France, Germany, Italy and the United Kingdom from 1800 to the present day

But in the 1940s there was a rapid rise in the French birth rate, from fifteen to twenty-one per thousand, and between 1946 and 1962 the nation grew by no less than six millions.

An upsurge of this speed and magnitude gave fresh heart and drive to a people just emerging from one of the most calamitous decades of its history. It also created immediate difficulties in the fields of education, health, housing and the care of the old. A working population born in the demographically lean years of 1880–1940 has had to provide for comparatively large numbers of old, retired people, and of children and adolescents not yet in productive employment. The French are proud of having raised national living standards spectacularly in such testing circumstances, as Pierre Massé affirmed when presenting the fourth post-war National Plan to Parliament, in 1962:

> The Fourth Plan . . . will enable France to emerge from what might be called the demographic defile. A more numerous generation will soon be reaching the age of employment. A rejuvenated France, strong in her greatest wealth – her men – will be ready to tackle the new tasks which will abound for them.
>
> Not that since the war we have spared our pains. On the contrary . . . we have increased our production considerably with a static working population, while undertaking the education of an increased younger generation, and we must continue our thrust to the end of the defile. . . .[27]

By the late 1960s, the birth rate in France had dropped back almost to the level of the mid-1930s (16·7 per thousand), but the post-war 'thrust in the defile' had meanwhile taken a toll. Schools and universities, in spite of rapid expansion, are badly overcrowded and under-staffed, though as much because of increased educational opportunities and greater length of schooling, as because of the higher birth rate.[28] A shortage of personnel trained in modern skills pushes up the top end of the salary scale and makes both for general inflation and for unemployment and unrest among the unskilled, and among those whose skills have become redundant in the hard managerial and technological pursuit of productivity targets for enlarged European and world markets. Though gigantic new housing schemes ring the main cities, there is still a great deal of overcrowding in antiquated tenements and lodging-houses,[29] while not all of the squalid shanty-towns (*bidonvilles*) erected after the Second World War beyond city limits by a sub-proletariat of immigrant workers from Southern Europe and North Africa have even yet been cleared.

The last hundred years constitute a period of massive gain to the French nation from one of its oldest sources of energy, namely foreign immigration. Between 1850 and 1951 France was quite exceptional among European nations, both by the large numbers of her immigrant population and by the comparatively small number of French emigrants leaving the country for New World or colonial territories overseas.[30] From 1850 to 1906, movements into the swiftly developing industrial districts of the north-east, and in and around Lyon, took the form of a spontaneous drift from the land across nearby frontiers: Belgians mingling in the factories of French Flanders with workers newly recruited from the countryside of northern France, for instance, and Italians spreading along the Mediterranean coast, and down the Alpine valleys to the Rhône. The second phase, which lasted from about 1906 until 1931, was a bigger and more organised response to the special need of France for extra manpower at a time when industrial activity was being boosted by the demands of Europe's last years of affluent peace and imperial expansion, by rearmament for and during the First World War, and by post-war reconstruction; while simultaneously, the national labour force was diminished by a low birth rate and, after 1918, by the toll of the Great War.

During these twenty-five years the number of foreigners living in France rose from 1,000,000 to 2,700,000, the largest contingents coming from Italy and Poland. Some of these men, engaged under contract, were sent home during the economic depression of the early thirties, thus relieving France of the mass unemployment that Germany, Britain and North America encountered. Many remained, however, and were absorbed during the next two decades, during which comparatively few new immigrants arrived. The huge expansion of industry and commerce in Western Europe since the early 1950s has attracted workers from the less well-developed countries of Southern Europe and North Africa to most of the countries of the Common Market and their nearest neighbours. France's share of this latest influx has brought the number of foreigners living within her borders back to the inter-war figure of 2,700,000, including particularly large contingents of Spaniards, Italians, Algerians and Portuguese.[31] Many political refugees have found a home in France since the First World War, the largest groups being Russian and Ukrainian families in flight from the Bolshevik Revolution of 1917 (about 20,000), Spanish Republicans exiled by defeat in the Civil War of 1936–9 (70,000), and white settlers from North Africa after Algeria and the former French protectorates of Tunisia and Morocco had won their political independence (over a million, quickly absorbed, mainly by the Midi, since 1954).[32]

2 Social Classes

THE MIDDLE CLASS

THE middle class has occupied the commanding heights of France's economy for more than a century, and the character of the modern nation as a whole has been broadly determined by this ascendancy. But the composition of the class, and its influence, have changed significantly since the Second World War. The old middle class, living by property, savings, manufacturing, trade and the professions, is still quite strongly entrenched in the provinces, particularly in the least industrialised ones. But its place is being taken, or challenged, everywhere by a new salaried, managerial and technocratic ruling class of what the French call *cadres* (originally an Army term meaning 'staff'). These 'new notables' keep many traditionally middle-class standards. They value good talk, good food, good manners and, above all, the best education for their children, on whose behalf they show traditionally intense concern for success in the long, hard steeplechase of qualifying and competitive examinations by way of which the modern Republic selects practically all its potential leaders. Generally speaking, the *cadres* share too with the old middle class a comfortable sense of privilege, and a sense of social responsibility that is real, though it may be limited in scope. In other respects, however, the young *néo-bourgeois* are producing fresh patterns for the French way of life.

An excellent standard definition of the traditional type of middle-class Frenchman states simply: '*Bourgeois* is he who has reserves.' Reserves, that is, of linen, wine and, usually, real estate, with glass and silver, antiques and pictures on display, hidden gold coin, cash and safe securities at the bank. But reserves also of moral strength and mutual support in what the French call *la grande famille*, family relations extending, that is to say, to every surviving branch and generation. The cohesive force of the well-to-do French farming and urban middle-class families is proverbial, and justly so, both for the stability it has brought to French society, and for the often excessively harsh demands it has made on freedom of choice in marriage and career. The part it played in the lives of dutiful daughters and *fils de famille* before and between the world wars is meticulously recorded in the family portraits of such twentieth-century novelists and memorialists as Jacques de Lacretelle, François Mauriac and Simone de Beauvoir. The latter's autobiography, *Mémoires d'une jeune fille rangée,* contains some particularly vivid descriptions of the décor, rites and dramas of the well-provided but thrifty, the *bon-vivant* but industrious and morally demanding households of the French upper middle class, as she remembers them especially from those long summer holidays spent in the country that are still a characteristic and strongly formative part of many a French child's upbringing, even in less palmy times, and in more modest social circles than she herself recalls. Thus the kitchen of her uncle's house in the south-western province of Limousin:

> The cast-iron cooking range threw out sparks and flames. The brasses shone: there were copper pots of all sizes, caldrons, skimming ladles, preserving pans, and warming pans; I used to love the gaiety of the glazed dishes with their paint-box colours, the variety of bowls, cups, glasses, basins, porringers, hors d'œuvre dishes, pots, jugs, and pitchers. What quantities of cooking pots, frying pans, stock pots, stewpans, *bains marie,* cassolettes, soup tureens, meat dishes, saucepans, enamel mugs, colanders, graters, choppers, mills, mincers, moulds and mortars – in cast-iron, earthenware, stoneware, porcelain, aluminium, and tin! . . . [In] the dairy . . . stood great vats and pans of varnished wood and glazed earthenware, barrel-churns made of polished elm, great blocks of pattern-patted butter, piles of smooth-skinned cheeses under sheets of white muslin. . . . I liked to visit the fruit loft, where apples and pears would be ripening on wicker trays, and the cellar, with its barrels, bottles, hams, huge sausages, ropes of onions, and swags of dried mushrooms.

Holidays for Mlle de Beauvoir usually brought a typical family drama: it becomes 'absolutely essential', say, for some girl to 'forget her cousin ... whose parents were against the marriage, and besides ... belonged to a very rich, dissipated and vulgar set which would not do at all'. But chiefly they brought

> never-ending picnics, tea-parties, and dances, festivities in the nearby country town. ... Singing, parlour games, charades ... and domestic chores. Flowers were picked and arranged in vases, and everybody took a hand with the cooking. Lili, Zaza, and Bébelle would make cakes, buns, shortbread, and brioches for afternoon tea; they helped their mother and grandmother to bottle tons of fruit and vegetables; there were always peas to be shelled, French beans to be strung, nuts to be cracked and plums to be stoned. The provision of food-stocks became a harassing and lengthy business.[1]

The comparatively late survival in France of a large farming population provides most French families with relatives in the country, and, apart from the really poor, summer visits to a familiar village. The 'extended' family (which, in the hard times of invasion and foreign occupation between 1940 and 1944, eased the strain of surviving for thousands of city-dwelling French families, by providing a village-based refuge, or source of unrationed provisions[2]) remains strong in post-war France, though its authority impinges less than it used to on the lives of the young. The *cadres* of today travel lighter than their parents in this as in many other respects. They tend to put efficiency and progress above the old *bourgeois* standards of continuity and security, though they seek to reconcile all four values where possible, since they are rarely radicals of either the revolutionary or the reactionary variety, but believe, after Alexander Pope (and unlike most of their elders, of the highly politicised 1930s) that only fools contest for *forms* of government: 'What e'er is best administered is best.' Their watchwords are *rationalité, performance, rentabilité* (i.e. profitability), *efficacité* (efficiency), *dynamisme, mutation.* Personal ambition is as highly rated as before, perhaps more so than in the settled sectors and regions of old

France, though the French *bourgeoisie* has, from the beginning of its rise to power, continuously thriven on the eagerness of its families to send their sons after the prizes of literary, scientific and medical prowess, and of parliamentary or forensic oratory, and on the pride they have drawn from high public service in one or other of the *Grands Corps de l'État*: Treasury, Council of State, Foreign Office or the Corps of Prefects.[3] Nowadays, exacting and responsible salaried work outside the civil and the armed services is also highly respected.

Néo-bourgeois pleasures include the traditional French ones of table, town and country: the luncheon prolonged by talk rather than gluttony, the *apéritif* hour, and dining in or out, at every level of price and refinement, though normally at higher ones than corresponding social strata in Britain or America; *la chasse*, comprising family expeditions that may involve no more than a gun-dog and a small car, and house-parties of forty or fifty guns perhaps, in good shooting country like La Sologne, which may hope to have the Prefect at the head of the list of guests. Wives and children continue to spend long holidays, and husbands shorter ones, at farms and country houses where the same *petite bande* of brothers, sisters, cousins and friends meet year after year till they in their turn become parents, aunts, uncles and grandparents. Traditionally the children must be 'restored' with large meals, long walks, tennis, table-tennis, swimming, riding or sailing, 'decontracted' by means of well-planned excursions, highly organised picnics, impromptu parties and theatricals; but they are left alone also, to idle (often most profitably) with books and friends and to pore (or dream) over holiday tasks (which are more or less severe according to the tensely awaited June–July examination results).

Where a *cadre* is also an *héritier* (commonly the case in higher income brackets), then property and antiques will continue to be acquired. But newer trends are for mechanisation in the kitchen and laundry (now that the reservoir of cheap, loyal and skilled domestic labour is drying up in even French villages); for holidays touring Spain, Sweden, Scotland, Greece, Morocco, far from the old family home; for ski-ing, sailing, swimming and sun-basking in company that is much more mixed than in previous generations;[4] and for a 'secondary residence', a converted weekend and holiday cottage in Ile-de-France or Bourbonnais, a mountain chalet in Savoy, a seaside villa on the Atlantic or the Mediterranean coasts.[5] A recent spate of promoter's rhetoric on behalf of certain new 'multi-sport' country clubs near Paris seeks to seduce 'doctors, industrialists and upper *cadres*' even further from the twin cults of property and propriety to which, it suggests, their class still enslaves them. The shareholder or subscribing member of such a club will enjoy 'a sort of secondary residence he can share with his friends': 'bucolic charm', but no repair bills, or cooking or making beds for visitors; Sunday lunch, without Sunday best, or the carving to do; company of his own age, free from the 'accepted' class rules for behaviour and the keeping-up of appearances; above all, the company of his own children, 'getting to know' them in a relaxed atmosphere (which is nevertheless doing them good) amid the shared delights (and sweet disciplines) of active sport and *le fair-play*. Beneath the meretricious appeals to fresh varieties of conventional middle-class snobbery and status-seeking, such emphasis on the *petite famille*, on travelling light, on informality, on spontaneity, on physical fitness, the open air and the playing-field (in reaction against an excessively accumulative and hierarchical way of life, and a traditionally over-drilled and over-bookish education) reflects a real change of direction in France towards some of the new social norms and values already predominant in North America and, broadly speaking, the rest of Northern Europe. The process also seems to be bringing the French *bourgeoisie*, its younger salary-earning categories at least, nearer to some of the characteristic attitudes of working-class life. The *néo-bourgeois* tend to be less stiff and distant towards each other, to show more spontaneous affection than was customary in the old *bourgeoisie*. They are more neighbourly, less wary and formal with strangers. They have learned to take more pleasure in passing good fortune (as the poor have always had to do), and rather less pride in close-fisted calculating for the long term. Most younger middle-class French men and women share at least some of the unpretentious tastes of their less privileged compatriots, in clothes, entertaining, holidays, magazines, books, records, films and television programmes. Middle-class women are becoming less pampered and protected; and increasing numbers of them go out to work, as working-class women have had to do for many generations.

THE WORKING CLASS

There are approximately fourteen million employees in French mines, factories, offices and shops, comprising just over 70 per cent of the total working population. Of course, no hard-and-fast line divides the French working and middle classes. Where they meet, at the level of, say, local government clerk and the proprietor of a small garage, skilled craftsman and small shopkeeper, their respective styles of living are not so very different, and individuals are constantly moving across an indefinite boundary from one class to the other.

French industry and commerce are to a considerable extent manned, as they are owned and managed, by an urban population which is still comparatively close to its rural origins. Because of the comparatively late development of large-scale industry in France, a high proportion of the French working class is only one or two generations removed from the soil. True, there are proletarian strongholds where the town-dwelling tradition is much older: the silk-making district of Croix-Rousse in Lyons, for instance, and Belleville, in the East End of Paris. 'In Belleville,' wrote Eugène Dabit, a pre-war novelist of working-class life, 'ties of any sort with a village are rare . . . all roots are Parisian, memories go back to the Commune of 1871.'[6] But this was Belleville of the 1930s. Since that date, rearmament for the Second World War, the convulsions of defeat, invasion and liberation, and, above all, the unprecedented speed and scale of industrialisation since 1945, have all combined to sweep hundreds of thousands of country people into the factories and tenement-houses of Marseille, Grenoble, Toulouse, Dijon, Orléans, Bordeaux, Le Mans, Rennes – and Paris itself, though rural recruits for industry usually work a stage in their local town or provincial capital before migrating to the metropolis.[7]

A novel by Roger Vailland, *325,000 francs*, published in 1955, gives a vivid picture of modern life, leisure and piecework in one such small industrial town in the Jura which specialises in the mass production of cheap plastics, in a region formerly known best for its fine watchmaking and other precision work. Bernard Busard, the hero, who has persuaded a friend to share a three-man shift with him, day and night, for eight months, in order to earn enough to set up on his own as a café proprietor, muses as the machine in front of him spews out its production of plastic toys, and puts his personal experience in the wider historical, moral and ideological context of the French working class:

> On one side, the ejection mechanism and the electronic eye, on the other Bernard Busard, his big, lean body, his racing cyclist's muscles, his brain, his love for Marie-Jeanne Lemercier; of the two, Bernard Busard was the less valuable article.
>
> He was worth a bit more than an injection piston and its servo-motor, since the manual press had been replaced by a semi-automatic one. But he wasn't worth the price of a semi-automatic press and a fully automatic one added together. His price was somewhere between these two precise limits. If the price of fully automatic presses should come down, down below *his* price. . . . Nine workers out of ten won't have a job . . . and the tenth will accept a lower wage. . . . Chatelard would tell him that he had just described one of the contradictions of the system, that the workers had a solution, and only one: change the system. But when?
>
> He raised the press, pulled, lowered it. . . .
>
> He remembered the arguments between his father and Chatelard.
>
> 'You missed the bus in '36,' old Busard would say. 'And you missed it again in '44.'
>
> 'The necessary conditions were not present,' Chatelard would reply. 'If we'd seized power, we would have been beaten and the working-class movement would have been wiped out for years to come, like after the Commune.'
>
> The memory of that interminable discussion made him sick with irritation.
>
> He raised the press, pulled, lowered it. . . .

Busard will have nothing to do with the life his father had led or with Chatelard's. He won't kid himself that he's a free man by making articles that are no longer in fashion at a loss, or by going out for a bit of fishing, while the womenfolk polish their stint of spectacle frames; the age of the craftsman is over and done with. But he won't sacrifice the present, which is all he has, for a revolution which is for ever being put off. He has found his solution to the problem, the only one for him.

'Me, I'm getting out of here,' he said out loud.[8]

Busard's ambition for a little business of his own expresses an independent and property-loving disposition that is characteristic of the French people. But the times are against him. The modern escape route from proletarian status passes through the increasingly important élite technician grade, into the rising *néo-bourgeoisie* of engineers and *cadres,* rather than through savings, into the shrinking class of small shopkeepers. By acquiring special technical skills and qualifications, some French workers and their families succeed in climbing to a higher level of society.[9] A politically militant minority also learns to look outwards, across national frontiers, to world-wide proletarian solidarity. Both processes are slow, however, and there is frustration and xenophobia in contemporary Belleville, though no more so than in industrial Britain or America.

The gap between the earnings of skilled and unskilled workers (*ouvriers professionnels* – O.P.; *ouvriers spécialisés* – O.S.) is particularly wide in France. And high above the most skilled technician or experienced foreman, a salaried executive earns on the average seven or eight times more than a female workhand, while paying less personal income tax than his British counterpart.[10] Extremes at both ends of the range are, of course, much wider apart still, and regional disparities are also particularly large in France.

Spiritual rewards are harder to measure than material ones. On the credit side of French working-class life there is family feeling without undue subordination or over-demanding discipline; morals without cant; the conscious exercise of old skills, at work, at home, in the kitchen-garden, on the cycle-track and bowling-pitch;[11] the growing use of many new utilities, from launderettes to supermarkets; comradeship, which not only sustains the rather uneven activity of French trade unions ('militancy' and 'solidarity' being strongest among the skilled men, and massively effective only in times of sharp political crisis or exceptional financial distress), but also brings warmth to other scenes of French working-class life: the shopping-street and market, the café-restaurant, the football ground, the table-tennis and cycling club, the camp site, the summer beach and riverside lido. There is a guaranteed minimum wage adjusted approximately to changes in the cost of living.[12] There is a general contributory scheme of social security giving old-age pensions, and maternity, sickness and death benefits, and covering approximately three-quarters of medical expenses. There are good family allowances,[13] and a statutory paid annual holiday of four weeks. For the skilled workman and his children, there is a slow but continuously wider access to greater leisure, better education, broader horizons, larger means to the good life.

On the other hand, recent improvements in purchasing power have favoured the industrial worker less than the white-collar employee, and the latter less favourably than the technician, engineer and *cadre*. Unchecked, such disparities widen the gap between the beneficiaries and the victims of France's mid-century 'economic miracle'. Marxists were quick to denounce, and to exaggerate, an economic fact of the 1960s, 'the relative pauperisation of the working class', which was certainly one good reason for much proletarian unrest, and a brief but massively effective general strike in May 1968.

Among the enduring hardships of French working-class life must also be reckoned the widespread inadequacy of housing in France. The Government's housing programme (though spectacular and massive) has not kept pace with the decay of old buildings, the movement of population into urban areas from the countryside (and from abroad), and the steep rise in population.[14] Some workers find even subsidised rents for government-built H.L.M. (*habitations à loyer modéré,* flats to let at a moderate rent) too high.

Though the working class is, generally speaking, housed less well in France than in Britain, more of its wages is spent on food; more wisely too, to judge by the choice of ingredients, the standards of cooking, the amount and quality of good bread, fresh vegetables, cheese, meat and sausages that the French worker looks for at his canteen (or in his lunch-pail), at his local or his holiday restaurants, at his home table. It is true that the French slums, together with rural Normandy and Brittany, hold the grimmer world record for alcoholism, based on widespread regular over-drinking, from childhood on, not on the exceptional bout of drunkenness, which is comparatively rare.

The politics of class solidarity, militant protest and, periodically, open revolt have, for more than a century, provided a nobler cure than *le pinard*,[15] for what Georges Navel, fitter, navvy, farm labourer and novelist, called in 1945 'la tristesse ouvrière', a kind of pervasive depression induced by the claustrophobia, monotony, fatigue and insecurity of factory labour, and by a continuing nostalgia for country ways and a plot of one's own that Navel perhaps feels more keenly about than most of his workmates, but which is probably more genuine and widespread in France than in nations more thoroughly urbanised, such as England:

> A peasant, even in a bad year, can feel his strength when he looks at his field. His field, his house belong to him. If he is a tenant, he has an agreement in his pocket, he is assured of the means of production. He may lack money, but not what he needs to stay alive.
>
> The worker, on the other hand, as soon as he has to look for work, faces catastrophe. If he cannot find a job quite quickly, he soon comes to the end of his savings. . . .
>
> There is a sadness in working-class life that can only be cured by playing one's full part in political action.[16]

France is not the only country where an industrial working class, native-born and immigrant, is cut off from the social amenities and economic privileges attached to property and the luck of birth or patronage. None of the Western democracies is classless, and the parliamentary institutions and social legislation of the French Republic are in many ways advanced and liberal. Yet the class war in twentieth-century France, though never as bloody as in Germany, Spain and Russia, has been a bitter one. National temperament may partly account for this. The history of France certainly can: the longest and most exciting revolutionary tradition in Europe (and correspondingly deep-rooted and recurrent movements of counter-revolution); a persuasively articulate intelligentsia reared on ideological abstractions and historical parallels; misfortune in war, foreign invasions and occupations, and consequent civil strife of both the shooting and the shouting kinds; constitutional instability; above, or rather beneath all, the fact that the wage-earning, mass-producing and city-dwelling industrial proletariat has until very recently remained a comparatively small and isolated class, in a country dominated by the economics and politics of small towns, self-employed businessmen, non-earning *rentiers* and a large and geographically widespread class of agricultural smallholders. Nor does the ascendency of *bourgeois* and rural France belong merely to the past. There are, it is true, many fewer peasant-proprietors every year. Every year more of those who do stay on the land become involved in the habits of production and consumption, and the ideological climate, of industrial society. Yet France is still Western Europe's largest food producer. Compared with Western Germany, Holland, Great Britain and the United States, its farming community constitutes a high percentage of the national labour force.[17] The number of self-employed persons of every occupation also remains high in France. Moreover, in France, as elsewhere, the latest varieties of industrialisation have created a swelling *néo-bourgeoisie* of managers, engineers, technicians and other white-collar employees which tends to reinforce the already formidable alliance of town and country property-owners and professional men, an alliance which is disposed by upbringing and self-interest to distrust and resist the proletarian minority, and to drive it into correspondingly rigid and mistrustful positions of defensive class warfare.

The French cannot be simply divided into two social categories, the middle class and the working class. Broadly defined, and added to a dwindling though still large farming community, these two classes do constitute the greater part of the nation, and they alone are growing. But other categories besides these two large ones still have a part in the modern French way of life, despite shrinking numbers.

The character of present-day France continues, in particular, to owe much to the distinctive and enduring influence of such formerly dominant types as the nobleman, the craftsman and the peasant.

THE ARISTOCRACY

The turbulent history of France from the sixteenth to the nineteenth centuries left behind it a complicated class of aristocratic families with various origins: the ancient feudal landowning and military caste, *la noblesse d'épée*; the *noblesse de robe*, or 'robed' civil and legal aristocracy, created by royal favour and the purchase of heritable offices of state and magistracy; the new imperial nobility founded by Napoleon Bonaparte at the beginning of the nineteenth century; and the peers created by Louis-Philippe, after this so-called 'Citizen-King', from the Orleanist, cadet branch of the French royal family, had mounted the throne in 1830. The French Revolution made all men equal before the law, but it took nearly another hundred years before the Republic was made secure against the pretensions of aristocratic dynasties old and new to govern as a class, or, at the least, to occupy an exalted position in the hierarchies of society, Church and State, alongside, and frequently intermarried with, the great *bourgeois* dynasties.[18]

Republicanism, triumphant after 1870, ensured that the allied ruling classes of yesterday, who, in their long struggle against the heirs of the French Revolution, had developed a doubly defensive philosophy of political conservatism and Catholic orthodoxy, should be very largely debarred from promotion in the civil administration of the country. Some aristocratic families were content to remain on their lands, especially in strongly Catholic provinces where they often continued to hold positions of influence and patronage. The *Office Central de Landernau* in Brittany, for instance, inspired by the paternalistic social Catholicism of Albert, Comte de Mun and René-Charles-Humbert, Marquis de La Tour du Pin Chambly de La Charce, and under the local leadership of the Comte de Guébriant, kept benevolent but tight control of the peasantry through the distribution of seed, tools and other supplies, and the marketing of farm produce.[19] Other old families did well in business. A few individual noblemen distinguished themselves in politics, e.g. Albert de Broglie (1821–1901), Albert de Mun (1841–1914), Colonel de La Rocque (1886–1946), Emmanuel d'Astier de La Vigerie (1900–69); in literature, e.g. Antoine de Saint-Exupéry (1900–44); in science, e.g. Maurice de Broglie (1875–1960) and Louis de Broglie (b. 1892). The diplomatic corps continued to have a fair sprinkling of the nobility and the gentry. But it was chiefly in the Army, and the vast overseas empire it was busy winning for the Republic between 1881 and 1926, that French aristocrats were now able to find a regular occupation congenial to their taste for glory, their love of command, their proverbial prowess and their tradition of public service. Not that they could pretend to a monopoly of command in the armed forces of the modern Republic. Marshal Lyautey, Generals Castelnau, Franchet d'Esperey, Leclerc de Hauteclocque, de Lattre de Tassigny, Castres, were born into an aristocratic officer class. Marshals Joffre, Pétain, Foch and Juin were not. General Charles de Gaulle was descended, through the male line, from a family of the minor 'parliamentary' (i.e. magisterial) aristocracy:

> The de Gaulles were not in any way *bourgeois* in the sense understood by Flaubert or indeed Marx. With a little *noblesse de robe* and *bourgeoisie d'épée* in their family tree, they lived by the pen, as secretaries, civil servants, *savants* and antiquaries. . . . Decent and threadbare intellectuals, with an uncle in the regiment of cuirassiers and a cousin in the priesthood. People who knew their grammar, their Latin and their Greek, who went to mass and served the state without asking for much in return, only regretting, in a dignified way, that they had to give of their talents and their virtues in the service of the Republic, rather than in duty to the heir of 'the forty kings who, in a thousand years, made France'.[20]

This recent family portrait reveals a long-held view of class distinction in France, contrasting material possessions (which are considered essential, and sufficient, for middle-class status) with the recognised obligations and attributes of an aristocratic tradition (however modest and attenuated): service to the Army, the Church, the State and, formerly, the Crown, developing and using such personal qualities as dignity, self-denial, reticence and refinement. Such an exemplary pattern of the gentlemanly (as opposed to the *bourgeois*) way of life no

11. Infantrymen, 1914

12. De Gaulle at Saint-Lô, 1945

9. Conversation at Deauville racecourse, about 1900

10. Jaurès in 1913

individuality and a love of independence that have become part of the fabric of French civilisation.

SHOPKEEPERS

Through the skilled crafts of baker, pastry-cook and *restaurateur,* the French *artisanat* merges into the category of *limonadier,*[22] café proprietor and small shopkeeper, which has similar standards, notably the personal touch and a reputation (with a small but regular clientele) for friendly and honest dealings and a high quality of goods and service. It breeds a similar spirit of egalitarian independence. It is also in these circles that one of the most vigorous of social traditions in France may be best seen – an equal, working partnership between husband and wife.

Generally speaking, the small shopkeepers, like the master-craftsmen of France, are now on the defensive, their *petit-bourgeois* living-standards threatened by the universal, attacking, modern forces of concentrated capitalism and mass production. Despite the brief, spirited, counter-attack of Pierre Poujade's 'Union for the Defence of Tradesmen and Artisans' ('the backbone of the country'), founded in 1953, only three occupational categories lost a bigger proportion of their men during the next decade, namely fishing-fleet skippers, agricultural smallholders and farm labourers.[23]

FARMERS

French farmers cultivate the most extensive and variegated farmland in Europe. 'Tillage and pasturage, these are the two breasts of France, her true mines and treasures.'[24] So it has been said since the beginning of the seventeenth century. The area of pasture in France grew faster than arable land, doubling its acreage between 1892 and 1938, and standing in 1969 at about thirty-four million acres of grassland to forty-two million of arable (approximately 25 per cent and 31 per cent of French territory respectively). Nearly a quarter of the country is forest (as against only a fifteenth of the United Kingdom). Most of this is in upland areas, and in the Landes (pine forests on the coast of Aquitaine), but there are many small plantations of privately owned fruit-trees and nut-trees doubt flatters reality, and is almost as unfair by implication as Molière's famous caricature of the *Bourgeois Gentilhomme* aping his betters in the age of Louis XIV. But it reflects the best of what modern France owes to its *noblesse de robe*.

Among the distinctive traits that the *noblesse d'épée* evolved for their historic roles of warrior, commander, judge, squire and courtier, and which, through continuous processes of emulation and infiltration, have been acquired in a measure by today's French élites of common birth, are daring and panache, quick contempt, prickly pride, tact, finesse, fine manners, formality, the will to excel, excitability in action, a fluent and cool tongue, traits which for many foreigners serve to identify the essential France.

CRAFTSMEN

The class of 'master-artisans' was legally defined in 1925 as 'workpeople of either sex exercising a handicraft, on condition that they do the work themselves, or with the help of their spouse, members of their family, or companions or apprentices, and that they do it without being under the orders of an employer'. Subsequent modifications of this definition, to include the use of machines and electrical motive power, to specify that the artisan is his own principal salesman, and to limit the number of 'companions' and apprentices working under him to a maximum of ten people, have not touched the three essential features of the artisan's status: manual skill, apprenticeship training and self-employed independence. All three are highly valued in France, and special measures have been taken in the present century to protect them against the mounting competition of salaried mass production. Apart from the large numbers of Frenchmen and women still involved,[21] apart from what they produce, and the reputation of French (and especially of Parisian) cabinet-makers, jewellers, furriers, dressmakers, leather-workers and of many other traditional crafts practised in every province of the country, *l'artisanat* remains in the view of many, even of those who recognise the inevitability and the advantages of large-scale, mechanised and impersonal production and distribution, a class worth preserving because it stands for and helps to keep alive a sense of quality, a striving for excellence, a respect for

13. Leaders of the Popular Front at the *Mur des Fédérés*, 1936, commemorating *Communard* prisoners executed in 1871

14. President de Gaulle and Premier Khruschev, 1960

15. A debate in the Chamber of Deputies of the Third Republic

16. Student demonstration, Paris, 1968

in the vicinity of villages, and along roadsides. The great variety of French regional climates and soils makes for a range of products that is 'probably greater than in any other European country', from 'meadow grass, potatoes, sugar-beet, fodder crops and wheat' to 'maize, olives, vines, peaches, citrus fruits and tobacco', also rice and hops.[25]

Since the beginning of the present century the pattern of settlement, land tenure, labour, production and markets has become ever more complex, as scientific, capitalist and co-operative methods of growing, processing and selling have pushed some areas into large-scale and specialised agriculture, while others are left unchanged, at the stage of mixed farming (polyculture) for subsistence or the local market, on family-run smallholdings, very often split up into a dozen or more tiny, scattered plots and strips which are time-wasting to work and impossible to cultivate efficiently with modern machinery.[26]

Napoleon's Code of Civil Law, sometimes called 'the machine for chopping up the land', usually gets the blame for the excessive number of smallholdings in France, since it is supposed to have introduced the equal division of heritable property among all the children of a deceased landowner (*le morcellement*). But, as Professor Gordon Wright points out, 'the abolition of primogeniture affected no one but the aristocracy. For commoners, equal inheritance had been customary in most parts of France long before Napoleon's time – and so had peasant devices for evading that principle' (e.g. arranged marriages between neighbouring families, and one brother buying out the others' shares). The subdivision of holdings into small scattered plots in such a way as to give each heir an equal portion of the different qualities and kinds of land available (*le parcellement*) stems from traditional polyculture.[27]

Farmers who employ no paid labour still constitute the largest category; there are approximately four times as many *exploitants* (that is, self-employed farmers and their families) as there are agricultural wage-earners.[28]

That this heterogeneous pattern of agriculture has created a rich diversity of human types is generally a matter of conviction and some pride among Frenchmen. Thus Jean Giono, the Provençal novelist:

> The natural laws which determine the shape, colour and temperament of a region, also determine the temperament of its inhabitants. . . . The master of an apple orchard could not be master of an almond grove. Vast horizons create one kind of human soul; deep valleys and narrow dales create another.
>
> The kind of happiness sought by the farmer settled on the loamy soil of a river bank is very different from what satisfies the farmer on the stony high ground, amidst his lavender bushes. The moods of wind and rain, when you've been exposed to them for a lifetime, lend a peculiar shape to the moods of this kind of life.[29]

In Giono's own, dour, empty, High Provence 'there is no such thing as a village community. There are individuals, each living by himself.'[30] By contrast, on the 'Generous Earth' of the Dordogne valley, in south-western France, nature's bounty is sociably harvested and expansively shared:

> On reaching the vineyard, which was on the lowest slope of the hillside, Foussac halted his oxen at the bottom, so that all the produce would be carried downhill, and proceeded to unload while we took baskets and set to work cutting the grapes with secateurs or sharp knives, for the bunches do not break off readily, unless they are very ripe. The fully able-bodied of us, so to speak, each took a row. The old men and children shared a row between two, while the smallest sampled the grapes and found them good enough to eat! When anyone had a basket full – and that does not take long – he called for another. This was the little ones' duty to supply, while Foussac came, carried the glowing contents of the full baskets down to the bottom and emptied them into the barrels that he had brought in the cart. There was so much chatter and laughter all the time that one had to shout for an empty basket in order to be heard. The work was not done in a hurry nor on the contrary was time wasted.
>
> On reaching Foussac's farm, the *comportes,* loaded with grapes, were dumped on the ground. We mounted the stone steps, carrying our baskets, which we had filled

with apples, pears, figs, melons and a few late peaches, collected from odd trees dotted about in or near the edge of the vineyard. . . .

The fruit that we brought was put on great dishes to keep company with half a dozen bottles of red wine, already there, and Madame Foussac proceeded to ladle soup out of a huge tureen. In it were, as usual, large pieces of bread, pumpkin, onions, some white haricots, herbs and some garlic and I cannot say what else. On to the table came a large home-cured ham and with it potatoes baked in their jackets, followed by salad of chicory and sliced onion with a dressing of walnut oil and red wine vinegar. Finally there arrived a number of small, round, flat cheeses, made of goat's milk and . . . the fruit. Everything was, of course, the produce of the holding – plain, fresh, good.[31]

The extreme diversity of livelihood and life-styles in the French farming community has not deterred either foreign or domestic observers from attributing two well-defined sets of characteristic traits to the 'peasantry' as a whole: thrift, vigour, tenacity, prudence, independence, on the one hand; and avarice, coarseness, obstinacy, backwardness and materialism on the other. In print at least, the good set seems still to be the dominant one, even as the numbers of this once preponderant French class decline (from over eight million in 1906 to seven in 1936 and three in 1968), and the contrasts between country ways and town ways everywhere begin to fade. Thus: 'The eyes of the village child reflect what there is of gravity and tenacity in our race';[32] 'the peasant class still constitutes the strongest and most stable element of the population';[33] 'Agriculture, when it is not just a matter of dull routine, civilises. Daily in touch with plants and animals, peasants learn that you can change nature's ways, but not without long and careful toil. . . . For proper balance, a people needs the good influence of a numerous peasantry';[34] 'The family farm is a school of will-power, energy, endurance and patience . . . it ensures, better than anything else, the continuity of nations and of societies. . . . Its value from the social, national and human points of view is greater than its economic value.'[35]

Gordon Wright opens his fine study of *Rural Revolution in France* by quoting the still confident assertion of Professor Cobban in 1949 that 'In the last resort, and at bottom, France is a Peasants' Republic,' going on to give the best contemporary assessment of what this means, in terms of an enduring 'peasantist' dogma in the changing France of the twentieth century:

> Few Western nations cling so strongly to their agrarian origins, or extol the rural virtues with such ritualistic fervour. . . . No other industrialised nation has kept so large a proportion of its total population on the soil; nowhere else do so many city-dwellers regard their peasant ancestry as a mark of distinction.
>
> Perhaps this 'peasantist' dogma should be classed as an item of political folklore; but, even so, its shaping influence on French political and social attitudes remains quite genuine. A nation that continues to think of itself as peasant, and that exalts what it believes to be the rural virtues, is likely to confront some special problems of adjustment in the industrial age.[36]

What Professor Wright calls 'folklore' – 'the belief that peasant life possesses unique moral qualities, and that the strength of any society comes from its broad small-peasant base'[37] – is often more bluntly described today as studied political humbug: the big landowners, it is said, are prompted to lay claim to kinship with the smallholders in an allegedly united family of good old French countryfolk, because the survival of a peasant class gives them a lever with which to prise open state coffers for their own advantage – a foolproof lever because, even with government protection, the independent peasant farmers cannot put up serious competition to the big farmers' efficient style and scale of food production; and a powerful one, because the peasantry is spread widely over most of the country's political constituencies and because its reputation as the traditional custodian of old-fashioned French virtues and vigour commands a broad area of ready-made sympathy.[38]

Whether observed as folklore or condemned as a piece of cynicism, the 'myth' of French peasant unity certainly ignores many factors: the long-standing differences between hired labour, tenant-farmers, sharecroppers (*métayers*) and owner-occupiers, between a minority of large landowners and a majority of small peasant-proprietors, between the economy and customs of 'open-field' and *bocage*,[39] between the archaic and declining agriculture of most of the south (where nearly half the *exploitants* left on the land are over fifty-five years old)[40] and the prosperous north, between remote or closed village communities, and semi-urbanised wine-growing or market-gardening districts near big cities, and between predominantly clerical or conservative areas and predominantly anti-clerical or 'red' ones. The concept also ignores recent changes: group farming, processing and marketing; consolidation of smallholdings and scattered plots to make viable farms (*remembrement*); improved research and advisory services, educational opportunities and credit facilities (to encourage more scientific and mechanised farming). Great pressure to innovate has been put on the central authorities by the technocratically-minded and sometimes angry young leaders of opinion in the middle range of farmers, strongly supported and guided by radical Catholic organisations like the *Jeunesse agricole chrétienne* (J.A.C.). These young farmers are determined to improve their standard of living against the double threat of what they call *clochardisation* (being reduced to beggary on farms too tiny to survive in today's economic climate) and *salarisation* (being reduced to the status of a capitalist's or banker's hired hand at the production lines of industry or industrial farming).[41]

Other changes in the French countryside spring from improved communications and other independent features of economic change. Thus market towns, or a nearby city, are replacing villages as commercial, service and social centres, emptying large tracts of country of all but those who actually work the land, or who are travelling through to deliver goods, solicit custom, collect and return workers and schoolchildren, or taking time off, *procul negotiis*, in a farmstead converted to weekend or summer cottage. On the other hand, growing knowledge of a world beyond village horizons comes to the men and women who do stay on the farms (and who are no longer part of a complete, fully structured, rural community) through contact with weekenders and holidaymakers, through military service, through television programmes of news and current affairs, through mass advertising. Thus the tastes and desires of townspeople and country people mix and are evened out. Before the Second World War, French peasants stubbornly saved gold and incurred heavy debts so as to buy land, sooner than spend money on improving the techniques of farming. The typical young farmer today is less interested in owning land at any price, more so in raising productivity so as to improve his standard of living. Since fertilisers, tractors and other machinery (including kitchen aids) have come on to the market, he is more than likely to get into debt through hire-purchase commitments for such items as these, the prices of which have tended to rise faster than his own profits. A fascinating account of one chain of cause and effect in the French countryside is given by Professor Laurence Wylie:

> On the farms in Chanzeaux the effects of using bottled gas are much deeper than simply increased comfort. Chanzeaux is in the *bocage* country, where each field is surrounded by a thick hedge of bushes and trees which for centuries have been harvested about every ten years for the wood. Curiously enough, bottled gas has made the hedges all but obsolete. The farmer used to spend a substantial amount of his time in the winter sawing wood and making bundles of faggots, for the family depended completely on wood for fuel. Now on many farms piles of faggots and logs are accumulating, for there is less and less need for firewood. . . . Therefore the most immediate practical purpose the hedges now fill is to fence in the livestock, but even this they do inefficiently since they not only take the nourishment from the fields but make it impossible to alter the size and shape of the holdings. So farmers are beginning to uproot the hedges, these relics of the past, and replace them with wire fences. When the size and shape of fields may be altered easily, it will become possible to attack the problem of regrouping the widely dispersed landholdings of Chanzeaux's farms, and with redistribution, the farms of Chanzeaux could be worked more efficiently with tractors. So the little

matter of cooking on a bottled gas range instead of with wood has important but unsuspected consequences.[42]

Such village scenes as this paint the detail of that wide, inter-locking composition of economic forces which are reshaping the society of mid-twentieth-century France.

3 The Economy

AGRICULTURAL PRODUCTION

ALTHOUGH the French agricultural labour force is shrinking rapidly (43 per cent of the working population in 1906, 37 per cent in 1936 and 15 per cent in 1968), this sector of employment is still proportionately larger in France than in Western Germany (10 per cent), Holland (8 per cent), the United States (5 per cent) and the United Kingdom (3 per cent).[1]

The nineteenth century, when the scale of British farming was already being drastically reduced by a free-trade policy leading to massive imports of food from the great new farmlands of the Americas and Australia, was for France a time when (except for an interlude of free trade during the 1860s) roughly speaking opposite policies led to an increase not only in the number of farms (which reached an all-time peak of nearly six million around 1890), but also in the acreage cultivated by a land-hungry peasantry, which had both fewer opportunities and less need to emigrate to factories at home and farms overseas. In a country so fertile and so extensively farmed, shielded by high tariff walls and with a comparatively sparse and stable population, virtual self-sufficiency was readily attained without increasing productivity. As a result, methods of farming and marketing improved only slowly, and when the world-wide depression and collapse of farm prices after 1929 led to the dumping of surplus produce from the more efficient farms of Eastern Europe and the New World, the French tariff system broke down and French agriculture entered a period of total stagnation: the number of tractors in use rose by less than 9,000 between 1929 and 1938, and the consumption of fertilisers actually declined.[2] After the Second World War, however, productivity was, on the contrary, raised dramatically, on the larger farms at least, with a fourfold increase in the tonnage of fertilisers and a thirtyfold increase in the number of tractors. By 1964, the production of wheat and vegetables was double what it had been in 1939, the maize crop was trebled, the barley harvest four times as big. France is the largest wheat grower in Western Europe (and the sixth largest in the world), producing nearly half the total crop of the Common Market countries (excluding Great Britain), and more than half of their barley (about the same amount as Britain). It makes just under a quarter of the world's wine (slightly less than Italy). Animal farming, including a famous breed of beef cattle, *le charolais,* and a very wide variety of good cheeses, accounts for 65 per cent of agricultural receipts.[3] Finding domestic and foreign markets for the abundance produced by the efficient sector of French agriculture, and phasing out thousands of small, inefficient family farms, with the least possible human distress and social disturbance, have become major preoccupations of French Ministers of Agriculture. They have not been able to prevent resentment boiling over into violence in some parts of the south and west, far from the main markets, and without adequate canning and food-processing industries, which suffer from too many middlemen, falling revenue and the belief that they are being treated by officials as second-class citizens.

Common Market partners on the Continent take about half the food that France sells abroad, but also compete strongly against the French in certain specialised fields of food production. The French farmers' next best customer is Britain.

INDUSTRIAL PRODUCTION

The pattern of industrial development in twentieth-century France is similar to that of agriculture: pre-war fragmentation and stagnation, post-war concentration into larger production units, and record growth.

On a world-wide stage busy since 1950 with 'economic miracles', the performance of French industry has been less spectacularly successful than the Japanese and the German, but more dynamic than the British. It is remarkable chiefly for having compressed into the last twenty years a degree of growth and structural change that it took the leading pre-war industrial nations more like half a century to accomplish, and, secondly, for what it owes to a new climate of confidence and innovation, fostered and exploited by a powerful new state planning agency, *Le Commissariat Général du Plan*, which was created in January 1946 with the object of producing a 'route map' of the nation's economic future based on objective information and round-table discussions between the representatives of all interested groups. This has worked well, enabling French public and private enterprises alike to plan ahead, for the middle and for the long term, within a coherent but flexible national programme of research and development.

French industry reached its present position from a pre-war and post-depression base-line that was well to the rear of Germany, Britain and the United States. Production in 1938 was still thirty-three points below the record level of 1929. Though the Second World War brought less wholesale devastation to France than to Germany, nevertheless her towns and communications, and her comparatively over-protected and run-down industries, suffered badly from German exactions, the collapse of overseas trade, severe aerial bombing and artillery bombardment, and the attentions of Resistance saboteurs, in and between the two Battles of France (1940 and 1944).[4] Seven years after the Liberation, as a result very largely of the imaginative and skilful deployment by the *Commissariat du Plan* of generous aid received from the United States through the Marshall Plan,[5] industrial production had fully recovered from the lost thirties and the destructive forties. The indices of industrial production since the war (1938=100) are as follows: 1951=143, 1958=213, 1965=310, 1969=390.[6] In 1959–61, for the first time for over thirty years, France enjoyed a favourable foreign trade balance. This was wiped out in the second half of the decade by rising imports, but the export cover, provided mainly by the sale of manufactured goods, stood at 86 per cent in 1969 (as against 82 in 1913, 86 in 1929 and 65 in 1938).

The First Plan (1947–50) gave a fresh start to the French economy by resolutely according priority to its six basic sectors: rail transport, coal, electricity, steel, cement, and the fertilisers and machines needed to restore and improve French agriculture. The French railway system, which now needed wholesale repair, had been nationalised back in 1937, and was one of the best achievements of pre-war French engineering and organisation. Industrial power, in the form of coal, electricity, gas and oil, had, on the other hand, always been one of the weak points of the French economy. By raising the domestic output of coal, gas and electricity, and by developing the Algerian oilfield and multiplying by twelve the capacity of French refineries to handle imported crude oil, the post-war generation of planners, engineers, miners and construction workers helped to put the country's manufacturing industries on a much better footing than ever before. Of the total power consumed, coal provides less than a third. If the French today use nearly two and a half times the power that was available to them twenty years ago, this is due largely to the expansion of the petroleum, gas and electricity industries.

A small amount of oil is produced from wells in Alsace and Aquitaine. But 94 per cent of the total refined has to be imported.[7] Altogether petroleum products provide over half of the total power consumed. Natural gas (which provides 6·4 per cent) is pumped in useful quantities from the Lacq field in south-western France. Hydro-electricity (which the French call *houille blanche,* white coal) and nuclear power together account for only 11 per cent of France's total consumption of energy (28 per cent of the energy *produced* in France). But they are spectacularly modern achievements, and they have played a big part in awakening public opinion to the industrial potential of France in the second half of the twentieth century. The great hydro-electric dams of the Rhône, Isère, Durance and Rhine, and smaller schemes elsewhere, in the Massif Central and the Pyrenees, have mostly been built since the Second World War, though some were planned in the thirties.

The subsoil of France has appreciable resources of iron ore, bauxite (used in the manufacture of aluminium), potash and salt.[8] A part of this mineral wealth is exported crude. But it also, of course, helps to sustain France's largest and most paying export trade, which is in manufactured goods:[9] notably aluminium, nitrates, cement, steel, textiles, clothes, leather goods, glass, perfumes, household equipment, fine wines, aircraft, cars and armaments. Although a smaller percentage of the working population is engaged in manufacturing in France than in Germany or the United Kingdom (29·2, 38·1 and 36 per cent respectively[10]), it contributes 42 per cent to the Gross National Product, and trade names such as Moulinex, Hermès, Caravelle, Mirage, Michelin, Renault, Citroën, Chanel, Courrèges, Guerlain, Dior, Courvoisier, Dubonnet and Veuve-Cliquot are known across the world.

THE STRUCTURE OF FRENCH INDUSTRY

This presents a pattern of extreme diversity, ranging from a few giant companies, some of them nationalised, to a very large number of family concerns. On the one hand, there are such firms as Rhône–Poulenc, Renault–Peugeot, Saint-Gobain, Péchiney, Michelin, which are among the biggest in the world; on the other hand, six out of seven of the 770,000 establishments registered in 1962 had less than six employees, and nearly sixty per cent of six and a half million factory, building and mine workers were in ones with fewer than two hundred on the payroll.

The survival of so many small industrial concerns in France is partly explained by a long history of taxation policies favouring the 'little man', and by the desire of larger firms to sustain their profit margins through the protection of less efficient small-scale competitors who set a generally high level of prices.[11] The bracing new climate of competition within the European Common Market, on the other hand, has brought pressures of a different kind. The necessity of concentrating research, production and marketing into larger units led to a number of mergers between big manufacturing firms in the sixties, some with international ramifications; several of the most advanced French producers have had to turn, both for capital and technical know-how, to foreign and, especially, American sources. This is true of Europe as a whole. But public opinion in France has proved to be particularly sensitive to the idea that American capitalism, aided by the foreign payments deficit of the United States, and armed with overwhelmingly superior techniques of invention, production and management, may somehow succeed in imposing 'colonial' status on the French economy. 'The American challenge'[12] and 'the balance of patents' are matters for continuing debate among French publicists, officials and citizens of every persuasion.

SERVICES AND COMMERCE

These, with the exception of private domestic service, in which the numbers employed are less than half what they were in 1911, constitute, generally speaking, an expanding sector of the French economy, though as yet they employ a smaller proportion of the national work-force than in Britain and North America. The number of civil servants more than doubled during the same period, while the number of state teachers trebled. French hotels and restaurants provide at their best a service rising to the level of art, which is assessed with rigour and reverence in the annual gastronomic guides published by Michelin and Julliard. The tourist trade is an important 'invisible' export. However, foreign visitors to France currently spend no more than French tourists abroad. Between 1964 and 1967 the previously favourable balance of tourism was eroded by stronger outgoing tides of prosperous French holidaymakers, heading mainly for Spain and Italy.

The trend in commerce is towards concentration in fewer, larger units, although in this, as in most parts of the French economic structure, the place of the small independent owner-operator, and his will and ability to survive, even into the 1970s, are exceptionally well entrenched.[13] There is also a high proportion of wholesalers to retailers in France, and a large proportion of the shopkeepers are self-employed without paid assistants. Many, it is clear, use no cash register either. For one of the ways by which so many small, family-run shops and services manage to survive in modern France is by tax evasion. The grocer, baker or ironmonger (the painter, upholsterer, locksmith or laundress), having been paid in cash, sadly reports an overall loss on the year's operations to the income-tax inspector, who, worldly wise, will settle for a compromise 'contracted' assessment: 'tout cela, voyez-vous, c'est une question de savoir s'entendre et de savoir vivre' – 'a matter of mutual understanding and not overstepping the mark'.

Besides personal income tax, which by tradition in France is low, unevenly imposed and inefficiently gathered, the state gets considerable income from indirect taxation, levied on tobacco, petrol, imports, and (through a value-added tax, *taxe sur la valeur ajoutée*, T.V.A.) on industrial and commercial profits. Industrial employers must, in addition to income tax and T.V.A., contribute heavily to their employees' social security benefits, family allowances, industrial injury compensation, annual holidays with pay, and even housing and (in Paris) transport expenses.[14]

The fragmentation of French commerce is, to a great extent, the natural consequence of a still remarkably even spread of settlement across the broad and rather sparsely populated hexagon of provincial France, counteracted only since the Second World War by widespread migration into towns, and by a rapid increase in the number of car-driving clients and vendors able to dispense with, or to cut out shops that are too isolated or over-specialised. Many small shopkeepers have learned to adapt, however, by joining chains served by a single large wholesale concern.

But although French commerce, like French agriculture and industry, has been comparatively late in adopting the habits and structure of modern Western capitalism, it is now, after a period of stagnation, fast developing a very modern sector. Since the range and mass of French consumption continues to rise with apparently little decline in the French shopper's traditionally critical discrimination, room for a wide variety of sales methods seems likely to continue, though some excessively wasteful channels of distribution, in vegetables and meat for instance, are increasingly exposed to attack by competitive trading and government decree. The whole pattern of domestic consumption is changing, moreover. Spending on house furnishing and household mechanisation, on health, travel, sports, books, photography, records and the like is increasing faster than expenditure on clothes, and much faster than expenditure on food and drink. The comparatively sluggish trades are the ones where the small man is most vulnerable to chain-store and supermarket competition. Year by year, the big organisations push up their share of the nation's retail trade, while the independent shopkeepers' turnover declines.

THE ROLE OF THE STATE

The modern French economy is a 'mixed' one. State guidance and management, government loans and partial or full nationalisation have all grown steadily since the Popular

Front reforms of 1936, at the expense of but not to the exclusion of private enterprise and the play of market forces. Neither the doctrinaire *dirigistes* and nationalisers of the period immediately following the Second World War, nor the more pragmatic planners of the 1950s and 1960s, nor the leaders of a recent *laissez-faire* reaction, stimulated by more open competition within the European Common Market, have set out to take over (or to take back) the entire economy. But government stimulus and control have been the dominant trends, launched by the Socialist founders of the Fourth Republic and reinforced by the technocratic leaders of the Fifth. The state as a successful entrepreneur, producing as well as purchasing goods and services, plays a bigger role in the French economy than in that of any other non-Communist country. The steady increase of government spending and influence characteristic of the last three decades has been brought about under the impetus of six National Plans prepared by the *Commissariat Général du Plan*, with the help of its thirty or more modernising commissions, and, since 1964, with the regional planning committees of the twenty-two Economic Regions (*Commissions de développement économique régional*, C.O.D.E.R.).[15]

The men who shaped the course of economic planning in post-war France (working for the most part in relatively calm, and politically neutral, waters, away from the storms of post-war parliamentary and constitutional crises) were given their immediate chance and inspiration by the war itself, which brought in its wake so many shocks to break down the old hidebound and stagnant 'Malthusian' order of French industry, trade and agriculture between the wars, so many trials to fire a new national temper, so many new openings for the future. Their first chief, Jean Monnet, head of the Plan from 1946 to 1952, had learned the value and art of international co-operation and industrial planning as a co-ordinator of Franco-British supplies in the war of 1914–18, as an official of the League of Nations and in Roosevelt's America, where he served on the British Supply Council in the Second World War. However, when he and his colleagues had to put dollar aid and government planning to work on the revival and reconstruction of France's economy after 1946, they were able to build upon deep indigenous foundations, in a country long used to strong, centrally directed state action for the promotion and protection of industry and trade, in the wider interests of the nation. Vital manufactures and commerce were officially encouraged, protected and regulated in France as long ago as the seventeenth century, under Colbert's administration, during the reign of Louis XIV; the Government of the Emperor Napoleon I, a century later, acted likewise. Throughout the nineteenth century the influential French Saint-Simonian school of paternalistic Socialism advocated the use of the most modern scientific techniques of the age, on the largest possible scale, under the direction of the most efficient bankers, industrialists, engineers and intellectuals available in the country, for the purpose of raising the standards of the largest and poorest class of its citizens. In the present century, besides Monnet, French reformers as different as the Catholic democrat, Emmanuel Mounier, the authoritarian technocrat, André Tardieu, the rather mysterious group of technocratic radicals out of *les grandes écoles* of the 1930s who were known as the Synarchy, and many like-minded supporters of Marshal Pétain's reactionary 'National Revolution',[16] during the Nazi occupation of France (1940–4), had all called for official planning of some kind or other to combat the 'established disorder' of liberal capitalism.

While investment in the basic power, mineral, manufacturing and transport industries, and in agriculture, remained the keystone of French economic planning even after the decade of immediate post-war reconstruction, the Second Plan (1954–7) already emphasised the importance of reforming the methods and structure of the French economy.[17] The Third Plan (1958–61) laid particular stress on priorities that would be socially beneficial, such as housing, schools, universities and hospitals,[18] and this ambition to plan for social reform was announced still more confidently in the Fourth Plan (1962–5):

> The overall increase of individual consumer income made possible by the growth of our economy runs the risk of being powerless, as the example of the United States shows, to ensure by itself the elimination of low standards of living whether they be tied to the economic situation in certain regions and to certain branches of

> activity, or whether they belong to certain groups of consumers – the poorly-housed, large families, those with small incomes, and old people . . . the Plan should give more attention than has been given hitherto to needs met by collective investment – town planning, education, public health – in order to fill the serious gaps from which the country suffers, to combat social scourges (alcohol, etc.), to face up to the consequences of population growth and ultimately to complete progressively the quantitative rise in purchasing power by a qualitative improvement in the French way of life.[19]

If the practical achievement of social and economic justice in contemporary France has not shown itself to be altogether equal to these generous aims, this might serve as a warning against overestimating the amount of idealism present in any great nation or new generation, and the amount of real power available to any so-called power élite. It should also serve as a reminder that it has proved difficult everywhere to make a post-war world that was both economically dynamic and socially just. The particular extent and the particular limitations of France's recovery from the static, indeed regressive, complacency of the 1930s and from the catastrophes and exertions of the 1940s, can best be understood in the particular contexts of French public opinion, institutions and history. The fields of action and of reference within which the planners and reformers of modern France have had to operate are examined in the chapters which follow.

4 Pressure Groups, Unions, Leagues, Creeds and Causes

THE LE CHAPELIER LAW

THIS law of 1791, inspired by the anti-feudal philosophy of the French Revolution, expressly prohibited all corporate organisations in an intermediary position between the state and the private citizen:

> No doubt all citizens must be allowed the right of assembly; but citizens exercising a particular profession cannot be allowed to assemble in defence of what they claim to be their common interests. The state no longer admits any kind of corporation, but only the particular interests of each individual and the general interest. No one is allowed to inspire citizens with any intermediary interest, to estrange them from the common weal through corporate loyalties.[1]

But associations of employers for the maintenance of prices and the protection of profits, and secret societies of workmen combining in self-defence against their masters, continued in despite of the law, and grew with industrialisation in the nineteenth century. In 1864, Napoleon III declared that peaceful 'coalitions' of workers would be tolerated (as employers' associations had in practice been tolerated for years). Twenty years later, under the Third Republic, a law of 1884 finally legalised all industrial and agrarian organisations formed for the protection of their members, including trade unions, though this did not end harassment of union members, and harsh repression of working-class strikes by the employers and their class allies in government and the public authorities defending property, law and order.[2]

BUSINESS INTERESTS

The extra-parliamentary defence of capitalist interests in France was for many years headed by that notorious bogy of the French left wing: *les deux cents familles,* a financial oligarchy composed of the largest shareholders in the Banque de France. Through its control of credit and of some influential newspapers, this central French bank, founded by Napoleon I, did at one time exert great pressure on Parliament, to the extent, it was alleged, of 'ruling the country over the heads of its chosen representatives'.[3] An example of its power and pretensions was its response to a pre-war Government's request for credit facilities: 'Our reply will depend on whether we are satisfied with the actions of the Government during the first respite we have given it as a reward for its present determination.'[4] The Bank was brought under more effective state control by the Popular Front Government of 1936. It was nationalised, together with the four largest French deposit banks, after the Second World War.

Before 1939, heavy industries and shipping were controlled by small, powerful committees of directors, the oldest and best-known being the *Comité des Forges,* founded in 1864, representing the boards of the largest iron and steel companies. These committees were united in 1919 as the *Confédération générale de la production française,* reconstituted as the *Conseil national du Patronat Français* in 1945–6. This pressure group lost its only big battle with Parliament after the war when the private iron and steel companies tried, and failed, to resist the Schuman Plan for a single European Coal and Steel Community (the first practical step in European unification). The steelmasters' defeat began a general, quiet conversion of French big business managers to the practice of co-operative planning with their peers and friends in the Treasury and other civil service departments, with the managers of the newly nationalised public sector of French industry (to which they were soon reconciled), and with the technocratic advocates of an integrated European economy.[5]

The *Confédération générale des petites et moyennes entreprises* (C.G.P.M.E.), led by Léon Gingembre, speaks for the 'little' businessman and shopkeeper, who has less to gain from modernisation and integration, who has indeed much to lose from the more efficient and larger units of production and distribution that the European boom (and American investment in it) has created. The numerical strength and economic difficulties of the class of small producers and *commerçants* were expressed more violently in the late 1950s through Pierre Poujade's *Union pour la défense des commerçants et artisans* (U.D.C.A.), and in a fresh outburst of neo-Poujadism in 1968 (including the blowing-up of tax offices, occupation of public buildings and seizing of official files). M. Gingembre's C.G.P.M.E. has had a more durable influence under more flexible leadership which, bowing to the inevitable, now concentrates on encouraging and aiding its members to form trading groups and chain stores in order to survive.

FARMERS' UNIONS

The Act of 1884 authorised farmers as well as industrial workers and factory-owners to combine freely in defence of their special interests, and led to the formation of thousands of so-called *syndicats-boutiques*, essentially co-operative purchasing societies, which thrived on the strictly practical desire of the peasantry for cut-price farm-supplies and insurance. The leaders of the movement were found not among the peasants themselves but in the local gentry and the *bourgeoisie* of the market towns. The movement eventually split along conventional French party lines into two large Central Councils, usually known by their addresses in Paris: the Rue d'Athènes (conservative and anti-Republican) and the Boulevard Saint-Germain (Radical-Socialist).[6] Both groups defended the ideal of the family farm and a protectionist policy of high tariffs against imported foodstuffs, and both, though for rather different reasons, favoured a farmers' union which would tend to unite all classes of the rural population:

> The Radicals' conception reflected their deep-rooted egalitarianism, which rejected the idea of economic or hierarchical differentiation. . . . The conservatives, on the other hand, clung to the doctrine that a kind of organic relationship bound all rural elements together into a harmonious whole; that behind the appearance of diversity there existed a single *classe paysanne*.[7]

Between the wars, and especially during the years of economic depression, the passive peasant masses began to receive the attention of more dynamic reformers and agitators. The conservatives' conception of a single, seamless rural society embracing landowners and tenants, rich and poor, educated and 'simple', was refurbished and remodelled as corporatism, a system that was at that time apparently flourishing in Mussolini's Italy (and attracting urban disciples in the French Royalist and neo-Fascist Leagues, then in their heyday[8]): parliamentary democracy and Republican individualism, which had always been disliked at the Rue d'Athenes, must be replaced by 'organic collectivities' including, in particular, a Peasant Corporation administered by and for an alleged community of all farming interests. A considerable tumult was worked up in rural France by agitators like Fleurant, self-styled Agricola, and Henri Dorgères. In 1934 a common 'Peasant Front' was set up to unite the various strands of agrarian corporatism, but it was a ramshackle affair, and soon fell apart in the tempest which brought the predominantly urban Popular Front to power in Paris two years later.[9] The reactionary leaders to whom most of the French turned for a while after the Nazi conquest of Europe in 1940 tried to put corporatism together again for the salvation of a people which had been destroyed, so they said, by the town-bred ideology of class war. Marshal Pétain dissolved all existing farmers' unions and set up in their place a single *Corporation Paysanne*. This in its turn was swept away by the restored Republic of liberated France (though some of its ideas and leaders remained active), and was replaced by an equally short-lived, purely left-wing, *Confédération générale de l'agriculture* (C.G.A.).[10]

The most serious opposition to the Rue d'Athènes came not from the equally conservative Radical-Socialists at the Boulevard Saint-Germain, nor from attempts by Fascists or Marxists to win the peasantry over, but from Catholic Brittany, where a turbulent and inspiring priest, Abbé Trochu, had begun the fight for 'peasant emancipation' at the beginning of the century. Trochu's movement was violently resisted by the conservatives, led by the Cardinal Archbishop of Rennes. These gained control of its newspaper *L'Ouest-Éclair*, and had the satisfaction of seeing its syndicates collapse in debt during the economic depression of the 1930s. But the 'grass-roots' tradition survived. The most radical and successful assault on rural conservatism since the Second World War has come out of Brittany: 'In no other part of France is agrarian syndicalism so solidly implanted at village level, so remarkably disciplined, so tough and effective.'[11]

But Catholic leadership of the post-war 'agricultural revolution' was not confined to Brittany. Half the members of the thousand or so *Centres d'étude technique agricole* (C.E.T.A.), which introduced farmers all over France to the idea of scientific food production, trebling revenue in some cases within five years, were *jacistes,* that is, members of the *Jeunesse agricole chrétienne* (J.A.C.), who also gained control of the *Centre national des jeunes agriculteurs* (C.N.J.A.) and secured its affiliation to the *Fédération nationale des syndicats d'exploitants agricoles* (F.N.S.E.A.), the principal farmers' union of post-war France.[12] From this position inside a movement up to now dominated by the large, prosperous farmers of northern France (and their very effective specialist pressure groups of sugar-beet and cereal producers), the young Catholic farmers have directly challenged the traditional union policy of fighting first and foremost for guaranteed prices, a policy which naturally benefits wealthy, large-scale *cultivateurs* much more than peasant smallholders, though it was often presented as a way of protecting the small family farm.[13]

Against this policy, the young *avant-garde* insists that, if the majority of French farmers are ever to enjoy a rising standard of living comparable with that of skilled urban workers, then radical 'structural' reform of French agriculture is imperative. So they campaign energetically for 'group agriculture' ('L'Individualisme, voilà l'ennemi', read the platform banner at the 1959 C.N.J.A. Congress); planned consolidation of holdings (*remembrement*); 'the organisation of production', including co-operative specialisation, and marketing on a European scale; a distinction to be made between ownership of land and ownership of the means of agricultural production; improved educational opportunities, including school buses to the larger towns (*le ramassage scolaire*); subsidies to agricultural social security; and improved medical care.[14]

THE LABOUR MOVEMENT

The industrial labour movement in France, unlike the early French peasant syndicates, rejected from the outset the upper-class patronage that it was offered, through paternalistic Catholic Workingmen's Clubs, started, in 1872, by Counts de Mun and de La Tour du Pin. It showed just as little confidence in the liberal parliamentary procedures for reform that were to be established, under predominantly middle-class inspiration and direction, in the constitution of the new Third Republic a few years later. In addition to the harsh conditions of daily living under nineteenth-century *laissez-faire* capitalism, the French urban working class had suffered repeated counter-revolutionary violence at the hands of the military, under orders from the middle class (1831, 1848, 1851, 1871), and this had led them to count on civil war rather than peaceful conciliation and compromise as the way to change society for the better. To the first General Council of the French trade unions, the *Confédération générale du travail* (C.G.T.), founded in 1895, it seemed that *bourgeois* and peasant, factory-owning and landowning France, united so often and so recently against them, now dominated the new French Republic quite as absolutely as it had formerly dominated the monarchy of Louis-Philippe and the Empire of Napoleon III. The extinction of the Paris Commune was the last large-scale action of open civil war in the 'Capital of the Revolution', but strikes and demonstrations, bitterly and often brutally carried out and put down, together with the daily frustrations and resentments of France's comparatively small, isolated working class, continued throughout the formative period of French trade unionism, and coloured its philosophy, known as syndicalism or anarcho-syndicalism. Syndicalist doctrine grew from the deep mistrust felt by an independent class of artisans owning little more than the tools of their trade, and a growing, propertyless industrial proletariat, for all parliamentary promises of reform: Parliament in France being, as they saw it, inevitably devoted to the interests of the property-owning majority of Frenchmen, the workers must build their own future independently of the established machinery of parliamentary government, within a self-contained urban wage-earning class, self-educated and self-organised for 'direct action' against wealth and privilege in the real world of factories and slums, not parliamentary action in the artificial, misrepresentative sphere of elected Assemblies. Direct pressure on the employers through strikes, boycott and sabotage would eventually reach the level of the revolutionary general strike, a concerted, universal withdrawal of labour which would bring about the transfer to the unions of the nation's entire means of production and distribution at one blow, on one cataclysmic *grand soir,* when capitalism would go down in darkness and leave the working class to inherit a new dawn of justice and prosperity.

The French labour movement had its political revolutionaries also. These believed that anarcho-syndicalism (as well as pure anarchism, which flared up in a series of individual terrorist attacks by bomb and knife in the early 1890s) was romantically out of touch with reality. In order to destroy capitalist injustice, the working class must undermine the political structures of capitalism with an aggressive political party of its own, under the strong leadership of a dedicated, disciplined, 'advance-guard of the proletariat'. Such was the lesson of Blanqui, the perpetual insurgent of 1830, 1848 and 1871, whose intransigence in despite of repeated failure, and whose long martyrdom as the political prisoner of three régimes (the monarchy, the Empire and now the Third Republic), gave French working-class militants an inspiring example. And such was the doctrine of Jules Guesde, an early French admirer of Karl Marx, and founder, in 1879, of the French Workers' Party, *Parti ouvrier de France* (P.O.F.).

Against the syndicalists, anarchists and violent revolutionaries, all set on some kind of cataclysmic change, stood 'possibilists' like Brousse, who believed that progress would and should come gradually, and parliamentary Socialists such as Briand and Millerand, who were prepared not only to collaborate with *bourgeois* colleagues in the Chamber of Deputies, but also to take ministerial office with them in reforming coalition Cabinets. And there was Jean Jaurès, the greatest French Socialist of the age. He was a true revolutionary, sceptical of the 'inevitability of gradualism' and of simply 'tinkering with the machine', and a profound humanist, looking forward to a radically new society willed by free men, yet he remained optimistically committed to attaining these objectives by peaceful persuasion and parliamentary action. His extraordinary determination and eloquence brought the various factions of French Socialism together briefly from 1905 to 1920 in a more or less united party, named the French Section of the Workers' International (*Section française de l'internationale ouvrière,* S.F.I.O.). But his assassination, on the eve of general mobilisation in 1914, at the hand of a fanatical French patriot scandalised by his fervent campaign in the international labour movement to avert the coming European war; then the war itself, and its revolutionary aftermath in Russia, with the effect the Russian Revolution had on popular opinion in France, all combined to break up the rather strained and superficial fusion of 1905, throwing the entire French left wing, in or against Parliament, in or outside the unions, back into its former state of intricately divisive controversy and mistrust – a state which endures to this day, and which has proved one of the greatest hindrances to the progress of practical democracy in France.

August 1914 showed the vanity of syndicalist hopes for an international general strike against warmongering capitalist governments (the policy known as 'revolutionary defeatism'). The war gave trade union leaders the chance to bargain more effectively than before on behalf of their members, from the new position of strength they came to hold in the expanded armament industries of a nation fighting for its life. As a result, anarcho-syndicalism declined in the unions (though less in the rank-and-file than among the leaders). On the other hand, the old revolutionary expectations of the syndicalists and Guesdists were revived when Lenin's Bolshevik Party, led by a small group of advance-guard revolutionaries, overthrew the Tsarist state by the very type of revolutionary action that had been advocated in France for years. This presented a new challenge to the heirs of Jaurès at the head of French parliamentary Socialism. A general strike in May 1920 failed completely, but when the French Section of the Workers' International, in congress at Tours later that year, received Lenin's conditions for joining the Third, Communist, International, the great majority of the militant rank-and-file responded sympathetically, and voted to accept them. The Congress of Tours then proceeded to found the French Communist Party (*Parti communiste français* – P.C.F.), in which 'the new Leninist faith was grafted upon the older Guesdist and Blanquist stems'.[15] Most of the leaders of the S.F.I.O., and all but a dozen of its sixty-eight Members of Parliament, remained faithful to the doctrine of parliamentary democracy, however, under the leadership of Jaurès's successor, Léon Blum.[16]

In 1921 the C.G.T., meeting at Lille, split along similar lines, but in different proportions: a narrow majority backed Jouhaux, their leader since 1909, *against* revolutionary strike action. The revolutionary minority of trade unionists was expelled, and set up a rival organisation: *Confédération générale du travail unitaire* (C.G.T.-U.), where the Communists soon took over the leadership from the anarcho-syndicalists and began the fight to win proletarian support away from the partisans of gradual reform still leading the old C.G.T.[17]

During the comparatively prosperous boom years after the Great War, the C.G.T., adopting a policy of participation ('No longer the brandished fist, but a presence in the nation. . . . We wish to be everywhere that working-class interests are discussed'[18]), flourished, though nearly half its total membership was now drawn from 'white-collar' office staff and teachers employed by the state. C.G.T.-U., meanwhile, denouncing Jouhaux's 'collaboration' with the *bourgeois* establishment, and maintaining an intransigently revolutionary position against the opportunity of mere partial amelioration, went through a short stage of stagnation.[19]

The economic depression and the rise of Fascism after 1929 brought the two groups together again in support of a political Popular Front, which won the general elections of 1936, The triumphant occupation of factories and mines by hundreds and thousands of workers on general strike in the summer of that year was an example of spontaneous French syndicalism, though largely without, on this occasion, a revolutionary aim.[20] The unions quickly brought the strikers under their control, however, and when, under the huge pressure of this unprecedented industrial action, the employers' representatives made substantial concessions, the unified leadership of the C.G.T. reaped a rich reward in enhanced prestige and authority. The so-called Matignon Agreement of 1936[21] contained a clause making collective bargaining between employers and employees compulsory, and this alone considerably increased the power and membership of the trade unions – for a time.[22]

It was the revolutionary *ex-unitaires*, however, who best reflected the mood of the French workers during the years of disenchantment and menace, at home and abroad, which led from the collapse of the Popular Front to the outbreak of the Second World War. By 1939, Communism had become a mass movement, commanding the spontaneous loyalty of most of the industrial workers, a fair proportion of white-collar workers, many intellectuals and teachers and, in some areas, the poorer peasants. It has remained ever since the best and the most stable organised expression of French working-class solidarity, which it represents, however, more effectively in day-to-day industrial action than in its rare attempts at the revolutionary general strike (in 1938 and 1947 this was no more successful than in 1920; in 1968, as in 1936, it produced positive practical results by cooling down the revolutionary mood to a point where negotiations might ensue), and more straightforwardly in defence of working-class interests on the elected municipal councils of its urban 'fiefs' in industrial cities and suburbs, than in the National Assembly or at the barricades outside. It is now a long way behind the *avant-garde* of the revolution. For the last quarter of a century, a revolution in France has been as unlikely with as without the P.C.F. and the C.G.T., and the main effect on French politics at the national level of the proletariat's scarcely wavering allegiance to the Communist cause has been so to divide the Left (into parliamentary and anti-parliamentary factions), while still scaring the Right (with a habit-forming rhetoric of violent revolution), as to keep the Left indefinitely out of power.[23]

After 1939, the alternative of unity or dissension in French trade unionism came to depend primarily upon national and international politics. Expelled from the C.G.T. after the Nazi–Soviet Pact of August 1939, the Communists recovered and increased their influence within it five years later, when trade unionism was restored in liberated France, and the Communist Party had earned a place of honour and influence in the nation as a result of its brave part in the French Resistance movement. For three years after the Liberation, unity in the French unions went hand in hand with party unity on the Left in Parliament, and in the 'tripartite' left-wing government coalition. But when, in 1947,[24] the Cold War between the Communist and anti-Communist powers began to divide Europe and the world, the Communist ministers were driven from office, and the Communist trade union leaders called out the industrial working class into systematic opposition to the parliamentary régime that had allegedly 'sold' France to Western capitalism and American 'imperialism'. This opposition took shape in a series of big, violent strikes against the rising cost of living, against the 'pauperisation of the workers', against the Marshall Plan (a 'trap' and an 'instrument of war'), against the Atlantic Alliance, and so on. The anti-Communists broke away and founded a new, second General Council: *Confédération générale du travail–Force ouvrière.* The schism of 1921 was reopened, but this time it was the Socialists who were in the minority and the Communists who kept control of the main organisation.

The as yet unmended breach between Socialist and Communist trade unions in France, and the gap dividing words from reality in much revolutionary or pseudo-revolutionary language still used by both groups, are not the only internal divisions that weaken the collective influence of French labour in local and national affairs.

The Teachers' Union withdrew in 1947 from both the rival Marxist confederations and set up its own autonomous one: *La Fédération de l'éducation nationale* (F.E.N.). There is also an autonomous *Confédération générale des cadres* (C.G.C.). Moreover, since 1919, when the strongly Catholic provinces of Alsace and Lorraine were returned to France, there has been an active confederation of Roman Catholic unions: *La Confédération française des travailleurs chrétiens* (C.F.T.C.). Its outlook is similar to the Catholic farmers' movement and to the left wing of the M.R.P.[25] It favours state planning and control, continuous discussions and co-operation between workers and employers under the arbitration of a democratic government, and the establishment of a new society embodying Christian-democratic ideals of personal freedom, economic and social justice and 'corporative' liberties. In 1964 the majority of C.F.T.C. members voted to drop the exclusively Christian basis of their doctrine, and, under the new name of *Confédération française démocra-*

tique du travail (C.F.D.T.), to seek to enrol all workers who are resolved to fight for social democracy 'independently of the state, the political parties, the churches, and all other outside organisations'.[26]

In 1966, C.G.T. and C.F.D.T. pledged unity of action at the national level, while in many local industrial disputes even wider unity was beginning to be achieved between all three of the big confederations. In May 1967, rising prices and unemployment, and authoritarian counter-measures by the Gaullist Government, provoked a one-day general strike. A year later, severe student riots in Paris seriously weakened the Government's position and self-confidence and signalled an opportunity for organised labour to mount a much longer and more effective general strike and occupation of factories (after the manner of 1936). This strong piece of 'direct action' by some nine million workers forced management and government to the negotiating table where (as at the Hôtel de Matignon thirty-two years before) big concessions were obtained by the established leaders of the main trade union confederations. The vanguard of the 'May Revolution', however, was small new groups of young anarchists, Trotskyists and Maoists,[27] who were in revolt as much against established trade union leadership (and especially against the allegedly fossilised bureaucracy and tame reformism of the current Communist bosses of the C.G.T.) as against de Gaulle's middle-class Fifth Republic (within which the Communist Party and union chiefs seemed to have forsaken their revolutionary vocation for the narrowly materialistic task of obtaining a gradual, negotiated rise of living standards for their members under capitalism). In the exciting revolutionary atmosphere that these so-called *groupuscules* of the extreme left wing succeeded in creating, there was some tactical outbidding by the old, mass organisations. The C.G.T. was wary of 'leftist adventures', but the former Christian C.F.D.T. was strongly attracted by the spontaneity and idealism of the young revolutionaries. Hopes of real unity for the French labour movement, which had begun to seem less improbable than at any time since the Second World War, faded once again into the future.

ROMAN CATHOLICISM

This is the oldest and by far the most widespread form of religious faith in France. When the French Revolution, which overthrew the old Catholic monarchy, had run its course, Napoleon I and Pope Pius VII signed an agreement, the Concordat, re-establishing the official union of the Catholic Church and the French State. Until 1905, the Church of Rome was again the established religion of the country. Today, more than half a century after its legal disestablishment,[28] one-sixth of all primary-school pupils and one-fifth of all secondary-school pupils attend private Catholic schools.[29] There are also Catholic university 'faculties' in Toulouse, Lyon, Lille, Angers, Marseille, and a 'Catholic Institute' in Paris, which gives university education of high quality (especially in philosophy and languages); but none of these institutions can award degrees and none can officially call itself a university.

Napoleon's religious policy was part of his overall plan to repair national unity after a decade of combined religious, social and political strife, and to get an incomparable instrument of social discipline firmly in the hands of his Government. The Pope was anxious to restore to the Church her 'eldest daughter', a nation with a tradition of Catholic service going back to the Crusades: *Gesta Dei per Francos*. When the *émigrés* returning after Waterloo clumsily attempted to revive the authoritarian pre-revolutionary alliance of landed aristocracy, royal throne and Catholic altar, the immediate result was to reinforce rather than to curb the free-thinking disrespect in which the Church was now held by many of the middle-class supporters and beneficiaries of Napoleon's post-revolutionary settlement. As the masses in the new factory towns began to grow restive, however, and to kick against the preponderantly *bourgeois* régimes of mid-nineteenth-century France, the new industrial governing class, like the old land-owning one, began to see the point of Catholic-inspired social discipline. Indeed they appeared more anxious for such a 'spiritual police force' than the long-established, over-confident, royal and quasi-feudal *ancien régime* of the eighteenth century, when *libertinage*, sceptical free-thinking, had flourished in the highest circles of the nation and state. Nineteenth-century France, on the contrary, would be led by a class which, outwardly at least, was the most devout part of the urban and manufacturing society it was building. And not merely outwardly: 'to start with', writes A. Dansette, in his *Religious History of Modern France*, 'the middle classes were anxious to give others a religion to which they were themselves prepared to pay no more than hypocritical respect. But the attitude became sincere as time went on and a growing proportion of the older middle-class families accepted Catholicism with steadily increasing sincerity.' After 1860 there was also a rapid revival of the teaching, nursing and contemplative orders: by 1877, total membership had reached 30,200 for men and 127,000 for women. 'There were, in fact, more nuns than there had been in 1789.' On the other hand, in Paris and the larger towns, the as yet fairly small industrial proletariat, and the numerous, vigorous and self-reliant class of skilled artisans, 'had no attachment to the Church'. Among the two and a half million inhabitants of the capital city, there were, by the end of the century, perhaps 100,000 practising Catholics, one woman in twelve and one man in fifty, coming mainly from the middle-class districts. The Catholic traditions of the French countryside altered more or less slowly depending on the historic strength of religion in particular regions: Léon, in furthest Brittany, for instance, remained 'deeply Christian', while the wine-growing district of Mâcon in Burgundy 'was almost entirely pagan'.[30]

Broadly speaking, the regional pattern of practising Catholicism on the map of France today shows much as it did a hundred or two hundred years ago. The *overall* fading of active faith continues as the country population moves into the cities, but the revivalist *équipes* of *jacistes* have scored most of their successes in traditionally Catholic regions. Thus the distribution for 1947, plotted by Canon Boulard, is still substantially correct, and differs little from Gabrial le Bras's for 1880: the bastions of Catholic faith are mountainous or peripheral, the regions of greatest indifference or hostility are open plains and river valleys, areas of movement and communication.

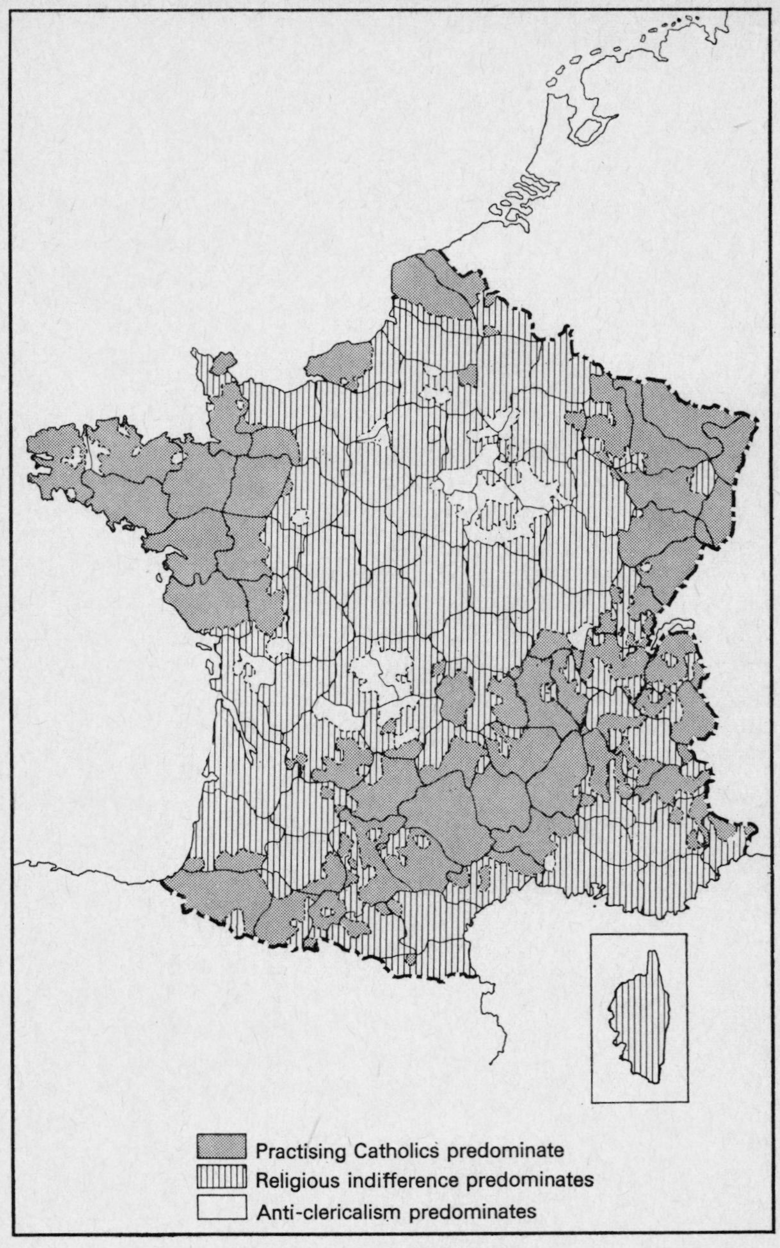

Map 12. Catholicism in rural France

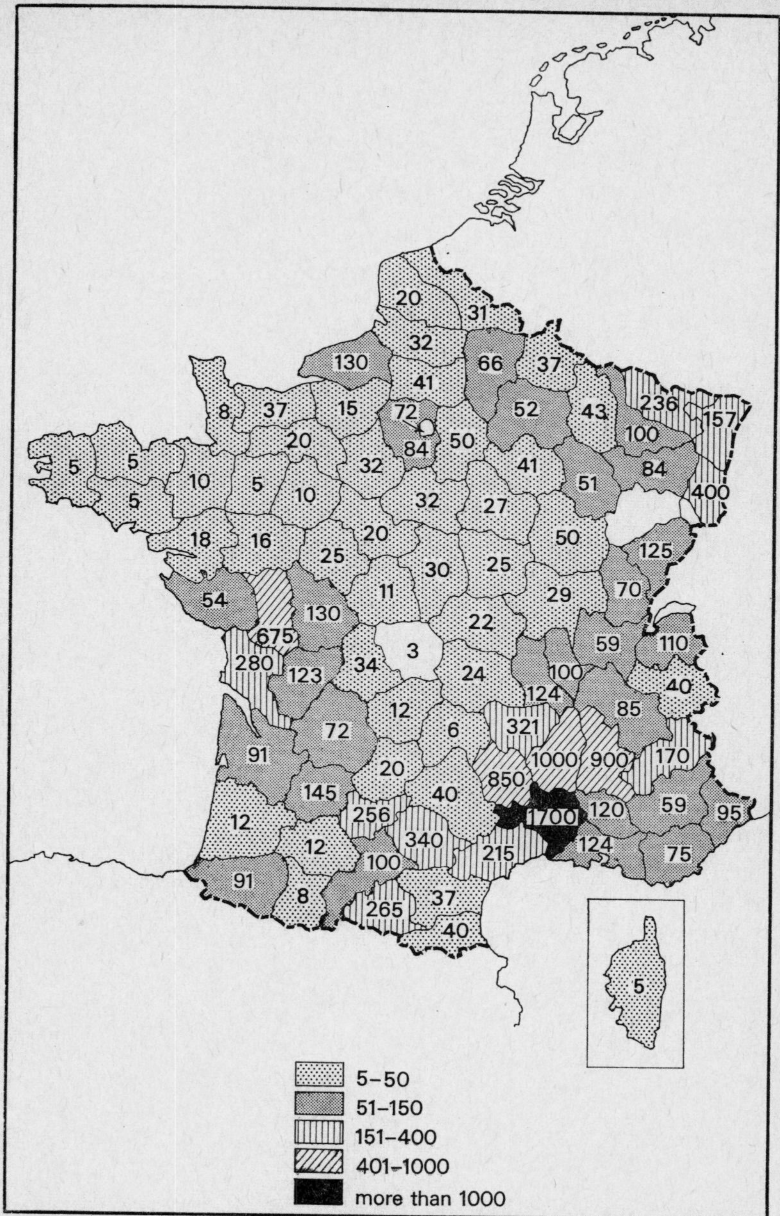

Figures show, for each *département*, the approximate number of Protestants per 10,000 of the population (1955)

D Map 13. Protestant France

THE PROTESTANT CHURCHES

There are about 800,00 French Protestants, most of them living in Alsace and northern Lorraine and the old Huguenot strongholds of southern and western France: the Cévennes mountains on the south-east margin of the Massif Central, the Dauphiné Alps, and the hinterland of La Rochelle, centred on the Atlantic coast *département* of Charente-Maritime, and covering part of southern Vendée, Deux-Sèvres, Vienne, Charente, western Dordogne and the north-eastern corner of the Gironde. Of the seven denominations, *L'Église Réformée de France* (400,000 members) and the *Église de la Conférence d'Augsbourg d'Alsace-Lorraine* (250,000) are by far the largest.

French Protestants have long been particularly active in industry and commerce. Protestant Europe gained much from the exile of hundreds of thousands of French Huguenots after 1685 (the year Louis XIV revoked the tolerant Edict of Nantes by which they had enjoyed freedom of worship, outside Paris, for nearly a century), A fresh 'Edict of Toleration' was accorded by Louis XVI, just two years before the revolutionary Declaration of the Rights of Man, which asserted that 'No one is to be molested because of his opinions, even religious, provided their manifestation does not disturb the public order established by law'. During the last two centuries, many French Protestants have migrated into the industrial areas of northern France, to the textile factories of Normandy and to such cities as Strasbourg and Nîmes, at the centre of old Protestant regions, each with more than 20,000 members of the Reformed Churches. There are also between five and ten thousand in Marseille, Le Havre, Bordeaux, Lyon, Toulouse and Saint-Étienne. In Paris they number some 100,000.[31]

The early anti-Catholic trend of the Third Republic gave French Protestants an influential part in the formation and execution of government policy, particularly in the state schools: 'For several reasons, the Protestant community was ready to provide the personnel required. Since it was not "clerical", it inspired confidence in the anti-clericals; since it was not atheist, it was accepted by the church-going *bourgeoisie*, if not as a good thing, at least as the lesser evil.'[32] On the other hand, the Vichy régime was hostile towards the Protestants, and their old redoubt in the Cévennes was a successful centre of resistance against Nazi occupation and oppression.

DEMOCRATIC CATHOLICISM

The conservative spirit of the hierarchy and most of the members of the Catholic Church in France did not go unchallenged even in the nineteenth century. In 1870, the traditional 'Gallican liberties', defining the special corporate identity and independence of the French Church, were undermined by the proclamation of Papal infallibility. But French Catholicism had already begun to acquire its modern reputation for producing unorthodox and progressive minority views from within its own ranks. Many individual members of the liberal and democratic *avant-garde* of the Church in France were to find themselves condemned by the ecclesiastical authorities in France as well as Rome, and some were to be excommunicated. But the cumulative inspiration they left behind thrust French Catholicism into the van of modern Christian thought and action, touching in particular the political and social responsibilities of Christians. Such were Lamennais and Lacordaire, who preached Christian democracy in the 1830s, Abbé Trochu, the Breton peasant leader,[33] and Marc Sangnier, who advocated a kind of Christian Socialism in the early years of this century, through associations of workers and students. Sangnier's review, *Le Sillon*, committing Catholics to the fraternal defence of the de-Christianised masses against selfish conservatism, was a direct forerunner of the Christian trade unions (united in 1919 in *La Confédération française des travailleurs chrétiens*); the associated young workers' and farmers' groups, *Jeunesse ouvrière chrétienne* (J.O.C.) and *Jeunesse agricole chrétienne* (J.A.C.), founded 1926–9, and the post-war French Christian Democrat party, *Mouvement républicain populaire* (M.R.P.).

In the most serious clash of recent years between the Vatican and the heirs of Lamennais, most of the leaders of the French Church came out on the side of its most daring *avant-garde* so far, the worker-priest movement. By 1940, many alert and sensitive French churchmen were beginning to be haunted by the knowledge that large areas of rural France and most of the larger French cities were as much a part of the 'mission field' as the distant continents of Africa and Asia, where, for the previous two hundred years, the missionary priests and nuns of French Catholicism had laboured most and to best effect: 'The modern world, with its great concentration of the working-class masses, hasn't become pagan; it was *born* pagan. Outside the Church. Just as, in China, one is, almost certainly, destined to be born pagan.'[34] And yet young priests who had served in the 1939–45 war as chaplains with the French Army, or in German prison and labour camps,[35] noted how genuinely fraternal and useful their mission to the proletarian and peasant masses had seemed, in contrast to ordinary parish life:

> There is something still separating us from the people. In the Army, we shared the life of the men; we were in the midst of them; they gave us their confidence and their friendship; at times we had the impression that they used to close up round us for comfort. They were happy to be with a priest, and said so, in their letters home.
>
> Now we are back in our parishes, each in his part of the city; we have put our cassocks back on again and taken up our religious duties once more. . . . And, once again, there is emptiness round us. *Why* should it be like this? What is it that still keeps us apart from the people, the masses?[36]

Instead of discovering the 'truth of proletarian existence' in order to bring the proletariat back to God, was not the French Church being reduced, by hidebound tradition, to 'trying to adapt to the workers the *bourgeois* expression of religion'?[37] Were not 'the classic forms of priesthood' out of date?

A Catholic mission to the dockers of Marseilles was launched by two Dominicans in 1940–1, and in 1944 the *Mission de Paris* was founded with the support of Cardinal Suhard (Archbishop of Paris from 1940 to 1949), who was as determined as any to break through the 'wall' dividing the Church from the working class. In 1949 there were about fifty worker-priests in France, of whom a dozen were in Paris. The principle governing the worker-priest movement was that the priest should not just try to serve the workers from within the sanctuary of his presbytery, his parish, his church and his ritual, but that he should abandon all these to become a worker himself, earning wages in a factory, living, praying and celebrating Mass in a slum, with a home-made altar and in a form and language his new comrades could share. Such devoted identification with the working class led normally to trade union membership (usually C.G.T., in Paris the strongest faction, rather than the Catholic confederation). Moreover, the independent spirit which had led the worker-priests into this new mission field made them specially sympathetic towards trade union militancy in the name of working-class solidarity, and their clerical training and zeal made them specially useful as shop-floor leaders of industrial action. So, by a natural progression from comradeship to office-bearing responsibility, and from collective bargaining to strike action, some were led to take part in political meetings, demonstrations and even, occasionally, riots against the enemies of the working class as designated by the ruling Communist *cadres* of the French proletariat, whose confident revolutionary philosophy, in their charitable enthusiasm and their isolation, they found difficult to resist.[38] The Vatican was soon alarmed, and the *Mission de Paris* was in 1954 at first curtailed and then, in 1959, condemned outright, as Lamennais's *L'Avenir* and as Sangnier's *Le Sillon*, and, to be fair, the counter-revolutionary Royalism of *Action Française*, which also proclaimed its allegiance to the Catholic Church, had been condemned.[39] In fact, small groups of worker-priests continued in secret. Six years later the prohibition of their mission was lifted, and, with certain restrictions, notably a ban on trade union membership, the movement was allowed into the open again with the official blessing of the Church. There were never more than a hundred or so French worker-priests during the fifteen pioneer years,[40] but their chosen destiny is representative of an important politically progressive trend in modern French Catholicism.

FRANCE OVERSEAS

The spread of Catholicism through French missions overseas was both stimulated and provided for during the first half of the twentieth century by two unconnected events in the history of the Third Republic. The first of these was a huge expansion of the French Empire. The earliest phase in the growth of overseas France took place in the seventeenth and eighteenth centuries, under the Bourbon monarchy. Algiers was added in 1830, but the most rapid spread came during the first forty years or so of the Third Republic, in North, West and Central Africa, the Indian Ocean and Indo-China. This final phase, in the golden age of European imperialism, greatly extended the field for which French Catholicism felt itself specially responsible. The second event, which at least initially provided the extra missionaries and Catholic teachers needed, was an anti-clerical purge of French education carried out between 1902 and 1905.[41] 'Religious orders', prescribed the law of 1904, 'are forbidden to undertake teaching of any kind, at any level, in France.'[42] The French Catholic teaching orders were forced to go abroad. They were allowed, indeed encouraged, to continue their already considerable work, in the French Empire.[43] Even Gambetta, who back in 1877 had called for an all-out attack on Catholic positions within the Republic ('Clericalism, that is the enemy!'), allowed that anti-clericalism was not for export.[44]

The French sense of mission in foreign, and especially in imperial fields, was not the monopoly of Christians. Ernest Psichari, for example, a grandson of the celebrated nineteenth-century rationalist, Ernest Renan, and an officer in the colonial artillery corps, was converted to Catholicism in 1912, and came to see his military and his Christian mission as forming, together, a real crusade. He was followed by many who thought likewise. The bitter rearguard action that many French officers and civilian administrators fought against pagan nationalism and atheistic Communism, in French Indo-China, Morocco, Tunisia and Algeria, was inspired by a similar crusader myth. But other military and civil servants of France's North African domains and protectorates saw themselves as the successors of the legionaries, colonisers and administrators of pre-Christian Rome.[45] And for others, the imperial model was Jacobin: to bring the 'Rights of Man' to all countries still stranded in the age of despotism and ignorance.

French civilisation, derived from classical antiquity, medieval Christendom and the revolutionary Enlightenment, is self-consciously universalist. Thus, ideally, the Republic could allow no particular differences of race, colour or creed to prevent the cultural and administrative unification of its overseas possessions and dependencies. But France's characteristic imperial policies of centralisation and assimilation (caricatured in the story of Indo-Chinese schoolchildren reciting from a textbook supplied by the Ministry of Education in Paris: 'Our ancestors the Gauls had long fair hair') were in the end fatally contradicted by geography and history: 'proconsular' government of far-flung territories by French soldiers and administrators over whom Paris in practice had too little control; second-class citizenship for natives and paternalistic or cynical contempt from their white overlords; the finally irresistible upsurge of revolutionary Indo-Chinese, African and Arab nationalism.[46]

POLITICAL LEAGUES AND CLUBS

Various persuasions of these have flourished vigorously, if in some cases only briefly, throughout the last hundred years of French history. The League of Patriots was founded in 1882 for the purpose of exhorting all Frenchmen, of whatever political party, to prepare for the next war with Germany, in which France would take her revenge for the defeat of 1870, and Alsace and Lorraine would be recovered: 'Republican, Bonapartist, Legitimist, Orléanist, these are with us only first names; the family name of all is Patriot.'[47] When the revenge (*la revanche*) came, in 1918, after horrors that the original *ligueurs* had failed to anticipate, the movement faded out. The French League for the Rights of Man and of the Citizen, formed to defend civil liberties threatened by militarist and clerical pressures during the Dreyfus Affair at the end of the last century,[48] has, on the contrary, survived, though on a reduced scale, and continues to voice articulate humanist opposition against those forms of prejudice and tyranny that still seek to deny the 'Immortal Principles of 1789'.[49] The Grand Orient Lodge of French Freemasonry was an extremely powerful anti-clerical pressure group of the Third Republic. *L'Action Française* was the name of a 'league' which campaigned from 1905 to 1944 for the restoration of a strong, hereditary French monarchy, seen as the 'integral', i.e. total, form of nationalism that was needed if the so-called 'real

France' was to react effectively against a century of soft-headed and debilitating democracy with which it was alleged to have been infected by Protestant, Jewish, Masonic and 'mongrel-immigrant' infiltrations. This is the declaration that postulants of Integral Nationalism had to sign:

> As a Frenchman by birth and sentiment, by rational conviction and deliberate choice, I shall carry out all the duties of an alert patriot. I undertake to fight any republican régime. The Republic in France is the reign of the foreigner. The republican spirit disorganises national defence and promotes religious influences directly opposed to traditional Catholicism. France must be given back a régime that is French. Our only future is therefore the Monarchy as it is personified by H.R.H. the Duke of Orléans, heir of forty kings who, in the course of a thousand years, made France. Only the Monarchy ensures the public good and, being responsible for order, prevents the public evils denounced by anti-Semitism and nationalism. The Monarchy, which is the necessary organ of all the general interests, restores authority, liberty, prosperity and honour. I associate myself with the work of monarchic restoration. I undertake to serve it with all available means.[50]

Charles Maurras, the founder and chief doctrinaire of the Royalist movement, and the editor of its daily newspaper (launched in 1908), with a gift for persuasive simplification and repetition, and an inspired partisan's capacity for imparting, and arousing, enthusiasm and hate, succeeded in mobilising against the Republic the emotional nationalism, the passion for political abstractions, and the love of verbal and physical violence of a small but politically active and disproportionately influential section of the French (and particularly the Parisian) landowning, professional and moneyed classes, petty, middle and upper *bourgeoisies,* with many intellectuals, students, serving officers and priests, through two generations, from the Dreyfus Affair, where he first made his name as a political journalist, to the Second World War, which brought him a brief, unreal triumph before ultimate disgrace. In 1945, at the age of seventy-seven, he was sentenced to life imprisonment by the Republican authorities of liberated France for having spent the last active years of his long career as high priest of French nationalism paradoxically collaborating with the conquerors of his country and, logically, supporting a French Government with views (at last!) almost as anti-democratic and racialist as his own: the so-called Vichy régime, headed by an aged reactionary, Marshal Pétain, under Europe's German overlords, between 1940 and 1944.

There had never been much chance of Maurras seeing his Dictator-King on the throne of France, and the Comte de Paris, the French Pretender, repudiated *L'Action Française* in 1937, in the name of constitutional monarchy. The League was strongest where it was most negative: ultra-nationalism – 'la France, la France seule' ('France only'); and counter-revolution – 'Marianne la gueuse' ('Marianne [the personification of the Republic, in her revolutionary Phrygian stocking-cap] is a slut').[51] The Second World War in Europe, and the accompanying French civil war between collaborators and resisters, did not quench either Royalism or Maurrasism completely, however, though the democratic and conciliatory Pretender and the authoritarian heirs of Integral Nationalism (of whom the readers of *Aspects de la France* – a new A.F. – were the most orthodox, Pierre Boutang, editor of a breakaway *La Nation Française*, was the most trenchant, and such small youth groups as *Restauration Nationale* the most violent) are as far apart as in 1937 from each other. Both are as far as ever from winning over a broadly popular following.[52]

In the Europe of Mussolini, Hitler and Franco, several Fascist movements sprang up in France, with no time for Maurras's nostalgic attempt to restore her royal past. Such were the anti-Communist *Jeunesses Patriotes* (founded in 1924), the anti-Semitic *Solidarité Française* (1933), the anti-Republican *Francistes* (1933), and the war veterans' association, *Les Croix de Feu* (1927). The last-named, after 1931 under a new leader, Colonel de La Rocque, who improved its discipline and gave its members a passionately nationalistic and vaguely anti-capitalist cause to march for, expanded fast and became, eventually, the largest and least extreme of France's pre-war Fascist organisations. The hooded 'Cagoulard' terrorists operated on a much smaller scale, with guns and dynamite, and funds supplied by Fascist Italy.[53]

Since the Second World War, a new class of political pressure groups has appeared on the democratic side. These are the so-called clubs. Though known by this old revolutionary name, they are essentially study groups (*sociétés de pensée*) concerned with peaceful reform, and have shown none of the fiercely sectarian violence practised in 1792–4 by *La Société* (or *Club*) *des Jacobins* and *le Club des Cordeliers*. Some of them date from the years of great expectation immediately following the liberation of France from four years of Nazi oppression and after fourteen years of economic depression, political helplessness and national decline. Others sprang up when the established political parties appeared again to be losing their grasp of reality and their grip on events, and the confusion and barely contained violence which ended the Fourth Republic and continued into the first few years of the Fifth. The earlier groups were mostly Catholic, part of the same post-war Christian Democrat movement that was sending reinvigorated teams of *jacistes* into action in the countryside, and *jocistes* (*Jeunesse ouvrière chrétienne*) and worker-priests into the factories and city slums. One of the most influential of the newer clubs, which tend incidentally to disprove the alleged 'depoliticisation' of the French by Gaullism a decade before the May Revolution,[54] is the Club Jean Moulin, named after a leader of the wartime Resistance, tortured to death by the Nazis. It was started, in 1958, by a small group of former *résistants* to combat what they discerned as a new threat of Fascist tyranny, from the white colonialist ascendency in what was then still French Algeria.

The clubs do not constitute a mass movement. They provide rather for a meeting of minds in a progressive élite drawn in great part from the teaching and other professions, from the administrative grade of the civil service, and from the managerial *cadres* of private and nationalised industries. In April 1965 about half of the one hundred and twenty clubs then in existence, in Paris and the provinces, combined to form a Convention for Republican Institutions, with the aim of bringing all 'democrats with a Socialist vocation' together in united opposition to the Gaullist ascendancy, and in support of left-wing candidates such as Gaston Defferre, Mayor of

Marseille, and, after his withdrawal, François Mitterrand, at the presidential election eight months later.

SOME PILLARS OF TRADITION

Independently of such transient circumstances as foreign occupation, overseas expansion and withdrawal, economic depression, the agricultural revolution and constitutional reform, such institutions as the *Institut de France*, the *Collège de France* and the *Comédie Française* remain upstanding in support of France's long and illustrious cultural and intellectual traditions. The *Institut* was founded after the French Revolution and incorporates the *Académie des inscriptions et belles-lettres* (founded in 1663), the *Académie des Sciences* (founded in 1666), the *Académie des Sciences Morales et Politiques* (founded in 1795, suppressed by Napoleon I, and restored by King Louis-Philippe in 1832) and the *Académie Française* (founded under the protection of Cardinal Richelieu in 1635). The French Academy's self-perpetuating membership of forty 'immortals' (writers mainly, but also scientists, churchmen, publicists, soldiers and statesmen) is the very picture of French cultural continuity. The *Collège de France*, founded by the French Renaissance king, François I, gives public lectures by some of France's most eminent and original scholars, philosophers, scientists and men of letters. The *Comédie Française* (1680), and the score of other state-subsidised theatres founded in Paris and the provinces since the Second World War, maintain the high style and reputation of French acting. Their foreign tours, and the French Institutes and branches of the *Alliance Française* and French schools established abroad, all help to spread French culture to most parts of the world.

Then there are the military and the civil services. The French Army has twice during the present century departed from its expected and generally respected role of 'Silent Service' (*la grande muette*), in order to take political sides, dividing the nation it exists to defend: over the Dreyfus case, between 1894 and 1905, and over French Algeria between 1958 and 1962.[55] Both times it was the officers who broke ranks. However, it is not in their traditions to take part in politics, and on both occasions the activists in the armed forces retired from the political arena once the crisis had been resolved, by the decisive reassertion of the primacy of the civil over the military power. The French permanent, professional civil service has an unbroken tradition of silent service to the state, and a long record of independent and powerful influence on government. It is indeed one of the most important constituents of French continuity and calm, beneath the repeatedly disturbed surface of French politics.[56]

Part Two: The State

5 The Constitution

ORIGINS

THE origins of the French Republic lie in the political philosophy and the dramatic events of the French Revolution, which asserted the rights of the nation as a whole against the sectional privileges and authorities established under the *ancien régime*, headed and held together by the monarchy.[1] At first the Revolutionary slogans 'Vive la Nation!' and 'Vive le Roi!' seemed not at all incompatible. It was in the name of the King that the Third Estate of the Realm, led by the politically conscious and enlightened middle class, in June 1789, set up a single, homogeneous National Assembly, in opposition to the two traditionally allied privileged estates of clergy and nobility: 'Vive le Roi! Vive l'Assemblée Nationale!' The inspired but inexperienced Assembly could not make constitutional monarchy work in France, however, largely because the weak Louis XVI was only superficially won over. After two years of growing hostility between King and court on the one side, and on the other an Assembly increasingly swayed by the democratic political clubs of Paris, Louis was arrested at Varennes-en-Argonne on his way to join *les émigrés* – French officers in exile with the army of his brother-in-law, the Austrian Emperor. The royal family was brought back to Paris, where Marat, in his newspaper *L'Ami du Peuple*, and Danton, President of the Cordeliers' Club, began to agitate for the traitor-tyrant's deposition. On 10 August 1792, while a large Austro-Prussian army under the Duke of Brunswick was massing to invade France and restore the authority of the crown by force, the revolutionary 'patriots' in Paris led a successful assault on the royal palace of the Tuileries and occupied it in the name of the people. On 20 September, at Valmy, in Champagne, the invasion force of the counter-revolutionary coalition was repulsed, and the following day, in the capital of the 'peuple libre', as Danton now proudly called the French nation in arms, the ancient monarchy of France was abolished. On 25 September the new French Republic was declared 'one and indivisible'. Its leaders in the Jacobin Club took up the task, proclaimed the year before by the monarchist Assembly, of 'abolishing irrevocably the institutions . . . injurious to liberty and equality of rights', namely the Church, the nobility, the *parlements*[2] and the trade guilds.

'At Varennes', wrote a modern French patriot, 'the French monarchy died in a road accident.'[3] Crudely speaking, this is true. But it was a long time dying. Not for close on a hundred years was the Republican constitution of France made secure. The First Republic, which lasted from 1792 to 1804, was followed by the ten-year reign of the Emperor Napoleon I. After his overthrow the monarchy was for a time restored: Louis XVI's two brothers reigned, successively, from 1814 to 1824 and from 1824 to 1830, when a second French Revolution placed the 'Citizen-King', Louis-Philippe d'Orléans (related to the Bourbon line through Louis XIV's brother), on a throne attached by charter to a parliamentary form of government. The Orléanist compromise was brought to an end, after eighteen years, by the revolution of 1848, which produced a short-lived Second Republic, overthrown by its own first President, Louis-Napoleon Bonaparte, nephew of Napoleon I. The Second French Empire lasted until 1870, when its armies were crushed in the opening campaign of the Franco-Prussian War. The Third Republic, which gradually established itself, through the remaining months of the war, and in the aftermath of defeat, as 'the form of government that divides Frenchmen least' (Adolphe Thiers), proved more durable than any other régime of post-revolutionary France. Although for several decades yet, there was a small but articulate minority still passionately committed to the restoration of the monarchy,[4] and although the numerical series of French Republics continued to grow, with a fourth version of the Constitution adopted in 1946 and a fifth in 1958, the general principles and the fundamental institutions of Republican government have been secure in France now for very nearly a hundred years.

The resistance to Republicanism put up by the First and the Second Estates of the old French monarchy, the Church and the nobility, was also tenacious. The Roman Catholic

Church of France was not disestablished until 1905, and for another forty years after that it continued to exercise a predominantly anti-Republican influence at home and in the then large French Empire overseas, mainly through the many French families still wielding inherited power and patronage as landowners and in local government, as officers in the armed services, and as diplomatists and colonial administrators, families which were church-going by tradition, and frequently by religious conviction also.

Because such convinced opposition and such entrenched corporate and class claims to privileged status and influence so long frustrated Republican reforms, and because industrialisation in the nineteenth and twentieth centuries had raised new obstacles to the advance of 'Liberty, Equality and Fraternity', the Republican tradition in France has been passed on to every generation since 1792 as a call to get on with still unfinished business, a faith militant, rather than a cause safely won. On the other hand, French Republicanism has acquired, with time, its own conservatives, left behind by the continuing leftward march of the Republican *avant-garde*. In particular, the political individualism of early generations, which put Liberty above Equality and Fraternity in the scale of Republican values, has served to justify *laissez-faire* resistance to the Socialism of later generations.

It was a middle class imbued with possessive individualism which had torn down the old society founded upon traditional corporate privileges. That an indefinite right to possess private property, accorded to all citizens in the first Charter of the Revolution, the 'Declaration of the Rights of Man and of the Citizen',[5] tends to create its own forms of unequal privileges, was a secondary consideration, the contradictory implications of which ('full individuality for some [is] produced by consuming the individuality of others'[6]) were only slowly grasped by the French peasant and middle classes. Not until 1946 were such social rights as education, medical care, employment, collective industrial bargaining for the wages and conditions of labour, 'material security, rest and leisure' added, constitutionally, to the individual legal and political rights of 1789. The principles of 1789 and 1946 were reaffirmed together in the Preamble to the Constitution of the Fifth Republic of 1958. 'Nowadays', writes Pierre Mendès

France, one of today's champions of militant French Republicanism, 'everyone recognises that . . . it is up to the state to fight economic crises and under-employment, to guide, stimulate and co-ordinate the efforts that are being directed towards general expansion and progress.'[7] Between the 'possessive individualism' of its liberal founders and the state control of society and the economy advocated by its Socialist heirs, French Republicanism has also found a characteristic 'middle way' in the present century. This is the policy of standing up for the independent proprietor of a small shop, factory or farm against the big estates, chains, trusts, cartels and joint-stock companies: *les gros propriétaires, les gros industriels, les sociétés anonymes.* There is theoretical authority for such a stand to be found in the 'Immortal Principles of 1789', if the fourth article of the Declaration of Rights ('Liberty consists of the power to do whatever is not injurious to others: thus the enjoyment of the natural rights of every man has for its limits only those that assure other members of society the enjoyment of those same rights . . .') is used to qualify the right to property averred absolutely in its second. In practice this Republicanism of the 'little man' has certainly helped to maintain the small-scale fragmentation of French agriculture, commerce and industry well into the second half of the twentieth century.

In 1792 the representatives of 'le peuple libre' offered to aid the other peoples of Europe to rid themselves of their own kings and priests and nobles. This gave French Republicanism an initially strong nationalistic bias which, fused with the doctrine of tyrannicide, became known as Jacobinism, after the political club to which the principal founders and the most radical leaders of the First Republic belonged. However, the rise of Marxism, a century later, tended to detach the French Republican *avant-garde* from its assertively patriotic antecedents, teaching that democracy was to be achieved not by the victory of one nation over another but by the emancipation of an international working class, through new, international, workingmen's associations. From the radical left wing of Republicanism, French nationalism, turning defensive, moved to the *bourgeois* Centre and Right, where the rising threat of the First, Second and Third Internationals (founded in London in 1866, Copenhagen and Amsterdam in

1901 and 1919, and Moscow in 1919–21), and the simultaneous challenge to France's position in Europe and overseas by her dynamic trading and colonial rivals, Great Britain, Germany and, later, the United States, were felt most keenly. But during the late 1930s the successes of counter-revolutionary Fascism in Italy, Germany and Spain caused spasmodic and contradictory shifts of feeling and policy in France: the Communist-led left wing abandoned their 'revolutionary defeatism' and called for arms to fight Franco, Mussolini and Hitler, while the French conservatives, on the other hand, were torn between their now habitual nationalistic reflexes and approval of the Fascist dictators' anti-Bolshevik posture: 'Better Hitler than Blum!'

After the Second World War, jingoistic patriotism in France (known as chauvinism, after Nicolas Chauvin, a naïve popular hero of the Revolutionary and Napoleonic Wars) was mainly to be found, if at all, on the extremes of both left-wing and right-wing opinion, where the established Republican 'system' was accused of giving way to a variety of obscure threats to the national interest, such as the hand of Moscow, international finance, the Vatican, Anglo-Saxon gold, United European (or American) technocracy. The flare-up of chauvinism among officers and colonists in Indo-China and Algeria during the colonial wars and retreats of the 1950s was narrowly based and, again, defensive, and hostile towards the parliamentary Republic: the National Assembly in Paris prattled while all over the Empire forgotten men held the crumbling bastions of Western and Christian civilisation. However, some of the old, outgoing missionary spirit of the Jacobin patriots has been recaptured and sublimated in the official ideology of contemporary Gaullism, as a claim that France is the natural leader of both Europe and the underdeveloped and non-committed nations.[8]

One predominant feature of French Republicanism is wariness of the use and abuse of power. In its extreme form, this doctrine, formulated for conservative Republicanism between the wars by the self-appointed and influential philosopher of the Radical Party, Alain, amounts to an almost unqualified commitment to the defence of the individual citizen against all the powers-that-be, including the power of the Republican state: *le citoyen contre les pouvoirs.*[9] More self-critically, it emerges as the demand that if the state, by planning and strong government, is to champion the nation as a whole against its privileged minorities (as the pure doctrine of the French Revolutionary Republicanism says it should), then it must do so by democratic *means* as well as for democratic *ends*. This is the position of P. Mendès France in *La République moderne* (1962), which is not only a fine statement of contemporary French Republicanism of the anti-authoritarian yet actively reforming variety, but also gives the best up-to-date account of why it is difficult in France to strike a constitutional balance between Republican democracy (with its traditional suspicion of power) and Republican government (with its traditional vocation for reform):

> If tomorrow we wish France to have a form of government that is capable of guaranteeing on the one hand the effective participation of citizens in the determination of policy and, on the other, of ensuring continuity and efficiency in carrying the policy out, then we must see to it that the powers in the state are in equilibrium, as Montesquieu two centuries ago showed they must be: '*Every man who exercises power* (and I would add: every constituted body which exercises power) *is inclined to abuse it; he does so up to the point at which he is checked.... To prevent the abuse of power, things must be so arranged that power checks power.*'
>
> Democracy resides in the balance of powers. Such a balance is the very beginning of democracy....
>
> The Constitution of 1946 was deficient in this respect. The Constitution of 1958 was no less so, while the use that has been made of it has aggravated this fault. When the time comes to correct the failings of the Fifth Republic, care will have to be taken to avoid backsliding into those of the Fourth.
>
> Men of the Left are readily convinced of the need to put checks on the abuse of the executive power. This is because the movement of emancipation and the conquest of liberty were first directed against the King and his ministers. These had to be resisted, their prerogatives had to be limited, they had to be made to submit to the control of a Parliament whose rights had constantly to be

> reinforced. For the whole of the last century there were ... governments composed of conservative notables whose inclination and whose mission were to contain and check the rising power of popular democracy. Working with and for this rising power meant, first and foremost, fighting against the established powers of government. These had to be weakened so that the people might speak.
>
> Thus was founded a still lively tradition. This is why so many Republicans and Socialists are still inclined to be reticent when an attempt is made to find a basis for firm and stable government.
>
> But it would be wrong to have the idea of extending democracy by methods that paralyse the action of the state, at a time when those who speak in its name must command the requisite means of standing up to private and sectional interests, and to economic and financial forces.[10]

A majority of French Republicans, in more than one crisis of this century, have for a time accepted government by an autocrat: Clemenceau in 1917, Poincaré in 1926, Daladier in 1938, Reynaud in 1940, de Gaulle from 1958 to 1969. But the general constitutional trend was towards weak administrations, at the mercy of overbearing Parliaments. Only during the last decade has the counter-trend against what is called 'Assembly régime' marked constitutional law to any effect. Minor constitutional changes in 1946 and 1954 had reflected broad recognition of the problem expounded above. But in 1958, and again in 1962, with de Gaulle in power, the balance between the executive and the legislative branches of the French state, that is between Government, Prime Minister and, especially, President of the Republic on the one hand, and the two Houses of Parliament on the other, was altered so drastically as to seem to many good parliamentarians besides Mendès France a quite unacceptably anti-democratic over-correction of the admitted failings of Assembly régime.[11]

The French habit of rewriting their political constitution from time to time does not preclude either gradual, pragmatic change, or reference to unwritten customs that can be used to bend statutes which prove impracticable. The French state 'moves with the times' and 'comes to terms with reality' more readily than it is sometimes given credit for. The written constitutions of Republican France (1793, 1795, 1799, 1848, 1852, 1875, 1946, 1958)[12] are like snapshots of a continuous process that is controlled both by the march of ideas and by constantly changing social and economic conditions. The process affects chiefly the relative positions and powers of the more or less permanently established offices and bodies of President, Prime Minister, Government, Parliament, the Council of State, the officials and elected councillors of local government. But the very determination of the French to record it precisely, in an apparently endless series of written constitutional Acts and amendments, does have the unfortunate effect of creating a permanent climate of constitutional impermanency which contrasts strongly with the constitutional consensus within which British and American politicians normally operate. Moreover, while most Frenchmen now assume that, broadly speaking, the Republic is the best of all possible forms of government for France, there is no general agreement over what particular forms and relations of power constitute the best of all possible French Republics. The marked constitutional dissensus in France means that each new team of politicians brought to office by a major shift in the political balance of opinion in the country is inclined to try out constitutional adjustments in order to try to make the machinery of government work better from their partisan point of view, Partisan revision of the electoral system (which is not fixed by the Constitution) is even more common: 'the classical terrain for partisan manœuvres'.[13] Thus the constitutional structure and the electoral systems of France tend to express the attitudes of the current political majority rather than permanent constitutional legality above party.[14] Opposing minorities, understandly identifying the state with the Government, tend for their part to inveigh against the 'system' (as the Gaullists did in the 1950s) or the 'régime' (as the anti-Gaullists have done since 1958) whenever their current political weakness or disunity keeps them from power. From 1951 to 1958 nearly one-third of the membership of the National Assembly consisted of extremists of the Left and of the Right who were not only against the Government and each other, but wanted to tear up and rewrite the Constitution as well (see Fig. 2).

The constitution of the Fifth Republic may be no more permanent, no less subject to continuous amendment and the eventual shock of replacement, than earlier versions. But its traditionally Republican aims at least are proclaimed unambiguously and with confidence:

> France is a Republic, indivisible, secular, democratic and social. It shall ensure the equality of all citizens before the law, without distinction of origin, race or religion. It shall respect all beliefs. . . .

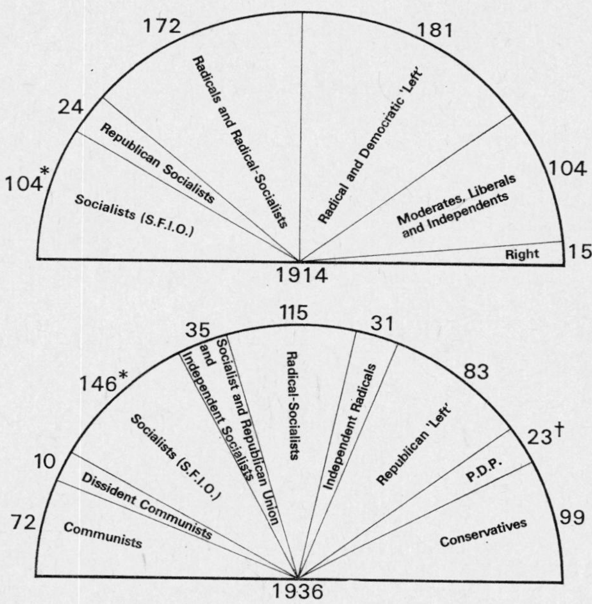

Fig. 2. Political party strengths in selected Parliaments. A. Chamber of Deputies of the Third Republic.

* S.F.I.O., *Section française de l'Internationale ouvrière.*
† P.D.P., *Parti démocrate populaire* (Catholic Democrats).

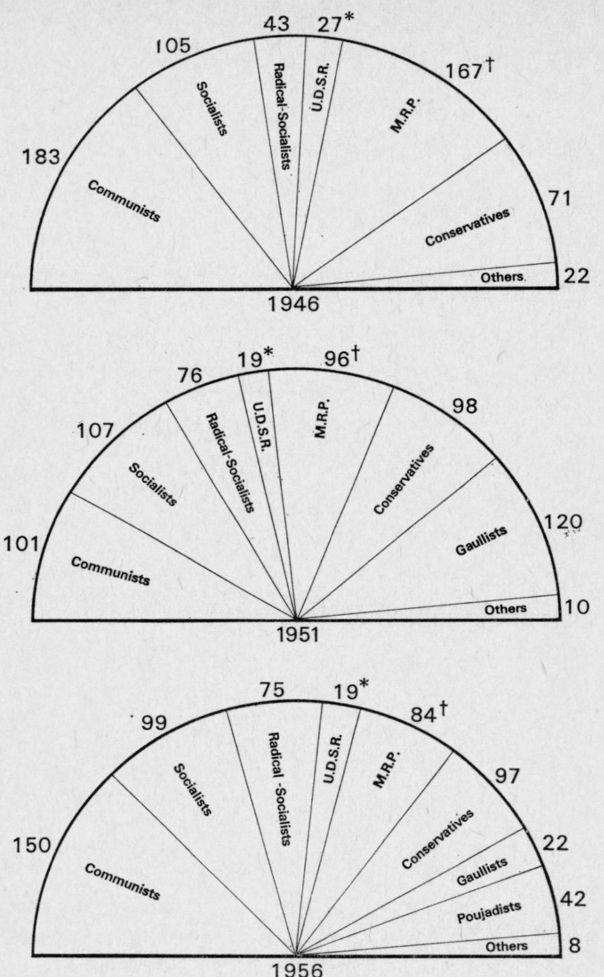

Fig. 2. Political party strengths in selected Parliaments. B. National Assembly of the Fourth Republic.

* U.D.S.R., *Union démocratique et socialiste de la Résistance* (Left-wing Radicals).

† M.R.P., *Mouvement républicain populaire* (Christian Democrats).

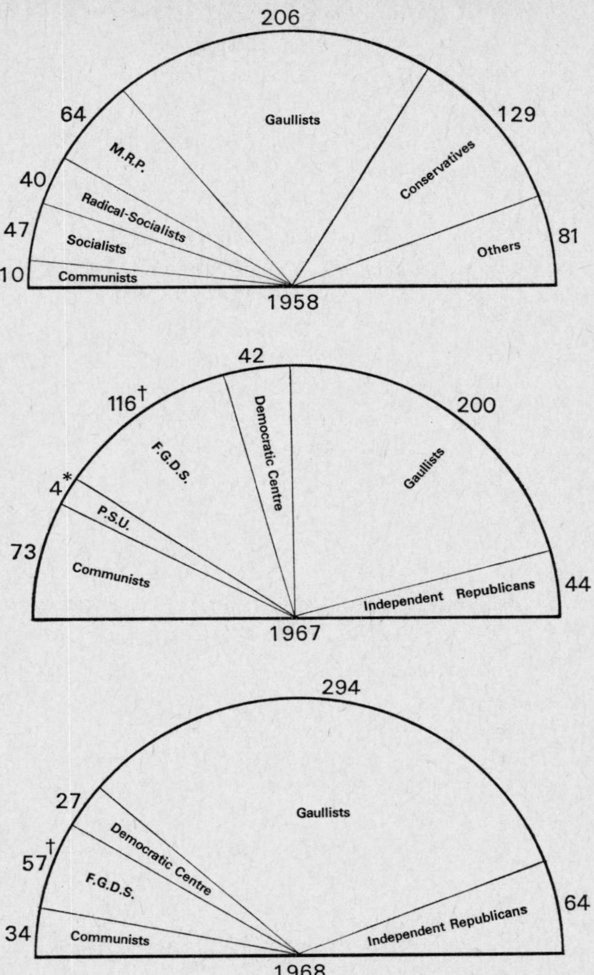

Fig. 2. Political party strengths in selected Parliaments. C. National Assembly of the Fifth Republic.

* P.S.U., *Parti socialiste unifié* (Left-wing Socialists).

† F.G.D.S., *Fédération de la gauche démocrate et socialiste* (Socialists, Left-wing Radicals, Clubs).

> The motto of the Republic is 'Liberty, Equality, Fraternity'.
>
> Its principle is government of the people, by the people and for the people.
>
> National sovereignty belongs to the people, which shall exercise this sovereignty through its representatives and by means of referendums.
>
> No section of the people, nor any individual, may attribute to themselves or himself the exercise thereof. . . .[15]

PARLIAMENT

The French Parliament is bicameral, consisting of a National Assembly, elected by direct universal suffrage, to which the political responsibility of the Government is 'pledged', and which may 'question' the Government's responsibility and bring about its resignation by passing a vote of censure or 'disapproving its programme or declaration of general policy' (Articles 49 and 50); and a Senate, representing the 'territorial units of the Republic' and Frenchmen living outside France, which is elected by indirect universal suffrage, that is, by a college of electors: men and women who are senatorial electors by virtue of their own previous election, to the Assembly or to a council of local government. As 97 per cent of them are the delegates of municipal councils, the Senate represents preponderantly the views and interests of France's tens of thousands of small country towns and villages.

The 487 deputies sitting in the National Assembly are elected for five years, the 283 Senators for nine. Before 1940, the Senate was as powerful politically as the popularly elected lower House of the French Parliament (then known by the more modest name of Chamber of Deputies), and it could and occasionally did overthrow a government. In the last twenty-five years it has lost much of its authority and is now in practice a consultative assembly only, though it has the power to veto bills passed in the National Assembly if, but only if, the Government wishes it to do so (Article 45).

THE EXECUTIVE

The Executive of the French Republic is a branch of government that is by tradition shared, in proportions which have varied greatly since the 1870s, between the President of the Republic and the Council of Ministers (or Government) under its Prime Minister (or, as he was called before 1958, *Président du Conseil des Ministres*). From 1875 to 1958, Presidents of the Republic were chosen by the French people only indirectly, like the Senate, but through an even smaller college of electors consisting solely of the members of both Houses of Parliament, meeting jointly in Congress at Versailles. Such Presidents were, generally speaking, the dependent creatures of the Parliaments that had chosen them. The effective Head of the Executive was the *Président du Conseil*, though his term of office, under the conditions of governmental instability which pertained for much of the Third Republic and all of the Fourth, was likely to be short. Presidents on the other hand were denied real power, though a politician of resource and drive at the Élysée Palace (the official residence in Paris of the French Head of State) could exert considerable influence behind the scenes during his seven-year term of office (*le septennat*) which might span the life-cycles of a dozen governments.

Presidents of the Fifth Republic serve for the traditional term of seven years (which may be renewed by re-election or, of course, cut short by resignation), but the form of their election was changed in 1962 from indirect to direct universal suffrage. The popularly elected Presidency is the 'keystone' of the new 'constitutional edifice',[16] and the correspondingly broader and more substantial authority with which it is intended thereby to invest the Head of the French State henceforth, is the heart of the Gaullist reaction against eighty years of Assembly régime.

The President's first duties, as laid down in the constitutional statutes of 1958, are to protect the Constitution, the state, the independence and the territory of France, and to ensure respect for treaties and for agreements of the 'Community' (which is the new name for what remains of France's overseas Empire). These duties set him above and apart from other 'governmental authorities', with the prescribed functions of 'arbitrator' and 'guarantor' and no constitutional right to 'determine policies', except in a declared emergency (Articles 16 and 20).[17] In practice, from the outset, de Gaulle gave these authorities a direct, positive lead in such important fields of policy-making and executive action as foreign and imperial affairs, defence and constitutional reform. Moreover, after the introduction in 1962 of presidential elections by popular vote, both de Gaulle and his political heir and presidential successor, Georges Pompidou, broke out of what had been alleged to be the presidential 'preserve' ('le domaine réservé – *dixit* J. Chaban-Delmas), and, without revising the rather imprecise *raison d'être* of the Presidency as defined in the written constitution of 1958, evolved a successful claim to 'inspire the general policy' over the whole range of the nation's affairs. Unrestricted in the scope of its application, the President's preponderant power within the Executive of the Fifth Republic is in no sense absolute, however, being limited in kind and degree by his obligation, under normal circumstances, to govern only with the agreement of the Prime Minister, whom he appoints (Article 8), but whose Government is responsible to the National Assembly, which may force it by a hostile vote to resign at any time. The revised system of checks and balances between Parliament and the Executive is completed by the restoration to the President of an earlier right (abandoned in 1877) to dissolve the National Assembly before the normal expiry of its mandate (Article 12). This presidential prerogative is also limited: the Prime Minister and the Presidents of the two Houses of Parliament must first be consulted; general elections must follow within forty days of the dissolution; the National Assembly convenes by right immediately after the elections; and there must be no further dissolution within the following year.

> Thus is established the balance between the executive power and the National Assembly, the Assembly having the power to dismiss the Government, the Chief of State having the right to dissolve the Assembly. The sovereign judge of this balance is the people, since, in the last analysis, it is they who arbitrate or will arbitrate the fundamental disagreements.

The principle of popular arbitration cited here by Pompidou in defence of the President's right to dissolve the Assembly, also inspires Article 3 of the new Constitution, which declares that the French people exercise their national sovereignty both through their representatives and by means of referenda, and Article 11, which authorises the President to submit to a popular referendum any Bill 'dealing with the organisation of the governmental authorities ...' Either Parliament or the Government may propose such a referendum. Thus a President acting in agreement with his Ministers has the power to by-pass the National Assembly, establish a direct dialogue with the nation over the heads of its parliamentary representatives, and hand over to the electorate the right of deciding for or against the enactment of possibly very important and controversial measures.[18] Like the restored right of dissolution, the introduction of law-making by referendum is the logical consequence of de Gaulle's policy of strengthening the Presidency to the point where it can rival the Assembly as a separate and equally direct and democratic expression of the popular will.

Article 16 gives the President almost unlimited emergency powers to enable him to carry out his primary mission of ensuring the safety and good working order of the state even 'when the institutions of the Republic, the independence of the nation, the integrity of its territory or the fulfilment of its international commitments are threatened in a grave and immediate manner and when the regular functioning of the constitutional governmental authorities is interrupted'. In such circumstances, only too familiar in France, and in de Gaulle's lifetime (1940–4 and 1958–62), the President is now authorised to 'take the measures commanded by these circumstances'. Before doing so, he must consult with the Prime Minister, the Presidents of the National Assembly and of the Senate, and the Constitutional Council, though he is not obliged to take their advice. He must inform the nation officially. Parliament meets by right and the National Assembly may not be dissolved. These are not very impressive safeguards against the possible misuse of vast powers for dealing with a state of emergency that is itself ill-defined. They might well tempt instead of dissuading an unscrupulous President who aimed at setting up a permanent dictatorship. But Article 16 has so far been invoked only once, by President de Gaulle, on reasonable grounds: the last-ditch resistance to Algerian independence of a white terrorist 'Secret Army Organisation', from April to October 1961.[19]

Besides the important and controversial new powers that were granted in Articles 8, 11, 12 and 16 of the Constitution of 1958 (none of which requires the countersignature of the Prime Minister), the following traditional presidential functions and rights were retained: chairing the Council of Ministers, signing ordinances and decrees that it decides on, promulgating laws voted by Parliament (there is no presidential veto – except in a declared emergency – but the President does have a fortnight's grace during which he may require Parliament to reconsider a law in whole or in part); ratifying treaties, appointing (and accrediting) ambassadors, appointing high civil and military officers. The President is also commander of the armed forces and chairman of the High Councils of Defence and of the Judiciary. He has the right of pardon.

The new, strong French Presidency was tailor-made for General de Gaulle (who was clearly, as he said, not the man for opening flower shows, and who had long attributed most of his country's ills to the constitutional weakness of its Presidents) and well adapted to the dramatic circumstances of his return to power in 1958 (a festering colonial war in North Africa and near civil war in the French homeland). Yet its status and powers, further enhanced in the years following, by what Pompidou described as 'evolution in broad daylight', which brought the authority of popular election and the fusion in one prestigious office of the functions of Head of State, Guardian of the Constitution and Chief Executive, appeared to be still generally acceptable to most Frenchmen more than a decade later, after de Gaulle's resignation and death, when the country was much more stable and prosperous. The anarchic uprising of students and young workers in May 1968,[20] provoked by de Gaulle's own high-handed paternalism in the exercise of his 'mandate', tended to convince their alarmed elders of the timely benefits of a Presidency made strong enough to restore order directly, while the conditions of administrative complexity and mass communications which underlie present-day politics everywhere and all the time, and which have personalised governmental authority in many countries besides France, have so far damped down any counter-swing against this most important chapter of the General's constitutional testament.

The Constitution prescribes that, in normal circumstances, the policy of the nation be determined and directed by the Government, under a Prime Minister whose duty is to 'ensure the execution of the laws' (Articles 20 and 21). In the double-headed Executive fashioned over a period of ten years by the reputation, personality and political philosophy of General de Gaulle, the Prime Minister's is the lesser role. Vis-à-vis Parliament, however, to which governments of the Fifth as of the Fourth and the Third Republics remain ultimately accountable, French Prime Ministers are in a much stronger position since 1958.

That year was not only one of exceptionally grave national crisis and alarming governmental paralysis but also the last of a long period of years during which French Ministries, under many different Prime Ministers, had been so repeatedly and heavily checked by constitutionally preponderant and politically fragmented Parliaments that coherent, long-term policy-making in the overall interest of the nation had become very nearly impossible, particularly in areas requiring decisive action against strongly entrenched sectional interests. Given the multiplicity of France's political parties, and the absence of a working majority in Parliament for any one of them, every Government of the Fourth Republic had been of necessity a coalition drawn from a reservoir of so-called *ministrables* (men of many different parties who were ambitious and likely to become Cabinet Ministers). Within this reservoir was a smaller pool of senior parliamentarians who served in many governments, most of them holding the Premiership once, and some of them more than once. The most vulnerable and unstable of Cabinet posts was that of Premier. Important ministries such as Industry, Foreign Affairs, Interior, were sometimes held for comparatively long periods by one man, or at least by one political party, under several successive Prime Ministers, and this made for some degree of purposeful continuity in these fields at these times. But throughout the twelve years of the Fourth Republic (1946–58), governments collapsed and were remade under new (or returning) Premiers, at the slightest strain, and on the average once every five or sixth months.[21] In spite of the constitutional weaknesses of elected government, and with the help of men and organisations working away from the parliamentary limelight, some things, such as industrial modernisation and expansion, and the first practical steps towards the unification of Western Europe, were successfully accomplished during these years. Other tasks, equally vital to France, such as financial and colonial reform, were shirked, or not tackled soon enough. The nation developed a chronic state of so-called 'immobilism', and the state itself in the end came near to collapse.

It was to be expected, therefore, on the long-term swing of the pendulum (which for nearly two hundred years of French history has oscillated between extremes of weak and strong government), as much as for the evident needs of the hour and because of the views of the man of the hour, that the Constitution of the new Republic would be designed to strengthen the Prime Minister and his Government, as well as the President of the Republic, against those statutory and customary prerogatives of the French Parliament as law-maker and Cabinet-breaker that the Executive as a whole had lately found most frustrating. On this, at least, most Frenchmen and French leaders were for the time being agreed. The missing but essential requirements of good government that Pierre Pflimlin, the last Premier before de Gaulle, demanded of the last Parliament of the Fourth Republic (in his investiture speech on 13 May 1958, the day the unity and authority of the French state were openly breached by the mob and the army of French Algiers), were 'authority', 'force', 'prestige' and 'duration'. And these corresponded clearly with the well-known constitutional objectives of Pflimlin's successor, who would steer the French Republic through and out of the crisis: 'discipline', 'cohesion', 'unity', and 'continuity'.[22]

LAW-MAKING AND RULE-MAKING

Laws in France are by definition texts adopted by the Legislature. In practice no Parliament can consider the mass of detailed regulations needed to implement legislation in a modern state, and this responsibility is assumed by the Executive, under 'rule-making' powers, known in France as *le pouvoir réglementaire*. Before 1958, however, the law-making prerogative of the French Parliament was technically unlimited. There was nothing to stop Parliament from legislating on detailed matters normally covered by governmental decree or ministerial *arrêté*, when this appeared politically expedient to a large enough group of deputies at a given time. When this happened, often the only way to free the machinery of legislation again was for the nation's official law-makers to unburden themselves of their responsibilities by delegating to the Government of the day the power to legislate over a wide area in their place, by decree (*décret-loi*). A government of the Fifth Republic retains the traditional *pouvoir réglementaire*, and may also still ask Parliament to authorise it for a limited period to take, through what are now called *ordonnances*, 'measures that are normally within the domain of law' (Article 38). But in addition, the 'domain of law' itself has been constitutionally restricted to exclude detail entirely from some fields. Parliament must still pass all laws, but laws which may still prescribe 'rules' concerning such matters as civil rights, legal status, justice, taxation, elections are now confined to the 'fundamental principles' of such others as national defence, education, property, unions and social security. Financial laws and laws pertaining to national planning are also required for determining the resources, obligations and objectives of the state in these fields (Article 34). Other business is dealt with as a matter of course by executive action of the Government, using its *pouvoir réglementaire*.[23]

Before 1958, the *order* of parliamentary business was determined by an all-party Rules Committee. Now it is firmly in the hands of the Government (though one meeting a week must be reserved for members' questions). Ministers are also able to exercise much stricter control than before over the *course* of parliamentary debates. Before 1958, the committee and report stages of Bills were completely controlled by powerful standing committees (*les commissions*). Each committee was recruited proportionately from all the political groups in the Assembly (or Senate): a miniature Parliament, but specialising in a distinct area of government, such as finance, foreign affairs, agriculture, defence, etc., and tending for this reason to respond rather narrowly to the pressures of sectional interests within the electorate. Moreover, the chairmen and vice-chairmen of these committees were usually ambitious and influential *ministrables* looking to succeed the reigning Minister in their field at the next government crisis. The committees habitually redrafted government Bills so drastically that when one came up for debate before the full House it might be changed beyond all recognition, no longer the Government's Bill but the committee's (and presented by the committee's *rapporteur*, not the Minister). Bills must still be sent to a committee for study before being debated in either the National Assembly or the Senate, but this may be an *ad hoc* one specially set up for the purpose, while the number of standing committees has been restricted to six for each House (though the size of the committees has grown correspondingly). In any case Parliament must now debate the Government's, not the committee's, text of a government Bill, and this is presented and steered through debate and divisions by the Minister, not the committee's *rapporteur*. Moreover, once the debate has begun, the Government may oppose the examination of any amendment which has not previously been submitted to committee, and it may close the debate by the 'guillotine' method, insisting on a single vote on all or part of the text under discussion (*vote bloqué*) (Articles 42 and 44).[24]

The reform of the legislative process outlined above reflects the crucial Gaullist doctrine of separation between the executive and the legislative branches of Government, in place of the alleged confusion of powers characteristic of Assembly régime in France. A further constitutional change is intended to reinforce this separation at the personal level: Article 23 obliges a deputy or a Senator to resign his seat in Parliament if he accepts a post in the Government. In terms of party politics, a correspondingly more clear-cut separation between supporters and opponents of the Government will, it is hoped, spring from changes in the statutes regulating the process and consequences of a government's parliamentary defeat.

GOVERNMENT AND OPPOSITION

Political parties and groups have the constitutional right and duty of freely and democratically giving expression to the people's suffrage (Article 4). Because of the large number of separate parties represented in French Parliaments since the founding of the modern Republic a hundred years ago, French governments have rarely enjoyed the support of a stable majority in Parliament, and never had to face a large, convincingly united opposition capable of providing a broadly based alternative government. As de Gaulle had predicted at Bayeux in 1946, and as Pflimlin confirmed in the National Assembly on 13 May 1958, the Fourth Republic, like the Third, failed to ensure executive 'duration' and 'continuity'. This was not so much because its Premiers had been unable to avoid or defeat the comparatively rare formal vote of censure that would oblige them to resign, or had been unable to obtain votes of confidence meant to confirm them in office (motions of both censure and confidence requiring, if they were to succeed, the backing of the absolute majority of the total membership of the Assembly), as because governments were vulnerable to constant attack from many directions by shifting alliances of small groups and individual critics opposed to particular aspects of its political programme, who could 'interpellate', i.e. question, challenge and defeat them on a succession of minor issues by a simple majority of those voting.[25] Harassed in this way, most Cabinets, after a few weeks or months, 'fell apart internally or resigned on defeat by a simple majority', without waiting to be overthrown by the procedure laid down in the Constitution.[26]

Under the new Constitution, the Government can make the National Assembly's acceptance of a Bill a question of general confidence, the Bill becoming law unless a vote of censure is proposed within twenty-four hours and is passed by an absolute majority of the Assembly. If the censure motion succeeds, the Government must tender its resignation to the President of the Republic, who thereupon terminates the functions of the Premier and may exercise his restored right to dissolve the National Assembly, with the automatic consequence that general elections for a new Assembly follow within forty days (Articles 8, 12 and 50). The Prime Minister, after deliberation in the Council of Ministers, is also permitted, but not obliged, to call for a vote of confidence in his programme or general policy, and the Assembly may, on its account, 'question the responsibility of the Government by the vote of a motion of censure', provided that this is signed by at least one-tenth of the total membership of the Assembly. Except on matters which the Government has itself made a question of confidence, the signatories of a motion of censure that has been rejected may not introduce a further one during the same session of Parliament (Article 49).

Though French Prime Ministers have, generally speaking, remained in office for much longer periods since these measures were introduced, it is still too soon to judge whether new internal arrangements for motions of confidence and censure in the Assembly have contributed significantly to the desired effect, for parliamentary elections since 1958 have produced unusually strong and united government majorities there. This development may owe something to the Gaullist version of presidential government, which works nationally, though not in local government, against the characteristically fine discrimination and fragmented loyalties of French party politics, by clearly encouraging the formation of a large 'President's Party' that is prepared to give the President's First Minister the long-term support in Parliament that he needs if his government is to survive. It has been facilitated by the reversion of the Gaullists, after a post-war experiment with proportional representation, to the traditional Republican system of parliamentary elections in single-member constituencies with the possibility of two ballots. Each constituency elects one deputy. A candidate winning an absolute majority of the votes cast at the first ballet is elected. Otherwise (that is, in most constituencies) there is a run-off (*ballottage*) a week later, when the least successful candidates drop out, leaving the field to the two men best placed locally to collect moderate or floating votes in a straight fight to 'bar the road', in the last resort, either to 'revolution' or to 'reaction'. The two-ballot, single-member electoral system tends, at least for the period of the election, and particularly during *ballottage* at the *deuxième tour*, to neutralise to some extent the deep-seated tendency of the French electorate towards multiple fragmentation. However, the persistent ideological divisions of the left wing, between Catholics and anti-clericals and, especially, between Communists and anti-Communists, have so far prevented the anti-Gaullist opposition from taking full advantage of this. In relation to the size of their overall poll at first ballots, the Socialists and more especially the Communists have been under-represented in the Assemblies of the Fifth Republic, and the Gaullists have been relatively over-represented.[27]

L'HÉMICYCLE

The semicircular debating Chamber of the Palais Bourbon, which is the principal public arena of parliamentary politics in France, suggests by its very shape both the novelty and the risks of the Gaullists' declared aim of separating more widely the powers of the Executive and the Legislature of the French Republic, and of sharpening the distinction between parliamentary parties supporting and opposing its Government.

The rectangular British House of Commons, where Government and Opposition members, Ministers and Shadow Ministers, confront and address each other across the 'Floor of the House', masking as it does many differences and rivalries on either side, epitomises a system of parliamentary government which works by simplification and separation, eliminating the finer shades of opinion, and exaggerating the division, at the centre of the political spectrum, between the supporters and the opponents of those who hold the executive power. The semicircular Chamber of the Palais Bourbon distributes the assembled representatives of the sovereign people of France fanwise in front of the President of the Assembly, who chairs its proceedings. His 'Speaker's eye' travels from the disciplined ranks of the Communists on his extreme left (the customary place of the most radically progressive group in French Parliaments, hence the term 'left wing') through the almost imperceptible nuances of the moderate Centre to the Conservatives and reactionaries on the right wing, and from the Cabinet Ministers and the spokesmen of the parliamentary committees who occupy segments of the front benches below his desk to the high back row of the *hémicycle* topped by an arc of deep boxes for the public and Press. The only 'floor' to cross is the space between the *hémicycle* as a whole and the rostrum (*la tribune*) just below the President's desk from which all set speeches are delivered. Deputies are allowed to put questions and to make short statements from their assigned seat in the tiered semicircle. But the most important and decisive confrontations take place between, on the one side, an isolated orator who, having left his place with party or Cabinet colleagues in the *hémicycle*, has crossed the floor and climbed to the rostrum, and, on the other, facing him, an audience embodying in theory the entire assembled nation. The very different line-up of two teams competing face to face in the Palace of Westminster is foreign to the French parliamentary tradition.[28]

Given the proved bent of the French mind, from Saint-Just to Charles Maurras, for constructing intransigent political theories, given the history of violent political strife in France, there is some reason for believing that it is advisable to separate Government and Opposition, as well as rival extremists, in the National Assembly with something more substantial than the conventional sword's length between the two sides of the relatively mild House of Commons game, and that this is an essential function of the characteristically indeterminate, flexible, shock-absorbing parliamentary Centre, where most of the governments of France for the last hundred years have been raised and have found their main support.

A case can be made against the attempt by the founders of the Fifth Republic to break with the spontaneously created French tradition of government by coalitions, growing from the Centre, or towards the Centre, and nourished by a continuous and easy coming and going between Committee Room and Cabinet Room, and between moderate Left and moderate Right. This has been the normal pattern since the final establishment of Republican institutions in France at the end of the last century; while the opposite, centrifugal state of political opinion and power has appeared mainly in times of national crisis, often as a threat to parliamentary institutions: the Dreyfus Affair at the beginning of the century, the economic depression and the rise of Hitler in the 1930s, and the aftermath of the lost Battle of France in 1940: German occupation of the country, the French Resistance movement, and Liberation by the 'Anglo-Saxons'. Professor Philip Williams points out that the spirit of cameraderie built up in the club atmosphere of the Assembly's Standing Committee rooms is 'a virtue and not a vice of parliamentary government'.[29] Professor Stanley Hoffmann demonstrates the inhibiting effect on present procedures for improving responsible government in France of the continuing reluctance of the French to narrow down the protective distance separating leader and led to anything approaching a face-to-face confrontation.[30] Both these outstanding historians of French politics since the Second World War are agreed, however, that such characteristic weaknesses of the French body politic as bureaucracy, irrelevance, procrastination, rhetoric, neglect of present realities and remembrance of battles past and best forgotten, were more often indulged than corrected by the manner of Assembly régime in the 'House without Windows' of the Fourth Republic.[31]

How many of the traditional procedures of parliamentary Republicanism in France, which have been cut back but not altogether eliminated since 1958,[32] ought to be finally abandoned, and how many ought to be maintained or restored for the good of the modern Republic, are matters of opinion.[33] How much, and what, can be changed depends partly on the Constitutional Council, set up in 1958 to pronounce on the constitutionality of all so-called organic laws (that is to say, laws governing the operation of political institutions) and of the standing orders of parliamentary assemblies (Article 61); depends largely, for the present, on President de Gaulle's legacy – the authority of a political idea and the preponderance of a political party; and will depend eventually on the new balance of power between the parties, and on the emerging pattern of social tensions and economic drives that the parties will succeed in representing on behalf of the sovereign people, in the open future.

6 The Civil Service and Local Government

THE ADMINISTRATIVE STRUCTURE

CHANNELS of communication, control and command are provided within the French state between the Government, which is responsible to Parliament for 'determining and directing the policy of the nation', and the permanent civil servants who carry out that policy in the daily life of the French people; and between the Ministries in Paris and the locally elected councils of provincial France, which have a limited responsibility for the affairs of their respective districts: the 95 *départements* and the 38,000 *communes* of the 'hexagon' (see Map 10).[1]

The modern French state derives from the centralised administration created by Cardinal Richelieu in the seventeenth century, to secure the rising political power of the French monarchy against the resistance and turbulence of feudal and religious factions, and perfected by Napoleon Bonaparte, as First Consul of the theoretically 'one and indivisible' First Republic, in 1800, in order to hold together the still highly fissile material of corporate, regional and personal ambitions released by the collapse of the monarchy. The Napoleonic state has been significantly liberalised over the last one hundred and fifty years, and elected local councils are now free to make many genuinely decentralised decisions on behalf of their constituents. But enough of its centralising force has survived into the middle of the twentieth century to check the healthy growth of corporate initiative in the French provinces, to promote much anxious planning of new schemes to improve regional independence and development and even to give some colour to the nevertheless exaggerated charge of Jean-Jacques Servan-Schreiber, one of the heads of anti-Gaullism in the 1970s, that Paris governs the French provinces as if they were its subject colonies. The decisions of even such important local representatives as mayors and departmental councillors (*conseillers généraux*) are subject to close supervision and control by officials of the central Government. This is known as administrative tutelage (*tutelle administrative*). On the other hand these officials are themselves subject to the checks and balances incorporated in two further important working parts of the machinery of French government: the *directions* and the *cabinet ministériel.*

The politically responsible Ministers of the elected Government of the French Republic are necessarily (and before 1958 were exceedingly) impermanent figures. The danger of undue power passing by default into the hands of permanent, but politically irresponsible, civil servants is correspondingly great. In consequence most French government departments have no chief administrator comparable to a British Permanent Secretary, but are divided into a number of separate directorates (called *directions*) each of which is headed, not by a permanent civil servant, but by a *directeur* who is appointed (and who may be dismissed) by the Government in office (though he is generally a career official seconded from his regular post in, maybe, quite another department).[2] As further reinforcement of the Minister's authority over the permanent staff in his department he personally appoints a small but powerful secretariat and brains trust called *le cabinet du ministre* which he has drawn from among political friends, from the universities, from journalism, from appropriate specialist branches of business, agriculture or technology, and, particularly in the Fifth Republic, from the administrative grade of the civil service itself. Whatever his background, no *chef de cabinet, directeur, directeur-adjoint, conseiller technique* or *chargé de mission* has security of tenure within the *cabinet.* The Minister may use him and promote him as he sees fit, and, naturally, dispense with his services, or take him with him when he moves to his next post, or recommend him to a colleague or successor.

The immediate subordination and personal loyalty of *cabinet* to Minister, and the multiple, mutable *directions* of French Ministries, are exact expressions of that wary mistrust of official power which, making the French such a difficult people to govern, paradoxically necessitates strong central government by permanent officials. Together with administrative tutelage, but finely biased in the opposite direction, the *cabinet ministériel* is an important part of the delicate self-regulating mechanism of compensation, between state control and parliamentary or local liberties, that is at the very heart of 'the reality of political power in France'.[3] Besides the surveillance of permanent officials on behalf of his Minister, the *chef de cabinet* looks after his contacts with the outside world – public relations, liaison with his constituency, collection of information of all kinds. The work is exacting, responsible and exciting. For a bright young man, it is also a swift and direct way to the top, giving access to places of real influence in both administrative and political spheres.

THE ADMINISTRATIVE GRADE

This grade of the French civil service was once recruited almost entirely from two sources: the Faculty of Law, and the privately-run, fee-paying *École Libre des Sciences Politiques*,[4] both of them more or less reserved for the sons of 'good families' in the ruling *bourgeoisie*: inheritors (*héritiers*, as opposed to *boursiers* – scholarship boys – for whom the path of success lay upwards through the Faculties of Arts and of Science, and the teaching profession). So the permanent state official's *esprit de corps* was reinforced by a similarly cohesive *esprit de caste*. To democratise the public administration of the country after the Second World War, *Sciences Po* was nationalised and, in addition, a new *École Nationale d'Administration* (E.N.A.) was set up, through which all administrative-grade civil servants would have to pass, after graduation from the University or one of the *grandes écoles*,[5] or after service in a lower grade of the administration. Entrance is by stiff competition, and intellectual and practical training are both thorough. After a first year spent working under supervision in a branch of the public service in France or abroad, two months with a private firm and thirteen months' instruction in the School itself, candidates sit an examination which tests and grades them, giving those at the top of the final order the first choice of branch. This training has brought a post-war generation of dedicated and skilled Keynesian planners to the top of the French civil service, a generation less politically conservative and narrowly juridical than its predecessors and more impatient with the sectional interests and the habits of inertia rooted in 'static', 'stalemate' France, which they see blocking the nation's progress towards general prosperity. But the new form of secular noviciate devised for *la haute administration* has not yet democratised the service.[6]

The men best placed in the final order at E.N.A. usually choose to enter one of the so-called *Grands Corps: Conseil d'État, Cour des Comptes, Inspection des Finances, Corps diplomatique, Corps préfectoral.*

LE CONSEIL D'ÉTAT

This has been described as the 'paragon of all French institutions'.[7] It is certainly one of the most ancient and powerful. It was modelled by Napoleon on the former pre-revolutionary *Conseil du Roi*, and has remained a nerve centre of the French state ever since, an excellent example of continuity and gradual evolution beneath the superficially sudden, revolutionary and counter-revolutionary peripeteia of French constitutional history. It is both an advisory and a judicial body.

The Council of State *advises* the Government on the drafting of new laws, decrees and ministerial orders, and resolves difficulties or disputes between Ministries and between departments over the interpretation of existing ones. For forty years French Parliaments have been delegating authority to governments to legislate by decree or ordinance or *loi-cadre* (that is, a general 'framework' law, the details to be filled in by the Executive); since 1958, the area in which executive action is to be regarded as proper and normal has been consolidated and extended by a further big bite out of the traditional 'domain' of parliamentary law-making. The Council's power of advice is correspondingly wide-ranging, and it is extremely influential. The *Conseil d'État* also *supervises* the working of the civil service departments, with power to suggest improvements and reforms, and, as one of the superior, central authorities of 'administrative tutelage', its *Section de l'Intérieur* (in close touch with the Ministry of the Interior) plays an important part in watching over and checking the local authorities either directly or through subordinate councils in the *départements*; its *prior* approval is required, moreover, in such matters as town-planning, long-term loans and boundary changes. Finally, the *Conseil d'État* is a court of administrative law (*Section du contentieux*), where local authorities, as well as private individuals and associations, can seek redress against undue interference in their affairs by state officials.

Many of the reforms promoted by the royal administration of Louis XVI in the last years of the *ancien régime* had been obstructed by reactionary opinion in the old French courts of common law (*parlements*). The revolutionaries therefore removed the official acts of government servants from the competence of the ordinary courts altogether, forbidding 'judges . . . to interfere in any way whatsoever with the operations of administrative bodies, or to summon administrators on charges connected with their duties' (Law of 16–24 August 1790). Napoleon's 'Constitution of the Year VIII' and (1799) transferred all such cases to the new *Conseil d'État,* and to subordinate courts in the *départements* called *Conseils de Préfecture*. At first, there were not many cases to try. But as the size of the civil service, and the incidence of government regulations on everyday life, increased during the next century and a half, the number of actions brought by aggrieved private citizens and corporations against officials alleged to have exceeded or misused their power grew, and so did the number of conflicts between local authorities and the central Government, which was also to fall within the competence of the *Conseil d'État*.[8] The courts quickly won independence from governmental or official pressure and throughout the next century and a half built up a body of liberally inspired precedents, and a respected tradition as the 'great protector of the rights of property and of the rights of the individual against the state' and the 'great redresser of wrongs committed by the state'.[9]

Since 1953, nearly all administrative cases are heard in the first instance by local *Tribunaux administratifs* (replacing the former *Conseils de Préfecture*), or by such specialist courts as *les commissions d'aide sociale* (public assistance) and *La Cour des Comptes*.[10] The *Conseil d'État* in Paris remains the final court of appeal for all administrative litigation.[11]

RUE DE RIVOLI, RUE DE VARENNE, RUE DE VALOIS AND PLACE BEAUVAU

The Minister of Justice holds the seals of state (and is known as *Le Garde des Sceaux*), but in practice the most important minister after (and at times before) the French Premier is the Minister of Finance, *le grand argentier*, because he holds the purse strings, and because his team of *inspecteurs des finances*, based at the Rue de Rivoli, where the French Treasury occupies a wing of the Louvre Palace, have an awe-inspiring reputation of cool brilliance. Nothing shows better the limits of pure technocracy, for finance must entail party-political decisions and is a familiar stumbling-block to French governments. But the authority and influence of France's men from the Treasury extends far beyond the walls of the Louvre: former *inspecteurs des finances* are to be found everywhere in French (and European) administrations, planning and deciding policy at the highest levels.[12]

Three French ministries reflect outstandingly important aspects of French life. The Ministry of Agriculture (Rue de Varenne) is a kind of paternalistic and all-embracing Home Office for rural France and, naturally, has far more weight and prestige than its British equivalent. The Ministry of Culture, in the Rue de Valois, maintains the strong French tradition of state patronage in the fields of drama, music, literature, painting, sculpture and architecture. De Gaulle's Minister of Culture was André Malraux, a close friend who shared with him not only the love of country they had proved in war but also a certain passionate and civilised 'idea of France'. With Malraux's driving temperament and creative mind in charge, official support of the arts was more than usually forceful and discriminating: in Paris, the galleries of the Louvre museum were extended, masterpieces of twentieth-century sculpture were added to those of earlier periods in the public gardens, the Opera House got a new ceiling by Chagall, and the classical streets and palaces of the historic centre, and the old aristocratic quarter of the Marais, had the grime of centuries cleaned off their honey-coloured walls and colonnades. Malraux's *Maisons de la Culture*, for the presentation, interpretation and discussion of literature and the arts, at Grenoble, Caen, Rennes, Amiens, Bourges and other provincial cities (and at Ménilmontant in East End, working-class Paris), supported and extended an already remarkable post-war renaissance of culture, and more especially of good theatre, in the French provinces.[13]

The Ministry of the Interior (Place Beauvau, nearly opposite the official residence of the President of the Republic, the Élysée Palace) is the key to government action throughout the whole civil service and every part of France. Its chief agents are the Prefects of the ninety-five *départements* into which the territory of metropolitan France is divided and the twenty-two Super- or Regional Prefects.

A Prefect has some five thousand listed duties, and four main fields of action. Within the area of his command (the military term is not inappropriate to the Napoleonic traditions of the *corps préfectoral*)[14] he is the sole representative of the state and the personal delegate of every Minister in the Government, so all government officials are directly subordinate to him, and the traditionally wide power of the French state to regulate society 'for the general purpose of assuring public order' (*police administrative,* as distinct from *police judiciaire* or investigation and repression of crime)[15] is his responsibility. Secondly, he maintains a two-way flow of information between Paris and his *département*. The prefectures are particularly valuable to the central Government as provincial listening-posts on which Ministers rely for up-to-date intelligence of prevailing economic and social conditions and current political opinion throughout the country. Thirdly, the Prefect represents his own Minister of the Interior, who is responsible for the supervision of all local authorities. In this capacity the Prefect is the tutelage authority of the communes and their mayors. Fourthly, he is the executive agent of the General Council of the *département,* and as such is responsible for putting into effect the decisions of an elected local authority. He is assisted by several Sub-Prefects posted to the *arrondissements* into which each *département* is divided.

The Prefecture is thus the focus of both central and local government at ninety-five points on the hexagon (twenty-two of which also represent the large-scale pattern of the Economic Regions). The Prefect must respond both to the voice of the elected local authorities – mayors (whom he must nevertheless overrule from time to time), municipal and departmental councils (whose decisions he may nevertheless have to fight on legal grounds, or send to the Council of State for a ruling) – and to the rein of the central Government, which hires and can fire him (but whose officials in his area, and sometimes in Paris too, he will often oppose on behalf of his mayors and councillors). Creatures of Napoleonic centralisation, Prefects have evolved significant counterbalancing faculties for the defence of local interests, and these have recently been reinforced deliberately by Paris, in the interest of what is called 'deconcentration' (as opposed to the direct expression of genuinely 'decentralised' autonomy by locally elected assemblies): for instance, in 1970 the control of the Prefectures over local expenditure was strengthened and rendered less dependent on decisions taken in Paris. In any case, the local councillors and mayors of provincial France, whom the Prefects and Sub-Prefects have to live with, are generally popular, and determined, men. Controlling them, in what the central Government decides is the national interest, is a subtle, creative and demanding art, which can bring great personal satisfaction and prestige. Prefects can stand up to Paris on behalf of their *administrés* all the better for their posts being less closely tied than in the past to party-political patronage, and less subject to the 'massacres' which used occasionally to purge their ranks when the government changed. A government can still summarily dismiss a Prefect, but since the Second World War the *corps préfectoral*, like the administrative grade in other government departments has been increasingly recruited from the alumni of the National School of Administration (E.N.A.), and offers a career which, at least up to the level of Sub-Prefect, is now reasonably secure.[16]

The Ministry of the Interior also directs *La Police Nationale* (formerly *La Sûreté Nationale*), headquarters of the state police, and supervises the deployment of the *gendarmerie nationale*.[17] In the towns (apart from Paris), the police are under the orders of the mayor, with some exceptions, which spring from the French people's long history of political turbulence. For instance, in towns with more than ten thousand citizens, it is the Prefect (appointed by the central Government) and not the mayor (a locally elected official) who is responsible for maintaining public order or repressing public disturbances, and Prefects can always take away control of the police from the mayor, in villages and towns of whatever size, if he fails to take the steps necessary to ensure order, or if the public peace is threatened over a wide area. The locally organised and paid *gardes champêtres* of small country places look after minor, routine matters, such as the checking of licences; though one, in the early years of the Fourth Republic, at Fontaine-de-Vaucluse (826 inhabitants), was ordered by his mayor, who had become exasperated by the Communist municipal councillors' persistent campaigning for peace, aid to China, and so on, to prevent infringement of a mayoral regulation making it illegal to carry or to make use of the atomic bomb within the town boundary.[18]

During the civil disturbances caused by the Algerian War, between 1956 and 1962, the special French riot police (*Les Compagnies Républicaines de Sécurité* – C.R.S.) were often in action, and the existence of a clandestine *police parallèle,* known popularly as *les barbouzes,* formed to fight anti-government terrorists with their own violent methods, began to be noticed and generally feared and disliked. The police once more used violence, frequently in excess, when disorder broke out again on the streets of Paris, Lyon and other French cities in the student rebellion of May 1968.

LOCAL AUTHORITIES

The feudal complexities of fief, charter town and ecclesiastical domain were replaced after the Revolution of 1789 by a more uniform territorial division of the country into small, contiguous areas called *communes,* a name recalling medieval struggles for municipal liberties. The *communes* were based on existing localities formed by nature and history, and these ancient entities have survived as the smallest units of French local government. By now they vary enormously in area, population and character. There are *communes* in the deep countryside extending over more than a thousand acres which have only 200 inhabitants. On the other hand, Marseille is a heavily populated *commune* of 62,000 acres, and there is a *commune* of 30,000 inhabitants embedded in less than 650 acres of the Paris suburbs. All, except the capital city itself, have the same structure of local government: a municipal council elected by universal suffrage, and a mayor (with assistant mayors in populous *communes*) elected by the municipal council from among its members.[19]

The mayor in his *commune*, like the Prefect in his *département*, embodies both central and local interests. He is the executive agent of his municipal council, responsible to it for administering the *commune*, for putting the council's decisions into effect, and for representing its views and interests before the courts and before the administration. In particular, he is responsible for maintaining local highways and directing municipal building operations; he also prepares the budget of the *commune* and, once this is passed, by his municipal council and the Prefecture, authorises payments from it. But he is, at the same time, the representative and an agent of the state in his *commune*, responsible for publishing and enforcing the law of the land and, in *communes* of less than 10,000 inhabitants, for maintaining public order; he is the registrar of births, deaths and marriages (a duty taken over from the clergy by the *commune* after the French Revolution), he provides the central Government with other statistical information (agricultural statistics, for instance, and the voting, school and military conscription-board registers), and he is responsible for public hygiene (*salubrité*) and morality.

As a state official, the mayor is at the end of a chain of command issuing from the Ministry of the Interior in Paris, and directly subordinate to his Prefect or Sub-Prefect. As the Executive of his local council, he is subject to central administrative tutelage. His budget must be approved by the Prefect, who can send it back for alteration and, finally, though this requires finesse and tact if it is not to lead to explosive or stagnant hostility between *mairie* and *préfecture*, alter it himself, if it fails to provide for some communal service required by law (such as a building for the state school in a strongly Catholic area). But within the bounds set by the hierarchical structure of the French state, and the standard codes of practice prescribed by the *Conseil d'État*, French mayors have great scope for decisive and authoritative action. Besides being agents of the local and the central powers, often re-elected time after time for long years of uninterrupted office, they are frequently prominent in national as well as local politics, linking the provinces with Paris as both chief citizen of a provincial *commune* and Member of Parliament. Many Cabinet Ministers, *ministrables* and opposition leaders of the last hundred years have also been mayors, some of them holding the office in large cities. In general, French mayors have 'considerably greater personal prestige and personal power' than British mayors.[20]

The *conseillers généraux* who represent the *départements* are elected by universal suffrage for a six-year term, half the council being renewed every three years. They meet for two short sessions a year only, and are not supposed to vote on 'political' issues. But the *conseils généraux* are political assemblies nevertheless, elected and seated by parties, 'a close reflection of the real political forces in the country', and containing many deputies and Senators among their members, with bases for action in both Paris and their *département,* providing yet another of the supple, personal links between French local and national affairs.[21]

The *départements* and the *communes* are the principal territorial units of Republican France, but they are not the only ones. Several separate overlapping administrative networks, for justice, education and defence, have existed for some time.[22] The *communes,* many of which are too small and poor to run their affairs independently, are encouraged to join forces in 'consolidated' groups or 'urban districts'. Since 1964, moreover, the latest of a long succession of schemes for overall, large-scale regional government has been put into effect, and is gaining influence steadily in the life of the nation.

Regional decentralisation was favoured at the beginning of the century mainly by political reactionaries, who were hostile to the Republic's practice of centralised national indivisibility, and who looked back nostalgically to the estates and provinces of the *ancien régime.* The Government of the wartime Vichy state (1940–4), which was warmly supported by such men, divided the country into eighteen administrative regions, twelve in territory occupied by the Germans, and six in the unoccupied south, each under a Regional Prefect. This was done for practical as well as for ideological reasons, but it was scrapped by the left-wing Government of liberated France. Then, in 1947, widespread revolutionary strikes by the Communist trade unions showed up the weaknesses in emergency of the uncoordinated information and police services of isolated Prefects. Eight civilian 'Super-Prefects', called *Inspecteurs généraux de l'administration en mission extraordinaire* (I.G.A.M.E.), were appointed to the eight existing Army regions to head security and communications over wide areas of country. They were also empowered to take charge of combined operations against floods, forest fire and other such disasters. Finally they were given the job of collecting information for the large-scale economic planning that has been an important priority for all the governments of post-war France.[23]

The primary objective of the present, Gaullist, scheme of regional administration is also economic planning, but more thoroughgoing: specifically 'the preparation and application of the regional sections of the Plan', and 'public investment by the Government'. Each of the twenty-two new regions is headed by a *Préfet de Région* who is assisted by an advisory body called *La Commission de Développement Économique Régional* (C.O.D.E.R.), which represents the people not through direct universal suffrage, as the councils of *commune* and *département* do, but by delegation, from local branches of existing social or economic associations, and the local councils themselves. This experiment in corporatism, of the kind long favoured in the social ideology of French Catholicism, and by pre-war and Gaullist technocrats, provoked some resistance from the old Republican notables, on municipal and departmental councils, as well as the predictable hostility of the extreme left wing: 'After having cut back the powers of Parliament, you are now attacking those of local assemblies by seeking to put carefully screened technicians in the place of democratically elected representatives . . . your Regional Prefects are to be veritable Proconsuls.'[24]

Because of its altogether exceptional size and importance, and its revolutionary history, Greater Paris has a special kind of local government. The reforms of 1882 and 1884 did not apply to the *Ville de Paris* (the central area, inside the nineteenth-century fortifications, which have now been demolished), or to the former surrounding *département* of Seine. Its general and municipal councils never had as much power as their provincial counterparts, and there has never been a single, elected Mayor of Paris. Routine administration is carried on by mayors without executive powers who are appointed by Government to each of the twenty *arrondissements* into which the city is divided. Executive power in the capital and its suburbs was until recently exercised by two very powerful government officials: the *Préfet de la Seine* (the senior French Prefect) and the *Préfet de Police*.

The whole Paris region was thoroughly reorganised in the late 1960s: Seine and nearby Seine-et-Oise have been abolished. *Ville de Paris* has become a *département*, and the rest of the former territory of Seine and Seine-et-Oise has been subdivided into six other new *départements*, whose Prefectures will provide so many fresh centres of supervision and control in the hitherto under-provided and formless suburbs (see Map 11). A *Conseil de Paris* replaces the defunct general council of the Seine and municipal council of Paris. The Prefecture of Police has been brought under the authority of the *Direction Générale de la Police Nationale* (which was created, in place of the *Sûreté Nationale* – that old rival of the Préfecture de Police – in October 1971) and its responsibilities, like those of the new *Préfet de Paris*, are confined to the city of Paris itself. Executive and police powers in the suburbs have been transferred to the new suburban Prefectures, and the whole *Région Parisienne* (which includes Seine-et-Marne as well as the seven new *départements*) is headed by a Regional Prefect.

Thus the state which gets its systematic and symmetrical organisation from a characteristically French *esprit de géométrie* continues to show enough equally French *finesse* to respond flexibly, if rather slowly, to changing circumstances.

7 Education and Justice

STATE SCHOOLS AND UNIVERSITIES

In France these form a single system springing from the same eighteenth-century revolutionary and Napoleonic policies of national unification and administrative centralisation that inspired the founding of the *Conseil d'État*, the *corps préfectoral* and the Institut de France. Teachers are civil servants of the central Government, and their pupils' entry to higher education (and so, generally speaking, to the managerial or technological *cadres* or to the liberal professions) depends on a pass in the public examination for the national school-leaving certificate, *le baccalauréat*, which is also organised and moderated by the Ministry of Education in Paris. The country is divided into twenty-three educational districts called *académies*, each headed by a *Recteur* appointed by the Minister of Education, and charged, as his representative, with administering all school and university education within his area. The *Recteur d'Académie* is also a kind of lay bishop, representing in his academic 'diocese', alongside the ranged temporal powers of the *corps préfectoral, conseillers généraux, conseillers municipaux, maires, députés et sénateurs,* the precious principles of the Enlightenment: reason, humanity, liberty of conscience and freedom of inquiry.

Napoleon's national teaching order, *L'Université de France,* has not stood still since its inception, in 1808, any more than the legal and administrative systems that modern France inherited from the same fertile brain and politically creative age. The Emperor wished to establish a state monopoly of education, as a means of directing political opinion and moral standards. The Roman Catholic Church, which he also sought to control, continued to take charge of all primary education, and to take a significant part in secondary education also. When, after Waterloo, the old French monarchy was temporarily restored to power, the Ultra-Royalists managed for some years to use the still solid organisation of the Napoleonic University as an instrument for reimposing the pre-revolutionary Catholic monopoly of public schooling. But of these two attempts to monopolise education in the name of State or Church, only the single, nationwide system of examinations remains. This has been in the hands of secular government officials since 1880. Monopoly of teaching had been renounced earlier, by both Church and State, between 1828 and 1850.

Throughout the second half of the nineteenth century primary and secondary education were expanded both by private initiative, mainly Catholic, and by governmental authority. The proportion of primary-school pupils educated free rose from one-third in the 1840s to more than one-half in the 1870s, but secondary schools charged a fee, and though the total number of secondary-school pupils was more than doubled between 1840 and the end of the century, nearly all of them were of the moneyed class, and as late as 1898 more of them went to Catholic *collèges* than to the state's *lycées*.[1] But the Third Republic, within a decade of its foundation, had launched a counter-offensive against the Catholic position in the primary schools. In the name of democracy, and national unity, and guided by the three fundamental principles of secularity, abolition of fees and compulsory attendance ('l'École laïque, gratuite et obligatoire'), the Radical Minister of Education, Jules Ferry, carried a series of great educational reform Bills through Parliament, between 1879 and 1882. Fifty years later democratic reform and expansion were extended to the secondary schools by the abolition of fees there also. In 1939 only a little over 12 per cent of French children between the ages of eleven and eighteen were in secondary schools. By 1965, 54 per cent were.[2] Schooling is now compulsory up to the age of sixteen, officially, though not yet in practice. Expansion and compulsion, together with free primary and secondary schools, and nearly free university tuition, have not, however, sufficed to bring the children of proletarian and peasant families into the French system of *higher* education in sufficiently large numbers to modify its still predominantly *bourgeois* character and recruitment. Clever pupils from poor families have, since the origins of state education in France, as previously in the Catholic *ancien régime*, been encouraged by free tuition and scholarships (and the democratic enthusiasm of their teachers), and many have risen high, but the proportion of working-class students (and of university scholarships) to the total student population is still a good deal smaller than it is in Britain.[3]

THE PRIVATE SECTOR

Private schooling, licensed by the *Loi Guizot* of 1833 for primary education, and the *Loi Falloux* of 1850 for secondary schools, was developed to meet the demands of the French Church. From the beginning it has been run almost exclusively for and by Catholics. For two rather brief periods – during the Dreyfus Affair (1898–1906) and the Popular Front (1934–7), when clerical reaction against the secular principles of French Republicanism appeared to constitute a real threat to Republican institutions – a counter-surge of private initiative in the educational field came from the predominantly anti-clerical left wing, bringing Socialists, trade unionists and volunteer teachers together in a co-operative effort to run evening and holiday classes for workers or their children, in so-called *universités populaires, collèges du travail* and *colonies de vacances*.[4] But the private effort by Catholics to sustain their creed in the minds of successive generations of French schoolchildren, in its own complete, independent system – *l'école libre* – and against the officially secular and at times, in practice, anti-religious education of the state schools has, perforce, been greater and more continuous. The great majority of the present nine thousand primary schools and five thousand secondary schools in the private sector of French education are Roman Catholic ones.[5]

Mutual hostility between the two sides of the French *question scolaire*, and the proverbial village bickering between *curé* and *instituteur*,[6] have abated since the beginning of the century, but the militant pressure groups of neither side have disarmed. In 1951 a practical compromise, giving limited state aid to the parents of children at Church schools, was embodied in the Barangé Law. This was not enough for the Catholic parents' association, *Union nationale des associations de parents d'élèves de l'enseignement libre* (A.P.E.L.), founded in 1930, which pressed for further official recognition and support. In 1959, the Debré Law conceded their point and instituted a contractual relationship between *l'école libre* and the state, with provision for state payment of teachers at most Catholic schools and additional subsidies at the discretion of the local government authorities. Since then there has been a corresponding intensification of the campaign against Catholic influence in education by such organisations as the *Comité National d'Action Laïque.*[7]

Although the French Church continues to reject the idea of complete educational integration within the state system, it has come to value the 'educational and apostolic possibilities' that it has already, in the public secondary and primary schools (for example, the right to operate a chaplaincy service for Catholic children in the state *lycées,* and the 'release-time' allowed every Thursday for voluntary classes in religious instruction). It tends to rely less than it used to on the survival of its own private establishments, which, seeming to perpetuate the division of France into 'two nations', does much to keep anti-clericalism alive. French secularists for their part are no longer so likely to be totally opposed to the right of priests to run any schools in France at all, nor so ready to insist that 'all French children should go through the same schools, just as all conscripts go through the same barracks'. All the same, the schools question may yet flare up again, dividing otherwise natural allies, such as the Christian Democrats and moderate Socialists and Radicals, and this, like the long rift between the Communist and non-Communist parties and trade unions, continues to impair the chances of political stability and democratic progress in modern France.

PRIMARY SCHOOLS

In the state system these take children at the age of six, after pre-school training at *l'école maternelle* (nursery schools). Their teachers, *instituteurs* and *institutrices,* have a strongly developed sense of responsibility for the mass of peasant and working-class children in their charge, stemming from their missionary origins in Ferry's *école laïque,* which was to be the torch-bearer of the Enlightenment in the supposedly benighted and certainly traditionalistic villages of nineteenth-century France. Their generally left-wing, often extremely left-wing, political sympathies are a measure of the disparity they observe between the boldly rationalist, democratically egalitarian ideals of the founding fathers of the Republic's educational system and the lagging practical achievement of enlightenment and equality in the Republic as it is.

SECONDARY SCHOOLS

Secondary education, from eleven to sixteen, is given in *collèges d'enseignement général* (C.E.G.) and in the newer, comprehensive *collèges d'enseignement secondaire* (C.E.S.), and from eleven to eighteen at the *lycées classiques et modernes* and newer *lycées techniques.*

To try to reduce the amount of primary-school talent that is still wasted, the whole of a French child's school career between the ages of eleven and fifteen (the so-called 'first cycle' of secondary education) has now been made a period of observation and orientation, during which teachers, educational psychologists and doctors regularly come together with representatives of the parent–teacher organisations to draw up advice for parents on the next most suitable stage of their child's education, as independently as possible of class background and financial resources. Sociologists and economic planners participate, bringing obvious practical advantages in the short term, such as knowledge of the labour market and of the requirements of local industries, but bringing also what some, from the broader viewpoints of open democracy and liberal education, see as equally obvious dangers, such as utilitarian child grading and the direction of labour.

French educational reformers hope also that the new technical, industrial and economics curricula for the *baccalauréat* examination will make higher education accessible to other kinds of ability and interest than the orthodox academic ones served in the traditional preparatory classes of the *lycées.* There has been some attempt, in *lycées* and in general and secondary colleges, to break with the rather abstract and authoritarian teaching that is customary in the French academic 'grammar' stream, and to put more emphasis on active learning and group learning, and on the desirability of observing facts before constructing theories.[8] But today's fifteen-year-old who chooses and is accepted for one of the *baccalauréat* courses is still likely to have to go through three years of intense intellectual effort. Hours in class are long (nearly thirty a week) and individual preparation during school hours and at home is heavy. There is not much community life or organised sport, and what there is tends to promote solo excellence or mass exercise rather than the team spirit. But a compulsory test of physical education (athletics, gymnastics, swimming) is now included in all *baccalauréat* groups.

The first object of the *professeur de lycée* is to use the still comparatively unspecialised *baccalauréat* syllabus (at least five subjects are examined by written paper or orally in whatever group is chosen) to develop his pupils' knowledge of general culture and capacity for general thought, to inculcate critical standards of appreciation of both facts and the relations between them, and to demand clearly articulate powers of self-expression in writing and speech.[9] Orals have always had a particularly important place in the French system of examination: 'it is practically impossible in France for any tongue-tied person to graduate'.[10]

The high intellectual performance required for success in the written and oral tests of the *agrégation* examination (the competitive method of entry to the highest teaching grades in secondary schools and universities[11]) can produce an over-exacting teacher who may weary and discourage the mass of ordinary pupils, and fail to make much contact at all with the *cancre* (the dunce), but it has also made a host of kindly and conscientious *professeurs de philo, de math-élem, de khâgne* and *de taupe,*[12] and many great ones who, by the example of their mastery and enthusiasm in the realms of literature, history, philosophy and science, by their creative and questing minds, and by the personal and friendly interest they take in their best pupils, awaken boundless admiration in an élite of real disciples, and keep the heights of French civilisation occupied from generation to generation; not without the risk, however, of driving some adolescents too hard and too high: *surmenage* (overwork), brought on by spontaneous emulation, as well as by pushing and demanding parents, is a continuing problem.

There is no sharp dividing line between secondary and university education either for teachers or for pupils and students. University lecturers have normally begun their teaching careers by taking a post at a *lycée* while preparing their doctoral thesis (though there is a trend against this now). Much university teaching is done by *chargés de cours* who are *agrégés* mainly employed by a *lycée* but released to lecture to students on one or two days a week. The intellectual qualities and the academic approach required from pupils of seventeen and eighteen, in the senior, post-*baccalauréat* forms of a *lycée*, are very close to what is expected of undergraduates at a university. *Lycéens*, moreover, get personal tuition, unlike the great majority of French university students. 'It is still true . . . that the better French students are fully formed intellectually when they leave the *lycée*.'[13]

HIGHER EDUCATION

Intensely concentrated in the capital city for the last two hundred years, higher education has created a great modern university quarter, on the left Bank of the Seine, opposite the cathedral of Notre-Dame, on the site of the forty or so colleges of the medieval University of Paris (Latin-speaking, hence the name Latin Quarter). Here the Sorbonne (originally the name of a residential college founded in 1253 by Robert de Sorbon, and used familiarly since the sixteenth century as the collective title of the Paris Arts and Science Faculties), and the powerful old-established Law and Medical Faculties of the University of Paris, took into their overcrowded libraries, lecture-halls and laboratories nearly one-third of all the university students in the country – until the policy of dispersal, to new campuses in the suburbs and in neighbouring cities, began to take effect, just before the student riots of May 1968. A small élite of French students, some 70,000, out of a total which increased from 300,000 to over 600,000 between 1963 and 1970, attend one of the specialist colleges of higher education called *les grandes écoles*, many of which are also in or near the Latin Quarter, and to which the best scholars of each generation are admitted at the age of eighteen by competitive examination, to prepare, under closer tutorial supervision than the anonymous mass of Paris undergraduates, and in a stimulating atmosphere of keen emulation, the degree and other examinations which will open their way to the best careers in France. The most famous of these *grandes écoles* are *L'École Polytechnique and L'École Normale Supérieure*. The first produces mathematicians, scientists and engineers, and its alumni constitute a formidable 'old-boy' network of influence, decision and mutual support. Celebrated *polytechniciens* (known familiarly as 'X's') include the mathematician Henri Poincaré, the motor-manufacturer Citroën, Marshals Joffre and Foch, Jules Moch, Valéry Giscard d'Estaing. Jean-Jacques Servan-Schreiber,[14] Pierre Massé and René Montjoie.[15] The second is the only *grande école* where the liberal arts are studied in a broad, non-specialised sense. It admits forty students a year on the results of an entrance examination consisting of three essays: French, philosophy and contemporary history, a Latin translation and prose, a Greek translation or a composition in a modern language, followed by several oral tests, all designed to show a capacity for general ideas and the quick improvisation of balanced, comprehensive and lucid *exposés*. *Normale* also admits an equal number of science students and, with stiff and specialised entrance qualifications and good laboratories, the science section is one of the most important centres of teaching and pure research in France.[16] The college is residential (all students getting free tuition, board and a grant[17]) and it has an excellent tutorial system. But no lecture or class is compulsory. The good *normalien*, from his omnivorous reading and interminable discussions in quadrangle and study (*turne*), and from a sense of pride and shared privilege, develops a characteristically self-confident brilliance in analysis and argument, together, it is generally admitted, with a tendency to abstraction and rhetoric. The school produced many of the outstanding French writers, philosophers and politicians of the nineteenth and twentieth centuries, among whom are Jaurès, Bergson, Alain, Péguy, Romains, Blum, Herriot, Giraudoux, Sartre, Soustelle and Pompidou.

Polytechnique and *Normale*, both founded in 1794, are contributions that the First French Republic made to the undoubted glory and fascination of Paris as a centre of learning and intellectual excitement – and to the problems of the French Ministers of Education in the second half of the twentieth century. So also are the more highly specialised arts colleges of *Langues Orientales* and *Beaux-Arts*, and *L'École des Mines*. Napoleon added the Military Academy of Saint-Cyr, near Versailles, now removed to Brittany; the restored monarchy and the Second Empire added *L'École des Chartes* (palaeography, 1821) *L'École Centrale* (engineering and technology, 1828) and *L'École Pratique des Hautes Études* (research in all fields, 1868); the modern Republics added the *École du Louvre* (archaeology and history of art, 1881) and the *École Nationale d'Administration* (E.N.A., 1945).

This historic concentration of higher education in Paris (in which must be included the post-*baccalauréat* work done at some of the finest French *lycées,* with four of the most famous in the Latin Quarter itself: *Saint-Louis, Henri-Quatre, Louis-le-Grand* and *Fénelon*) is sustained by the centuries-old attraction of the city for ambitious students and teachers as a centre of culture and of power unapproached by any other in France, and unsurpassed in Europe.

Universities in the French provinces were in general decline by the eighteenth century, and were not revived until the latter part of the nineteenth, and then only in the much diminished form of 'faculty bodies', at some of the cities where university studies had flourished independently in the Middle Ages and the Renaissance. In the 1890s these began calling themselves universities once more, but they remained state institutions, like the University of Paris, under the tight control of the Ministry of Public Instruction. Generally speaking they were kept short of funds and prestige until the middle of the present century, since when encouragement and grants have gone out in abundance from central Government to the *Académies.* Many of the provincial universities are now very large and busy indeed, e.g. Lyon (with 36,000 students), Aix–Marseille (36,000), Toulouse (33,000), Bordeaux (33,000), Montpellier (26,000), Lille (27,000), Rennes (21,000), Strasbourg (22,000), Grenoble (23,000), Nancy (19,000), Caen (12,000). There are also thirteen new University Institutes of Technology.

But two post-war decades of university expansion in the provinces failed to relieve the mounting pressure on accommodation, teaching facilities and tempers in the University of Paris. It was indeed at the new Arts and Social Sciences campus of Nanterre, built on the outskirts of Paris to relieve the Latin Quarter, but badly sited in a bleak industrial suburb, and planned for maximum numbers (about 11,000) with minimum regard for elementary human susceptibilities, let alone traditional French individualism and sociability, that the first riots against the cumbersome and paternalistic management of university expansion flared up in the spring of 1968, to ignite the 'May Revolution'.

The purpose as well as the facilities of higher education in France also became a burning issue at this time, between officials and academics, and between rival schools of educational reform. The crux of the matter was to decide whether the traditional *baccalauréat* should be retained as the sole university entrance qualification, or whether university entry should be made *more* academically selective (so as to cut down much wastage of unsuccessful undergraduates) or *less* so, in the alleged interests of democracy (by breaking down the still predominantly *bourgeois* monopoly of the *lycées*).

Gaullist attempts to change the system met opposition from all sides, and particularly from those many French teachers who are politically left-wing but professionally conservative. The students' uprising of 1968 found the Government in the middle of a frustrated and confused process of reform which was intended to create more university openings for technological, economics, management and 'modern' linguistic and literary studies, so bringing students with a culturally or intellectually underprivileged background or upbringing more readily into the sphere of higher education ('minds salvaged and vocations developed independently of the traditional run of the mill') and at the same time tying the orientation of university studies more closely to the needs of industrial production ('liaison between the university and industry', 'scientists are also producers in the service of the nation').[18] The latter aim was bitterly contested by the radical left wing as being repressively élitist and crudely utilitarian, in the service of capitalism. There was also well-grounded fear of unemployment among students preparing to graduate in swollen arts and social sciences departments.

Four months after the riots, which seriously weakened de Gaulle's authority, his new Minister of Education laid a comprehensive Higher Education Reform Bill before Parliament. Motivating the proposals, he stressed the duty of all concerned to abjure the rigid and authoritarian type of education that the University of France had inherited from the past, and to try to create better personal relations between teachers and students, as well as closer connections between degree courses and career prospects, and between universities and the world outside, particularly their regional environment.[19] 'Autonomy' of individual universities and 'participation' of students and junior members of faculty in the running of university affairs were to be warmly encouraged, though within fairly strict limits, so as to avoid 'anarchy'. These limits included the maintenance of a single national system of degrees, degree courses and examinations, the purely consultative functions of regional educational councils, and the customary subordination of the new educational establishments to central administrative tutelage. The Bill was passed by a large majority on 7 November 1968. Turning its good intentions into practicable new methods and institutions proved difficult. Some headway was made by the beginning of the academic year 1970–1, but not without considerable confusion and contention. The University of Paris was divided into thirteen groups of *unités d'enseignement et de recherche* (U.E.R.). The directors of these new centres complained that they had not been granted enough funds to make the operation a success, while the Government countered with the claim that public expenditure on education was rising faster than any other outlay.

JUSTICE

'Civil rights and the fundamental guarantees granted to the citizens for the exercise of their public liberties' constitute the first specifically named area within the 'domain of law' that is protected by the French Constitution from encroachment by the Executive (Article 34). It is for Parliament, therefore, to see that the law preserves the French citizens' rights and liberties, which were defined in general terms in the 'Declaration of the Rights of Man and of the Citizen' of 1789, and in the Preambles to the Constitutions of 1946 and 1958. Justice under law is dispensed in France by two separate judicatures: one for administrative law, headed by the *Conseil d'État*, which has already been described,[20] and another, which is quite distinct, dispensing justice according to the codes of civil and penal law.

The most important French appeal judges are nominated

by a High Council of the Judiciary, whose President is the President of the Republic and whose Vice-President is the Minister of Justice, with nine ordinary members appointed by the President of the Republic. All other judges are proposed directly by the Minister of Justice, though the Council gives its opinion concerning such appointments. It is also the disciplinary council for all judges, and has the duty of assisting the President of the Republic to protect the independence of the judicial authority from any kind of interference, including that of the Government. Judges are declared 'irremovable'; thus, once appointed, they cannot be threatened with dismissal for some decision or attitude unpleasing to the executive power.

As well as the so-called 'seated magistrature' of judges, there is, in France, a 'standing magistrature' (*la magistrature debout,* or *le parquet*) of Public Prosecutors whose career is also an official one.[21] Entry to it, as into the higher civil service, is by public examination, after training at a single postgraduate *Centre National d'Études Judiciaires* in Bordeaux (C.N.E.J.), opened in 1958, from which nine out of ten of all judges, Public Prosecutors and officials of the Ministry of Justice will in future be recruited.

Barristers (*avocats*), who represent parties contesting a civil case and who, in criminal cases, plead as defending counsel against the Public Prosecutor, exercise an independent, private profession. They do not become judges; the Bench is not, as in Great Britain, recruited from their ranks.

French law and legal procedures are expounded systematically in a series of statute books called *codes,* originally drawn up under the supervision of Napoleon I. The two most important of these are *Le Code Civil* (or *Code Napoléon*) and *Le Code Pénal,* which embody for civil and criminal law respectively the mixed legal inheritance of Napoleon's France: Roman law, customary laws of the *ancien régime,* the liberal spirit and lucid ideas of the eighteenth-century Enlightenment and the French Revolution, and a certain amount of the property-owning and anti-feminist prejudices of the dominant middle class. The original codes are continually being brought up to date, however, and a body of case law has also been built up over the last hundred and sixty years. Precedent is often invoked to justify a particular interpretation of the

Code, though no French judge is bound by precedent. French law is both taught and applied with, generally speaking, less respect for precedent than in Britain, and rather more attention is given to the original principles and purposes of the written statutes.

Minor private lawsuits are heard and petty offences (*contraventions*) tried in one of 454 *tribunaux d'instance*,[22] and there are also special *tribunaux de commerce* (for disputes between businessmen) and *conseils de prud'hommes* (for disputes between employers and employees).[23] The ordinary law-courts are the 179 *tribunaux de grande instance*, at least one to each *département*, and more in heavily populated areas.[24] These are collegial courts with three judges, and deal with major civil suits. Minor infractions of the law are dealt with by the *tribunaux d'instance* acting as *tribunaux de police*, and more serious offences (*délits*) by the *tribunaux de grande instance* acting as *tribunaux correctionnels*. Appeal from these courts is to one of twenty-eight *cours d'appel*,[25] and thence to *la cour de cassation*, which quashes (*casser*, from old French *quasser*) the judgement of a lower court if it finds that there has been misapplication of the law, but is not concerned with the facts of the case. Quashed cases are sent back down to a different lower court, to be heard again. Crimes (*crimes*) are tried at Assize Courts, the only kind of trial by jury in France, and the only recourse against a judgement of the 'sovereign jury' is to the *cour de cassation*.

All cases involving penal law are presented to the appropriate judge by an examining magistrate (appointed by the Ministry of Justice from the bench of the ordinary courts, for three years at a time). This is the *juge d'instruction* to whom is entrusted the preliminary work of detaining suspects, interrogating them, collecting and examining witnesses and other evidence, and deciding if there is a case to be made. The preliminary 'instruction' of criminal proceedings in France is the centre of some rather melodramatic speculation by foreigners, and of a common misconception, reinforced by the freedom of the French Press to comment on cases still being heard before judgement is passed, that in France a person is officially guilty until he is proved innocent. This is quite untrue. A fundamental and explicit assumption of the 'Declaration of the Rights of Man and of the Citizen' of 1789 (Article 9) is that 'every man is presumed innocent until declared guilty', though French jurists *are* aware that, in the words of Professor Duverger:

> On the whole, the French system of public liberties is fundamentally concerned with liberties as means of opposing the powers that be, and especially, with freedom of thought and freedom of expression in every form (religion, education, the Press, books, theatre, etc.); also with freedom of political action (demonstrations, meetings, associations). The so-called civil liberties (protection against arbitrary arrest, the *habeas corpus* of the Anglo-Saxons) are somewhat less well developed . . . because the fight for public liberties in France during the nineteenth century was essentially one of the forms taken by the fight to establish a democratic state . . . a fight for the rights of the citizen rather than for those of the private individual . . .[26]

On the grounds that the *juge d'instruction* is, being a judge, impartial, he is not compelled to bring a suspect into court, and cases of abusive arrest and prolonged preventive detention without trial have occurred.[27] But the right of suspects to protection by a legal adviser when appearing before the *juge d'instruction* has since 1897 been an essential part of French law, and this right has recently been extended to prevent suspects being treated as witnesses (and so denied such protection). Further, there is a right of appeal against detention during the preliminary examination, such appeals being heard by a special section of the Court of Appeal, the *Chambre d'Accusation*.

At the trial, French and British forms of justice, particularly the procedure for hearing criminal cases, differ considerably. The British judge is rather like a referee. Assuming that the best side will win provided the rules are kept, he stays out of the fight between counsels and witnesses, simply ensuring that order is maintained and reminding the jury of their duties. In civil cases French judges behave similarly. But in the French criminal courts, the more paternalistic and philosophical Roman tradition influences procedure (rather than medieval trial by single combat – *duel judiciaire*), making it the duty of the presiding judge to lead the court actively in a combined search for truth that nothing must be allowed to obstruct. To this end he freely applies his authority and his knowledge of the law of crime and of life to the full. The interrogation of the prisoner at the bar is practically his exclusive prerogative, and he participates actively, Code in hand, both in the examination and cross-examination of witnesses, and in the jury's deliberations.

Since 1941, the three judges and nine jurors sit together to consider the facts of the case, and the legal issues raised, and to decide not merely whether the prisoner at the bar is guilty or innocent, but also, if guilty, how he shall be punished. But the jurors have the last word, and the system is biased in favour of the accused, since although the 'college' of bench and jury does not have to reach a unanimous opinion, any decision unfavourable to the accused must be taken by a majority of eight votes.

Besides the ordinary courts of law and appeal there are special courts for children and for minors aged between sixteen and eighteen. In 1963, after a court set up to try Army officers implicated in a plot to overthrow the Fifth Republic had failed to convict, a new court, the *Cour de Sûreté de l'État,* was formed, under very dubious constitutional authority, though later ratified by Parliament, to try such cases in future.[28] There is also a Parliamentary High Court of Justice for considering accusations of high treason levelled against the President of the Republic, and charges of treason, crimes and conspiracy brought against Ministers and their accomplices.

Part Three: The Last Hundred Years

8 The Establishment of the Republic

THE FRANCO-PRUSSIAN WAR

AFTER two attempts (1792–1804 and 1848–52), the Republican form of government was finally established in France during the last quarter of the nineteenth century. France's seventy-year-long Third Republic was founded in the bitter aftermath of unsuccessful foreign war and consequent civil strife between Frenchmen, a dramatic pattern of events that was destined, with some variations of scale, timing and cast, to be repeated twice during the next hundred years, at the birth of both the Fourth and the Fifth Republics.

The Republicans who formed the chief opposition party during the Second French Empire (1852–70) did not seek the war with Prussia that would lead to its overthrow. The immediate cause of the war was a German claim to the succession to the Spanish throne, an apparently outdated quarrel of princes. Moreover, when French arrogance and Bismarck's diplomatic skill turned the prospect of settling this quarrel amicably into the reality of armed conflict, most French Republicans, like the great majority of their compatriots in all parties, and popular opinion abroad, were convinced that Louis-Napoleon's army would have a walkover, and that the imperial régime they opposed at home would gain strength from an easy victory on battlefields across the Rhine. Thus neither the cause of the war nor its expected outcome appealed to Republican opinion in France. But within two months of the French Government's confident declaration of war, Napoleon's armies had been crushed, the Emperor had surrendered with 83,000 men at the French frontier fortress of Sedan, and both Metz and Paris were besieged. After two centuries of French preponderance, the balance of military power on the continent of Europe had shifted to the advantage of a new master: the united German Reich.

The defeat of Louis-Napoleon led logically to the restoration of the Republican form of government he had destroyed eighteen years earlier. The Republic was proclaimed in Paris on 4 September 1870, and the Foreign Minister in its first 'Government of National Defence', Jules Favre, went to open peace negotiations with Bismarck outside Paris. Unfortunately for the future of Europe, neither side could, or would, grasp the reality of the new European power system. Favre 'found himself regarded by Bismarck not as the spokesman of a temporarily misled people, but as the representative of a nation with a record of constant aggression which it could not be trusted not to renew at the first opportunity'.[1] The Germans insisted on a strategic barrier between themselves and the nation that had declared war on them 'thirty times in the last two hundred years'. . . . 'We must have land, fortresses and frontiers which will shelter us for good from the enemy attack.'[2] Alsace, with Strasbourg, and the northern part of Lorraine, including the fortress of Metz, must be ceded to the German Empire. Favre knew that such conditions would be rejected out of hand by Paris, where the invasion had aroused the old fervour of Jacobin patriotism, and he broke off the discussions, prophesying 'an endless struggle between two peoples who ought to stretch out their hands to each other'.[3]

This struggle, which in three stages (1870–1, 1914–18, 1939–45) was to kill and maim several million Frenchmen and Germans during the next eighty years, besides some millions more of their allies, began almost at once. The Franco-Prussian War which had been, up to that point, a matter of comparatively sane, even polite, sieges, conducted by professional armies who honoured the old-fashioned rules of war, and the comparatively limited horror of gallant cavalry charges (mostly French) breaking themselves against modern guns (mostly German), gave place to what Professor Howard calls 'a savage war of peoples'.[4] Gambetta, the Republicans' firebrand, tried to revive the old revolutionary device of victory by mass levies; and his hastily formed French citizen armies fought back against the German invaders in sorties from besieged Paris, and along the line of the Loire, for a further six terrible winter months. They were backed by the guerrilla attacks of irregular *francs-tireurs* (which brought the inevitable retaliation: hostages executed and civilian populations bombarded), but all to no avail. French bravery and ingenuity were no match for Germans equally brave and much better trained, equipped and led.

Ironically, the aggressive Jacobin spirit of 1792 and 1793, for fear of which, very largely, Bismarck had demanded the amputation of France's eastern borderlands, now failed to work its old magic. The prospect of losing Alsace and Lorraine fired France's new Republican leaders in Paris to proclaim total war ('la guerre à outrance'), and to wage it with heroic energy. But the nation of peasant-proprietors, rural tradesmen and provincial notables that was the real France (outside Paris, at least), eighty years after the Jacobin revolution, had not the force to throw back the invader, grown stronger in every way in the sixty-four years since the Battle of Jena. Favre had finally, at the end of January 1871, to accept Bismarck's terms for an armistice. On 8 February, at the first general election since the fall of Louis-Napoleon's Second Empire, a *bourgeois*, rural and provincial majority of the electorate returned a majority of conservative gentry who were for ending the war at all costs, and all the sooner because of the Republicanism it was stirring up in Paris, which looked more dangerous than the Germans to the Catholic and landowning leaders of the French countryside.

A conservative, Adolphe Thiers, was elected 'Head of the Executive', the Assembly was brought back from Bordeaux to Versailles (not Paris), and the peace was negotiated and eventually signed at Frankfurt on Bismarck's terms: the French to give up the north-eastern part of the two former Lorraine *départements* of Meurthe and Moselle, and all Alsace except Belfort; and to pay an idemnity of five thousand million francs. The Germans would occupy northern France until they got their money.[5] Before he could sign the peace and liberate French territory, however, Thiers had to deal with a revolt of Parisians both against the peace and against the predominantly rural, reactionary and Catholic majority in the Assembly, who clearly wanted to overthrow the Republic and were daring to speak for France from Bordeaux and Versailles.

THE PARIS COMMUNE

The population of Paris had suffered greatly during their long siege by the Prussian Army, from starvation, frustration, enforced idleness, futile sorties, bitter cold, and now unemployment. They were ready to flare up if the *Versaillais* handled their grievances and bruised pride roughly. This is exactly what happened: before business could revive, the moratorium on debts and rents was annulled, and many *petit-bourgeois* Parisians were threatened with bankruptcy; the pay of the volunteer National Guard was threatened, and the regular Army was sent to take away its artillery at Montmartre. Two generals attempting this final assault on the dignity and independence of the capital were shot by the mob. Thiers pulled back his men on Versailles and the second siege of Paris began.

Paris in 1871 was still a city of workshops and of skilled artisans, and the Commune was not, in fact, the proletarian forerunner of the Soviet Revolution later to be celebrated in Communist mythology. The name, *Commune,* harked back to the revolutionary dictatorship of Paris over rural France in 1792, rather than forward to the dictatorship of the proletariat. Its rank-and-file came from the lower middle as well as labouring classes, and the leaders of its Committee of Public Safety were Federalists (believing in a loose-knit nation of self-governing towns), and Radicals nurtured on the pre-Marxist doctrines of 1848 and the Jacobin legends of 1792–4. Its motives were mixed: economic distress, anti-Catholic and anti-rural traditions, emotional patriotism, mob excitement. It was weakened by petty and abstract quarrels over authority and doctrine, and soon degenerated into anarchy. But it was the gentry and peasantry of the avenging army that Thiers sent against the Commune, who set the example of indiscriminate brutality amid which this brief but horrible civil war was concluded.

The last stand of the *Communards,* on 27 May, was made in the Cemetery of Père-Lachaise, after a week of savage street fighting. One hundred and forty-seven insurgents were shot there the next day, against the wall known to subsequent generations of Socialist and Communist pilgrims as *Le Mur des Fédérés.* During *la semaine sanglante,* the Tuileries Palace.

the City Hall and many other buildings were burned, and the Archbishop of Paris and many other hostages, especially priests and police officers, were shot. The number of real or suspected *communards* killed fighting at the barricades, beaten to death as they lay wounded, or summarily executed in the 'expiation' that followed their defeat, is thought to have been 'not less than 20,000'.[6]

The extinction of the Paris Commune, followed by the deportation of those *communards* who survived the battle and the flight of thousands of workers from the capital, weakened the French labour movement for some years.[7] It was in a mood of defensive conservatism, formed in the shadow of mob violence put down in blood, that the new Republican ministers took over the government of France and that the new Republican Constitution took shape. In 1872 the International Workingmen's Association was outlawed and several trade unions, tolerated since 1868, were dissolved or driven underground. Not until the return to France of an exiled supporter of the Commune now converted to Marxism, Jules Guesde, who founded the French Workers' Party, in 1879, did the movement against capitalism get under way once more, helped by an economic depression, lasting from 1882 to 1894, which brought unemployment, strikes and renewed violence (and the legalising of trade unions).

THE SIXTEENTH OF MAY

The Republic faced its first important crisis six years after the Commune. It was a bloodless, constitutional one. The Monarchist majority of 1871 dwindled away rapidly, its cause discredited by quarrelling between rival Legitimist and Orléanist factions and, in particular, by the impossibly out-of-date conditions for restoration dictated by the Bourbon claimant, the Comte de Chambord, who insisted among other things on remounting the throne of his ancestors under the white flag of Henri IV and thus banishing the tricolor of Valmy and Austerlitz. Meanwhile, the fortunes of the Republicans rose steadily, in the country and in Parliament, and the democratic institutions and procedures by which (with some adjustments to meet changes in the balance of political power) France would be governed until 1940, were gradually established. In August 1871 Thiers had been made 'President of the Republic'; in 1873 his successor, Marshal MacMahon, was confirmed in office for seven years by the 'Law of the Septennate'. Finally, in 1875, the deputies agreed to the suggestion of one of their number, M. Wallon, that France be permitted to 'escape from the provisional', and passed, by one vote, his amendment to the effect that 'the President of the Republic is elected by the plurality of votes cast by the Senate and Chamber of Deputies united in a single National Assembly', thus regularising the presidential succession in an officially established Third French Republic. Further detailed constitutional laws followed in February, July and November of 1875.[8]

The Monarchists hoped that the conservative bias of the new institutions – a strong, preponderantly rural Senate, and a strong Presidency, filled for seven years by one of their own leaders – would give them stability and enough time to prepare a more modern and accommodating kind of monarchical restoration. But the Republicans were playing the game of moderate conservatism more successfully. In the general election of 1876 they had a crushing victory, returning over 360 deputies to the Chamber, more than twice as many as the anti-Republicans (who included 80 Bonapartists).

The Royalist and Catholic President MacMahon was soon in open conflict with the new Republican majority. On 16 May 1877 he forced the moderate Premier, Jules Simon, to resign, and replaced him with the Monarchist Duc de Broglie. When the Republicans disapproved, the President exercised his constitutional right, with the support of the Senate, to dissolve the Chamber at once. For the ensuing general election, a whole new right-wing *corps préfectoral* was appointed, in order to put official pressure on the electorate to vote against the Republicans. Gambetta, the eloquent leader of the Radical left wing, promised that the Republicans would 'return four hundred strong'. In the event they won 320 seats, a comfortable majority, which reflected a real triumph over corrupt official attempts to muzzle and bully Republican opinion in the constituencies. The conflict between the Presidency and the popularly elected Chamber of the French Parliament was then fought to the finish; the President, said Gambetta, would have to 'give in or get out'. In fact he did both. He appointed a Prime Minister acceptable to the majority of the Chamber of Deputies; he publicly recognised that political responsibility belonged, under the Constitution of 1875, to the Cabinet and not the Presidency, and that the President's 'right of dissolution . . . cannot be set up as a system of government'; and two years later, in January 1879, he resigned.[9]

Le seize mai established the preponderance of Parliament over the Presidency, which was to last until 1958. After MacMahon, it was always the Executive which had to climb down in a quarrel with the Legislature. Eighty years of mild Presidents and weak, unstable governments stemmed from the crisis of 1877. This also immediately consolidated the political strength of the Republican party: during the next decade, the Republicans would 'take over the Republic' from the Catholics and dukes.[10] In order to do so, however, they would for the time being abandon their more radical demands, such as the separation of Church and State, the introduction of income tax, the suppression of standing armies,[11] and generally go slow on economic and social reforms, thus collecting *bourgeois* votes from the Monarchists and Bonapartists and building up a so-called 'Opportunist' group of middle-of-the-road *ministrables*.

Anti-clericalism remained a rallying-cry, however, and egalitarian, anti-Catholic educational reform survived vigorously from Gambetta's so-called Bellville Manifesto of 1869: 'Free, compulsory, secular primary education with competitive examinations for children of greatest intelligence for admission to higher education, which shall likewise be free.' The *question scolaire* hampered reconciliation between Frenchmen in the new Republic by keeping the Catholics doubtful. When the liberal Pope, Leo XIII, in 1890–2, called on French Catholics to 'rally' to the Republican régime, he met with a poor response.

The rise of *opportunisme* at the centre of the parliamentary *hémicycle* inaugurated a typically Third-Republican pattern of coalition government growing from a political Centre where moderates attain power by combining against the extremists of both Left and Right, on the basis of expedient compromise. This system was put to the test between 1886 and 1889 by a brief assault on the Centre mounted by both extremes, temporarily united behind a popular but politically naïve soldier-hero, General Boulanger.

BOULANGISME

Like President MacMahon's *coup* of the *seize mai*, this was a complete failure.

Unrest at the extreme edges of French political opinion against big business and industrial interests, and against the 'Opportunist' Republican deputies and ministers now in league with them, had been aggravated by several years of recession and unemployment, and at first the Boulangist 'syndicate of the discontented' was weighted on the side of left-wing Radicalism.

The General was recommended for the War Ministry in 1886 by the Radical, Clemenceau, and he quickly gained notoriety as a friend of the masses and an enemy of the upper classes by declaring that his soldiers, sent to break a miners' strike at Decazeville where a manager had just been lynched, would share their rations with the strikers, and by removing the names of a number of royal dukes, and of the Bonapartist Prince Murat and his son, from the Army list. When Bismarck referred to him in the Reichstag as a threat to Germany, and a minor frontier incident was concluded in France's favour, apparently because of the French War Minister's firmness, then popular patriotic fervour combined with democratic enthusiasm to promote the handsome soldier to the status of national hero. *Le brav' général* became *Le Général Revanche* ('the General who will avenge us') and the idol of all Paris. Royalists and Bonapartists now thought that they could use Boulanger to carry out an anti-parliamentary *coup d'état*, and, after a plebiscite, restore the monarchy. Boulanger was dropped from the Government, posted to a provincial command, then relieved of it and put on the retired list, but his 'martyrdom' only increased his popularity. There were hysterical mass demonstrations for him in Paris, led by the League of Patriots, and he won a number of by-elections both in the provinces and the capital. The Royalist Duchess d'Uzès poured out millions for his election campaigns. Finally, in January 1889, at a by-election in Paris, he polled 245,000 votes, against 163,000 for the combined Radical and

Opportunist candidate and 17,000 for the Guesdist.[12]

The General's partisans now pressed him to lead a march on the Élysée and remove the President by force; but he would not cross the Rubicon, and Boulangism went into rapid decline. Boulanger was all 'image'. Galloping past the Arc de Triomphe on his favourite black charger, Tunis, followed by a cavalcade of staff officers, he *looked* like a modern Napoleon. He was a brave officer; he had the real 'common touch', but politically there was really nothing in him, and certainly not the makings of a dictator. He was all things to all men, and always compliant to the wishes of his adored mistress, Mme de Bonnemains. In the end, his shallow ambition was quite easily checked by a threat to try him for plotting against the state, and by timely electoral reform to prevent parliamentary candidates from winning several seats one after the other. Assailed by sincerely Republican scruples, thwarted of his unofficial plebiscite, Boulanger fled to Brussels with Mme de Bonnemains. When she died of consumption soon after, he shot himself on her grave.

THE PANAMA SCANDAL

The Republican Centre was shaken once more, from 1890 to 1893, by the exposure of a parliamentary scandal connected with an ill-planned scheme of Ferdinand de Lesseps, the engineer and entrepreneur who had built the Suez Canal twenty-five years before, to cut a new canal through the isthmus of Panama. An inquiry revealed that some thirty Republican deputies had received bribes to vote public loans for the Panama Company. The storm of excitement aroused by the Panama scandal was almost entirely confined to parliamentary and Parisian circles. Most of the French were still peasant or small-town realists who 'rather expected their deputy to feather his nest, and so long as he continued to watch the interests of his constituents . . . did not resent it'.[13] Only one of the deputies implicated (and dubbed *chéquards,* because of the counterfoils used in evidence against them) was defeated at the general elections of 1893. But the Socialists made big gains in Paris and its working-class suburban ring; their number in the Chamber of Deputies increased from twelve to fifty. The smell of corruption at a time of much urban unemployment and distress appeared also to stimulate two more sinister forms of political protest against the Opportunist Republic; the first was an outbreak of urban terrorism by anarchists, who threw their bombs in public places, indiscriminately, against the anonymous mass of capitalist exploiters and hangers-on, and once, pointedly, against the deputies in their debating chamber at the Palais Bourbon. The outbreak culminated in the assassination of the President of the Republic (with a knife). The scandals of 1893 also intensified anti-Semitic protest against the new Republican order. Among the chief intermediary agents of parliamentary corruption by the Panama Canal Company were some shady Jewish financiers.

Anti-Semitism in nineteenth-century France flourished on the popular belief that Jews played an inordinately influential part in international finance, and hence capitalist oppression.[14] It was genuinely a prejudice of the masses, particularly in eastern France (and former French Alsace) and in Algeria; but it was not confined to the mob. It was in fact moving up the social scale. The Duc d'Orléans was known to hate what he called the 'anonymous and vagabond wealth' of the great cosmopolitan Jewish families, and this was also the view of a Royalist and Catholic pamphleteer, Édouard Drumont, whose current campaign of abuse against French Jewry was widely influential in Catholic middle- and upper-class France. Drumont's works included *La France juive* (1886), *La Fin d'un monde* (1888) and *De l'or, de la boue, du sang* (1896). In 1889 he founded the 'Anti-Semitic League', and, three years later, an anti-Jewish newspaper, *La Libre Parole*.

The wild individual protests of anarchist terrorism faded out with the growth of organised trade unionism, but anti-Semitism remained, to swell and fester in the next French political crisis: the Dreyfus Affair.

LITERATURE AND THOUGHT IN FRANCE AFTER 1870

There was a sombre reaction to the double disaster of Sedan and the Paris Commune. Victor Hugo, returning in triumph from exile after the fall of the Emperor he had pilloried eighteen years before as *Napoléon le petit*, continued to celebrate the divinely ordained march of humanity towards a new dawn without kings or armies or priests or nations; but the events of what he called *L'Année Terrible* darkened even his sanguine inspiration, though they failed to diminish his even-handed compassion for all: 'good, evil, heroes, bandits' whom 'the hurricanes of history hurl together in one great blind confusion'. But Hugo was the patriarch, 'le Père',[15] a glorious survivor from the heroic age of Napoleon I and the spring-time of Romanticism. The *maîtres à penser* of the seventies, Taine and Renan, brought a colder spirit of quasi-scientific inquiry (called Positivism by its chief French exponent, Auguste Comte) to the causes of France's defeats and dissensions, and they came up with politically reactionary answers, in *Les Origines de la France contemporaine, La Réforme intellectuelle et morale* and *Caliban*. Equally critical of French society and morals was the reforming novelist, Émile Zola. He was also inspired by the scientific method and, in particular, by its application to experimental medicine (as expounded by Claude Bernard, in *Introduction à l'étude de la médecine expérimentale*). Zola's saga of the Rougon-Macquart family, in twenty volumes, is meant to combine the methods of social and of natural history, and he called his theory of literature 'Naturalism', though the work is more imaginative, epic and moralising than might be guessed from the way the theory emphasises techniques of social survey and laboratory experiment (*Le Roman expérimental*). Another self-appointed physician of the allegedly sick society of nineteenth-century France was Paul Bourget, whose first novel, *Le Disciple,* took a specimen of contemporary youth, a student taught by Taine to look on virtue and vice as products like sugar and vitriol, and imagined what kind of a disaster might ensue if such a convert to scientific determinism decided to test the theory in real life. Bourget's contemporary, J.-K. Huysmans, in a famous 'decadent' novel, *A Rebours* (1884), and a younger writer, Maurice Barrès, in *Le Culte du Moi* (1888–91), plunged the naturalist's probe into the secret corners of their own psyche, before both moving on, as Zola prescribed, from inward reflection upon individual behaviour to the study of collective man in his social environment, and from self-regarding aestheticism to religious traditionalism.

Émile Durkheim, the founder of the French school of sociology, and Professor of Education at the Sorbonne, taught that moral values are to be derived from the scientifically observed needs of groups and are only as strong as the 'solidarity' of the group. Other moralists favoured the combative individualism suggested by Darwin's discoveries, and for a while 'le struggle-for-lifer' became a French vogue word. The exaltation of the rights of the individual *against* the unjust law and order of established society was found concurrently not only in militant syndicalism and among the solitary terrorists of the 1890s, hurling their bombs and sharpening their knives in defiance of the social order, and at the risk of their necks, but also in some wealthy Paris salons, where anarchism was fashionably associated with a vague *fin-de-siècle* feeling that *bourgeois* society was doomed. One of the most lionised pure theorists of anarchism, Jean Grave, published *La Société mourante et l'anarchie* in 1893.

Ignoring the stern warnings of Positivist sociology and Naturalist fiction, and the desperate protests or disturbing dreams inspired by the philosophy of anarchism, the majority of France's urban middle class remained somewhat complacently attached to the creed of scientific optimism. This popular faith had its community ritual of periodical Universal Exhibitions: ceremonies of self-congratulation and of emulation, public demonstrations of the marvels and advantages of technology. Since 1851, when the first of such occasions took place, in London, they have spread world wide. Paris held Universal Exhibitions in 1855, 1867, 1878, 1889, 1900 and 1937. The Exhibition of 1889, which helpfully distracted attention from the Boulangist disturbances, had a huge, steel-framed Hall of the Machines, and it had the Eiffel Tower. Later Paris Exhibitions have also left traces in the capital: the Grand Palais and the Petit Palais, the Palais de Chaillot (which in 1937 replaced the earlier Trocadéro), but none has left standing a more compelling symbol of the soaring technological ambitions of the French or a bolder example of their skill and style with new materials than this 985-ft. tower which was for forty years the tallest man-made structure in the world.

Contemptuous of both the critical and the conformist varieties of late nineteenth-century *scientisme*, a group of poets – Verlaine, Rimbaud, Mallarmé, Laforgue, Moréas and others, whom literary history knows as Symbolists, were writing lyric verse which, reacting against the earthbound and eventful documentary literature of the Naturalists, moves through the scientifically observable plane of reality, glancing off objects, dissolving appearances, and keeping only so much of the material world in the reader's mind as to suggest some supernatural domain of evanescent or timeless being (or absence of being: *le néant*) which is inexpressible in pedestrian, non-musical prose.

A young writer who was an attentive listener in Mallarmé's charmed circle of disciples, who passionately admired Rimbaud, and for whom the iron laws of scientific determinism seemed to be making a veritable prison-house out of the 'grey 1880s' in Paris, was Paul Claudel. He found his way out, into the light of the spirit, through reconciliation with the Catholic faith of his forebears. Other poets, Verlaine, Jammes, Péguy, and the novelist Huysmans, had already or would soon follow a similar path, while a leading literary critic of the 1890s, Ferdinand Brunetière, proclaiming the 'bankruptcy' of current attempts to find in science a substitute for the traditional Christian view of man and morality, heralded the religious pragmatism of Barrès and Maurras, leaders of a new nationalist movement, who would come to see Christianity as a precious, irreplaceable asset of French civilisation that must be saved at all cost from the mounting wave of secularism in the schools and universities of the Republic.

Compared with Naturalist fiction and Symbolist poetry, the art of drama in France at this time was at a low ebb. Rostand's *Cyrano de Bergerac* was a bravura pastiche of the fresh colour and wit of the Romantic history play. New foreign works, by Ibsen and Hauptmann, and new Naturalist and Symbolist experiments in staging, together with a very few original French plays by young authors such as Maeterlinck, Jarry and Claudel, did little more than prepare an *avant-garde* audience in Paris for the renewed fusion of poetry and reality on the stage from which a great French theatrical revival was to spring later, in the first three decades of the twentieth century.

An accomplished glory of the young Third Republic was Impressionist painting, in which poetry and realism were already one. French Impressionism was born of the desire to paint reality as the eye sees it, in the changing light of natural day, and not as the artist reconstructs it in the studio. But on the canvases of Manet and Degas (even when their subject or their sitter is commonplace, and though both have a sharp eye for the world's miseries and imperfections), external nature has a glowing surface and a plenitude of form to which the painter has clearly responded with unmixed pleasure. Renoir, Sisley, Gauguin, Monet practically eliminate the seamy or gloomy side of life and paint simply what delights them. Cézanne and Van Gogh give all nature – blossom, corn, clouds in the wind, ancient hills – an elemental calm and inevitability that is perhaps even more exhilarating.

Writers, painters, thinkers and musicians influenced each other all through the nineteenth century. Now Fauré was inspired by landscape painting and by Symbolist poetry, notably Verlaine's. Debussy's musical Impressionism owes more to literature than to painting, but some of his most exciting pieces are musical landscapes as responsive as Manet's or Monet's brush to what the rising philosophical star of the period, Henri Bergson, called 'the immediate date of consciousness'.[16]

Towards the very end of the century, there was a reaction against the languid, misty or morbid forms of escapism prevalent in minor Symbolist and so-called 'Decadent' writing and painting. André Gide, who was to become one of the leading spirits of the next generation, published in 1897 an ecstatic hymn of pagan praise to the earth, the senses and the precious irrecoverable present. But *Les Nourritures terrestres* did not have many readers yet, nor would it have for another twenty years. In 1898 a political crisis broke in France which brought a brusque change of climate to French literary circles.

THE DREYFUS AFFAIR

The early crises of the Third Republic – Paris Commune, Sixteenth of May, Boulangism and the Panama scandal – all had a centrifugal effect, tending to reinforce extremist factions at the opposite poles of political opinion. At one extreme stood the champions of 'order', believing in strong government from above which would preserve the *status quo*: Thiers and the *Versaillais*, MacMahon, who had named his platform *L'Ordre Moral*, the 'Caesarist' right wing of the Boulangist movement. From the opposite extreme there sprang the movement for revolutionary 'change', impelled from below, that is from those who do not benefit from the *status quo*. Against the banner of order (at any price) the *communards*, Gambetta's and Clemenceau's Radicals, Guesde's Marxist *Parti ouvrier*, anarchists, terrorists and syndicalists all cried out for progress (by one means or another).

The rise of Opportunism after 16 May 1877, and its success in holding on to power through the political storms and the economic depression of the eighties and early nineties, suggested that the Republic was developing a substantial enough Centre to avoid further head-on clashes between rival extremes. The Dreyfus case put an end to this 'brief period of political calm'.[17] It did so, not with a new cause for mass discontent or privileged alarm, but by raising to flashpoint the heat of an existing conflict between the new and the old ruling cadres of France, the politically conscious *classe politique*. In the resulting explosion the nation was split along old lines of cleavage which had been covered over by Opportunism, but not mended.

In 1894 a list of secret military documents, apparently delivered to the German Embassy in Paris by a French officer, was discovered by Major Henry of the French counter-espionage organisation.[18] Suspicion fastened on an Alsatian Jew, Captain Alfred Dreyfus, employed on staff duties at the War Ministry. Convicted by court martial, on worthless evidence, illegally witheld from the defence, Dreyfus would confess to nothing, declined to commit suicide, and shouted his innocence out loud at the macabre ceremony of degradation, on the square of the *École Militaire*, where he was stripped of his badges of rank, and had his sword broken in front of him, before being deported for life to Devil's Island, off the tropical coast of French Guiana. His family and friends started the struggle to have his case reopened and his name cleared. Two years later, a new head of counter-espionage, Colonel Picquart, became convinced that Dreyfus was innocent and that a certain, shady Major Esterhazy was the more likely culprit. He reported his conclusions to the Deputy Chief of the Army General Staff. He was told to keep quiet, and, when he refused, was posted to Tunisia.

Meanwhile, so as to save the reputation of the War Office, Major Henry, Dreyfus's chief accuser, had begun to manufacture evidence against him. Esterhazy was acquitted unanimously by a new court martial, but by now a number of politicians and the Press were involved.

The Dreyfus case blew up into the Dreyfus Affair in January 1898. Émile Zola, the most celebrated French novelist of his age, published an open letter in Clemenceau's *L'Aurore* under the editorial headline 'J'accuse', indicting Dreyfus's judges for violation of the rights of the defence, and Esterhazy's for acquitting a real traitor on orders from the War Ministry. Daring the General Staff to arraign him in the Assize Court for libel, he was tried and convicted, but escaped his sentence of fine and imprisonment by fleeing to England. Picquart was thrown out of the Army. The public 'revisionist' campaign to reopen the Dreyfus case then really got under way, headed by the specially formed 'League of the Rights of Man' and backed by a petition of prominent writers, scholars and politicians. On the other side, supported by all the pillars of tradition in France, and particularly by the Church, encouraged also by the Government which, after Panama, felt itself particularly vulnerable to scandal, the General Staff fought with cold fury against what they saw as a public affront to the honour of the Army and as a conspiracy, plotted by Freemasons, Protestants and, especially, Jews, to undermine the safety of the state. For Léon Daudet, for example, it was simply a matter of 'a Jew having betrayed France, and now other Jews and their friends continuing to do her harm'.[19] Anti-Semitism had been spreading in the French officer class, in which the influence of Catholic gentry was preponderant. Catholic officers and gentlemen tended to feel alienated from the new Republican establishment, based broadly on the *opportuniste* alliance of anti-clerical ideology and business interests, and which appeared pointedly disregardful of the 'natural' leaders of the old military, rural, church-going France. Such men were particularly prone to believe the fables of Drumont's *La France juive*, and to suspect corrupt Jewish influences everywhere in high places, and particularly in Parliament and the War Office.[20] That Dreyfus was originally suspected and convicted just because he was a Jew has been contested,[21] but there is no doubt that anti-Semitism was one of the driving forces of the movement to prevent a fair revision of the evidence and procedure by which he had been condemned.

In 1898 Henry's forgeries were discovered, and he was put under fortress arrest at Vincennes, where he cut his throat. Far from silencing the anti-Dreyfusard faction, now in full cry, this news drove them to fresh extremes. Henry was a martyr, his forgery was an act of high patriotism, wrote the young Charles Maurras, in the article which founded his reputation as a political controversialist.

By 1899, Radicals, Socialists and the Dreyfusard intelligentsia had mobilised public opinion sufficiently to force the Government to order a retrial. Dreyfus was brought back from Devil's Island, was accused once more before seven 'brother officers' at a fresh court martial in Rennes (away from the Paris crowds), and was again found guilty, though with extenuating circumstances, by five votes to two. Faced with the Army's stubborn *esprit de corps,* he accepted a pardon. But his supporters would be satisfied with nothing less than official recognition of his innocence. This was finally given by a ruling of the *Cour de Cassation,* but not until 1906, after the Republican left wing had been carried to power by the impetus of the Dreyfusard movement.[22]

The Dreyfus Affair divided those who considered themselves to be realists because they preferred possible injustice in a particular instance to a general breakdown of law and order (without which, they said, there could be no justice at all), from the idealists who held that the pre-eminent duty of the courts is to dispense justice to each individual at no matter what risk to society, and indeed that society is itself threatened by every injustice that it knowingly permits. Dreyfus became for one party the symbol of mankind's desire for a universally just society, while the Army represented for the other a vital bastion of the national heritage under attack by an international conspiracy of fanatical intellectuals and self-seeking materialists who threatened everything of value that France still stood for.[23]

The affair was also exploited for more narrowly political ends, by both sides, in a struggle for power which was won decisively by the Dreyfusard left wing, in the parliamentary elections of 1902. The Radical-Socialists then used their victory to break off relations between the State they now controlled and the Church whose influence in public affairs they had long opposed. Many priests had supported the anti-Dreyfusard cause. Such open meddling in reactionary politics was now to deprive Roman Catholicism of its official position in France. Under the Radical Ministry of Émile Combes (1902–5), most religious orders were dissolved and all were forbidden to teach. In 1904 the French Ambassador was withdrawn from the Vatican and the following year a Socialist Minister, Aristide Briand, carried a law separating Church and State. An attempt was also made to 'republicanise' and 'democratise' the armed services, but some of the methods used (e.g. spying on officers to see if they or their families went to Mass) discredited this policy and limited its effects. The French Church was, in the end, invigorated by disestablishment, and the Army command was improved by a measure of social levelling in the higher *cadre*; but at the time both the Catholics and the officer class were angered and demoralised. Such feelings were to the advantage of the counter-revolutionary Integral Nationalism with which Maurras would now stiffen the ideology and revive the fortunes of the traditionalist and authoritarian right wing.[24] The Socialists also renewed and strengthened their organisation on a broader front, uniting to form a single *Section française de l'internationale ouvrière* (S.F.I.O.) in 1905. The dividing line between a working-class movement for democratic change (internationalist, anti-clerical and anti-militarist) and a middle-class party of law and order (nationalist, Catholic and authoritarian) was sharpened by the great debate over a crucial miscarriage of justice. French literature was also marked by it, although the leading writers on either side – Zola, France and Péguy, Barrès and Maurras – had all begun to involve themselves in political controversy before 1898.

Zola had never thought of his naturalist's laboratory as an ivory tower, but in *Les Trois Villes* (*Lourdes, Rome, Paris*), which followed his great 'natural and social history' of the Rougon-Macquart family (terminated by its twentieth volume in 1893), he was much more openly partisan and moralising than he had ever been before. *Les Quatre Évangiles* (*Fécondité, Travail, Vérité, Justice*), begun in 1899, express a still greater ambition to edify and prophesy. Zola's notes for the final volume, *Justice*, which was to point the way to the United States of Europe through 'the great kiss of peace', but which was interrupted by his accidental death in 1902, reach a paroxysm of shrill protest wrung from the author's involvement in France's great crisis of conscience:

> Only through France can humanity be born. . . . If other countries seem wiser, cleaner, that is because they lie, they cover up, they live on the past. When France has made truth manifest, and ordered justice to be done (*her painful calvary*), then everything will crack open and collapse in the nations round her. France the Messiah, the Redeemer, the Saviour, Queen.[25]

Between 1876 and 1898, Anatole France moved from harmonious antiquarian poetry (*Les Noces corinthiennes*) and sentimental private *rêveries* (*Le Crime de Sylvestre Bonnard*) to the first in a long gallery of ironical portraits of self-deluded fanatics and genial sceptics which was to make his reputation as the oracle of early Third-Republican urbanity and liberalism. Barrès and Maurras had begun to abandon self-culture and aestheticism and to devote their literary skills to the service of *Énergie Nationale* and *Action Française* several years before 'J'accuse'. The young Charles Péguy flung himself into the Dreyfusard vanguard with all the fervour of a newly recruited Socialist crusader.

The affair did not decide the political vocation of these four writers, but it did forge and temper their originality (whereas Zola's genius flowered before the affair, and faded during it). in *L'Affaire Crainquebille* (1901), which ironically reduces the *Affaire Dreyfus* down to the vulgar, but no less pathetic, dimensions of an elderly barrow-boy wrongly convicted of insulting a policeman, and in the hilarious parodies, cruel histories and irreverent fantasies of 'justice' which fill *L'Île des pingouins* (1908), *Les Dieux ont soif* (1912), *La Révolte des anges* (1914), France composed a witty sequence of variations on the central theme of the Dreyfus controversy. The last page of the sequence, which records Lucifer's renunciation of the revolutionary method in the name of inner reformation ('The victory is Spirit, and it is in ourselves, and in ourselves alone, that we must attack and destroy Ialdobaoth'), reflects the author's enduring anti-clericalism and hatred of established authority; but it does also express a certain sceptical detachment from the Dreyfusards' political triumph. Charles Péguy reached a similar, though more openly hostile position after a more painful process of disillusionment. The high Dreyfusard *mystique* as he defined it, that is, a battle for the soul of France, put in mortal danger by the acceptance of 'a single illegality officially registered',[26] had been brought down, after the Radical-Socialist electoral victory of 1902, to the level of anti-clerical and anti-militarist *politique*. This degradation of Dreyfusism he saw as the work of parliamentarians, capitalists and academics opportunistically allied in what he called contemptuously *le parti intellectuel*. The counter-force of his blazing prose pamphlets, his verse of epic scale and his modern miracle play, *Le Mystère de la Charité de Jeanne d'Arc*, sprang from an increasing obsession with three interdependent orders of mystical faith upon which he believed that his spiritual salvation, and that of his country, must depend: Dreyfusism, patriotism and Christianity.

Barrès, like Péguy and France, reached the top of his powers during the decade which followed the affair. His already declared ambition was to 'formulate', 'illustrate' and 'educate' the sensibility of his generation,[27] and to these ends he wrote thousands of articles, scores of essays and speeches and a dozen widely read, mainly political, novels, protesting against Germany's continued occupation of Alsace and Lorraine and alleging the corruption of France's national traditions and the decline of her international position under Republican centralisation, secularism and pacifism. At the same time, Charles Maurras, the third leading patriotic writer of this generation (contemporaries of Kipling, D'Annunzio and Yeats), was winning souls and fighters for his more narrowly doctrinaire school of Integral Nationalism, with such tracts as *Une Enquête sur la monarchie* (1900–1), *L'Avenir de l'intelligence* (1905) and *Kiel et Tanger* (1910).

Finally, in 1913 and 1914, just before the outbreak of the Great War that would shatter the civilised order of society in which the Dreyfus Affair had raged, but whose underlying common consents and accepted rules it had scarcely disturbed, two writers hitherto untouched by the political passions and tensions of the affair were caught by the edge of the dying storm. Roger Martin du Gard wrote *Jean Barois*, a novel of ideas which rendered earnestly and clearly the central *crise de conscience* of the Dreyfus generation – tradition or reason? – and André Gide (who had read and recommended the manuscript of *Jean Barois* for the N.R.F.)[28] published his own first political novel the following year (1914). This was *Les Caves du Vatican*, in which zealots of traditional religion and fanatics of scientific humanism are alike represented as blundering puppets, on strings pulled by cynicism and chance, out of which only the careless genius of a single young fantasy-hero, Lafcadio, soars up freely – for a time.

COLONIAL EXPANSION AND WAR FEVER

The intensity of the struggle over Dreyfus, and the fascination of the ideas it involved, combined with a still unshaken habit of self-sufficiency, kept the French nation very much to itself at the turn of the century. The world watched France in the throes of the affair with largely unjustified smugness. Few Frenchmen took much notice of what was going on beyond the borders of their homeland. Delcassé, who became Foreign Minister in 1898, and who was to hold this office for the next seven years, worked for most of this time out of the limelight. His aim was to complete the policy, initiated by his *opportuniste* predecessors when they negotiated the Franco–Russian alliance (1890–5), of countering the vigorous ambitions of Imperial Germany with help from the West as well as from the East. This would lead to an agreement of co-operation and so-called 'cordial understanding' between France and Great Britain, signed in 1904. The making of the *Entente Cordiale* was a more tricky diplomatic operation than the earlier negotiations with Russia. Autocratic Russia's suspicions of Republican France were not reciprocated by more than a handful of French Republicans. But Britain and France were rival *nations,* not just opposite forms of *government,* close neighbours and traditional enemies who had fought each other too long and too well not to be thoroughly familiar with and sensitive to each other's competing ambitions and complementary faults. Paradoxically, the road to their unfamiliar new *Entente* lay through Africa, where, freshly arrayed as the two greatest imperial powers at the height of Europe's colonial expansion overseas, they appeared once more to be spoiling for a fight.

In 1898 France's 'Second Colonial Empire'[29] was in full progress, in spite of comparative indifference at home on the part of a people still predominantly peasant, 'wedded to the soil' (and having about enough good soil to go round) or occupied with small family businesses or independent trades which were neither threatened by foreign competition nor in need of overseas markets. Only the comparatively few big bankers and industrialists were interested in new markets and materials overseas; however, these men were influential in Opportunist circles and they found in the Opportunists' leader, Jules Ferry, an enterprising French imperialist.[30] French explorers, missionaries, soldiers and adventurers were ready to take the necessary action.

France already possessed a 'First Colonial Empire' dating from the time of her kings. This had been created piecemeal by Richelieu, Colbert and Law[31] for the protection of trade between France and the rich tobacco, sugar, coffee, cocoa and (after 1750) cotton plantations in the West Indies and the Indian Ocean. A 'New France' was also established in Canada and Louisiana. Smaller, isolated trading stations (*comptoirs*) were set up in India and West Africa (Pondichéry, Sénégal). Scattered Pacific islands, of which the most important is Tahiti, were explored by Bougainville in the eighteenth century but not annexed until the end of the nineteenth. The decline and partial dispersal of the old royal French Empire was due principally to the growth of free trade, the abolition of slavery, and losses (mostly to Britain) in the Seven Years and the Napoleonic Wars. Louisiana was sold to the Americans in 1803. The Indian *comptoirs* were signed away in 1956. Sénégal is now one of several independent African republics in a residual French 'Community'. Guadeloupe, Martinique, French Guiana and Réunion survive as *départements d'outre-mer*. The islands of Saint-Pierre et Miquelon off Canada with their small community of fishermen are overseas territories under French administration. There are about six million French-speaking Canadians on the mainland, mostly in the province of Québec.

The second period of French colonial expansion began with the conquest of Algiers in 1830. The revolt of Abd el-

Kader forced the French to choose between conquest of the interior or complete evacuation. An African army was created, the greater part of the country was pacified, and cheap or free concessions of land expropriated from Arab farmers or reclaimed from wasteland attracted a growing population of European colonists. In 1856 there were 180,000, and 2,300,000 Arabs. Both populations increased rapidly, and a century later totalled 1,100,000 and 8,500,000 respectively.

In 1881 the French established a protectorate over Tunisia, and its energetic first Governor, Paul Cambon, later Ambassador to Britain and an architect of the *Entente Cordiale*, began large-scale production there of olives, fruit and phosphates. At about the same time the extension of trading and mission posts in Indo-China involved the French in a war of pacification which was slow but steady, and downright unpopular only when a temporary set-back or rumour of one brought it to the notice of Parliament and public: then Ferry, dubbed derisively *le Tonkinois*, was accused of playing Bismarck's game by forgetting the 'blue line of the Vosges' and chasing mirages in the East.[32] But French influence continued to spread through Laos and Cambodia, and Annam, Tonkin and Cochin-China, the three most heavily populated parts of the peninsula, which became Vietnam after the Second World War. By 1911, French Indo-China had nearly 17,000,000 inhabitants, of whom less than 300,000 were French settlers, administrators or soldiers. French rule was indirect, through 'protected' native rulers and élites educated in French ways: Hanoi University was founded in 1918. Nationalist stirrings and an outburst of terrorism against European domination appeared during the second decade of the twentieth century.

The last two decades of the nineteenth century had seen the establishment of a French protectorate in Madagascar (which came under direct rule, as a colony, in 1896), and the extension of French influence by explorers (the foremost being Brazza) and soldiers (under, notably, Gallieni and Marchand) into West and Central Africa: Sénégal, Niger, Guinea, Ivory Coast, Dahomey, Sudan, Mauritania, Upper Volta,[33] Gabon, Middle Congo, Oubangi-Chari and Chad.[34]

French interest in the Middle East dates from the Crusades, and springs, in post-medieval times, from trade relations and missionary activity, and, since Napoleon, from military campaigning against the British and the Turks. In 1860 a French expedition was sent to restore order after the massacre in Syria of the Christian Maronites by Moslem Druses; then, after the First World War, Syria became a French mandate.[35] French is taught as a second or third language in the schools of Egypt, Syria, Lebanon and Israel. It was for long the *lingua franca* of the Levantine and European immigrant population in Egypt and the language of the Egyptian ruling class. In Syria it has lost the position it once held, but the Lebanon is still largely bilingual, though Arabic is the official language.[36]

In 1875 the British bought the Khedive of Egypt's holding of shares in the French-built Suez Canal. Four years later, joint Franco-British control was set up, but when the French Government failed in 1882 to obtain parliamentary support for the joint suppression of a nationalist revolt there (which threatened the safety of the Canal), the British entered the country alone and placed the government of Egypt under their sole authority, to the exclusion of France.

The bad feeling between France and Britain over their differences in Egypt continued for another two decades, breaking out with sudden violence when the British thwarted a French thrust to the Nile valley from Equatorial Africa. This was the Fashoda incident. In March 1897 Major Marchand had set out north-eastwards from the Middle Congo coast with orders to 'fire a pistol shot on the Nile' for which the French Foreign Office, he had been told, would 'accept all the consequences'[37] Sixteen months later, after a long and very difficult expedition through tropical forest and marsh, with a commandeered steamer which had to be dismantled and pushed on rollers where the rivers were not deep enough, he succeeded in establishing a small garrison in the Nile fort of Fashoda. The plan was to link up with the Abyssinians (who had lately beaten the Italians at Adowa) and the Dervishes (whom Kitchener was fighting in the Sudan), and, with their aid, to block the attempt to create an all-British route from 'Cape to Cairo'. But while Marchand's expedition was on its way, the British had beaten the Dervishes at Omdurman, and soon after Marchand reached Fashoda from the south the victorious Kitchener arrived from the north with five gunboats and a very much stronger force of infantry and artillery.

Polite visits between officers were exchanged. The French were able to read what the Dreyfusards were saying about their General Staff in newspapers supplied by the British, and the British tasted fresh vegetables from the French fort. Both sides held their fire until instructions arrived from home. When the Cabinet in Paris came to consider the facts it was plain they could not fight a war with the British, either at Fashoda in Africa, or on the intervening seas, and they ordered the adventurous but completely inadequate expedition to withdraw. Thereafter, Delcassé at the Quai d'Orsay and Paul Cambon, French Ambassador in London from 1898 to 1920, worked quietly, against popular dislike of the British, towards an accommodation with the power which had humiliated them on the Nile, but which was itself shaken (to the delight of the French) by the effort of putting down the Boer revolt in South Africa a year or two later, and which would also soon be looking for allies against the rising imperial and naval power of Germany.

The first step was a Franco-British agreement signed in 1899 dividing Africa into spheres of influence. France would stay out of the Nile valley, but westwards she would be free to explore, pacify and develop a huge area and variety of country stretching from the Congo to the Mediterranean. This was done during the next twenty-five years, the protectorate of Morocco being added to the French Empire in 1912, but not before the two great imperial powers, now on friendly terms and supported by Russia, had clashed with the Germans, who had ambitions in Morocco themselves.

The decade which followed the Franco-British *Entente Cordiale* of 1904 was a brilliantly inventive and expansive era of French civilisation, but it was marred by social unrest and punctuated by alarms of war. In France, the latter seemed to come mainly from the mounting colonial ambitions of Germany and, in particular, from her peremptory demand for a share in the carve-up of Africa. At Tangiers in 1905, the Kaiser intervened to stop Morocco going wholly to France and Spain, and insisted, against France, on a European Congress to decide the future of the Sultanate. This was held in 1906 at Algeciras, where the Franco-British position prevailed. Accordingly, when Morocco subsequently collapsed in anarchy and violence, a French army intervened. The Kaiser, however, sent the German gunboat *Panther* to Agadir in 1911 in a gesture of dissent and appropriation, indignantly interpreted by increasingly excited patriotic opinion in France as one more step, after Tangiers and Algeciras, towards a general European war.[38] In 1905 Britain had taken up the challenge of Germany's growing Navy, and a naval arms race ensued. In 1913 Germany reinforced her Army; France replied by increasing the period of military service to three years.

Colonial rivalry was one of the causes of the First World War. Another was the fact that, as a result of the Russian alliance of 1895, 'in August 1914 France was committed to a war undertaken by her ally on behalf of a Balkan state'.[39] It has been suggested also that war fever between the two great leagues lining up opposite each other – the Triple Alliance of 'Central Powers', Germany, Austria, Italy (with Turkey on the eastern wing), and the Triple Entente: Russia, France, Britain – was a convenient way for the ruling classes throughout Europe to avert labour troubles and revolutionary working-class discontent at home. The motives that Europe's ruling classes and restless masses had for going to war in 1914 are certainly too complex for any such simple Machiavellian explanation. But it is true that in France, as the younger generation of *bourgeois* became more war-minded (and, while waiting and preparing for the war, speed-mad and air-minded),[40] the French working-class masses, on the other hand, were being increasingly attracted towards violent action against both *laissez-faire* capitalism and chauvinistic nationalism.

SYNDICALISM AGAINST THE STATE

After the unification of the French Socialist Party in 1905, and the 'charter' of syndicalism adopted by the Trade Union Congress at Amiens the following year, which reaffirmed its 'independence vis-à-vis the employers, the political parties and the state', the French labour movement went over to the attack by 'direct action'.[41] There were threatening Labour Day parades in Paris, and several big strikes, by postmen, railwaymen and quarrymen, strikes which many, on both sides, believed to be the opening phase of the looked-for revolution. Clemenceau, opposition Radical turned ministerial strikebreaker, justified himself to a C.G.T. delegation in this light:

'You are behind the barricades. I'm in front. Your way is disorder. My duty is to keep order.'[42] In October 1910 Aristide Briand, one-time champion of the syndicalist theory of the general strike but now France's first Socialist Prime Minister, crushed a railwaymen's strike by arresting their leaders and conscripting the rank-and-file as Army reservists.

While the class war in France was making trade unionists violent and governments repressive, and alienating workers from earlier parliamentary champions and the parliamentary régime itself, Socialist repudiation of war between nations was gaining strength. The C.G.T. in congress at Marseille in 1908, recorded their acceptance of the doctrine that 'the working class has no mother-country', and recommended that workers 'reply to the declaration of war by declaring a revolutionary general strike'. Jaurès in particular laboured without pause or stint, in Parliament, Press and one international Socialist conference after another, to 'break', as he said (at Basle in 1912), 'the threatening thunderbolts of war'. But Europe went to war for all that. And in the atavistic excitement of general mobilisation (the day after the assassination of Jaurès by a young French nationalist), the workers of Europe, just like the peasants, the middle classes and the nobility, marched off obediently, and at first enthusiastically, to a battle between nations and not classes. In France, the so-called 'Sacred Union' between Frenchmen of all social ranks and political allegiances was practically unanimous.

LITERATURE AND ART, 1900–14

When André Gide looked back over the first half of his literary career to Paris in the 1880s, it seemed to him as if the Symbolist and Decadent generation had been indoctrinated when young to despise as mere 'contingency' everything that was not 'absolute', all the 'prismatic diversity of life', and, in a phrase, 'to turn their backs on reality'.[43] While the war of ideas between Socialism and nationalism was calling France, Barrès, Maurras and Péguy away from *fin-de-siècle* aestheticism, Gide, as he put it, was being 'saved by gourmandise', during three years spent, mainly in the Mediterranean and North Africa, 'unlearning' everything that he had previously 'learned with his head', as a boy in a puritanically Protestant home, and as a literary apprentice in Mallarmé's circle in Paris. It was the first stage, celebrated in the lyrical prose of *Les Nourritures terrestres,* of his relentless 'assumption' of the widest possible range of human experience ('assumer le plus possible d'humanité'), a voyage of discovery, guided by art, music, nature study, travel, a vast programme of reading and the special influence of Shakespeare, Blake, Nietzsche, Dostoevsky and Conrad, and logged with ironical detachment in a dialectical series of critical 'tales' (*L'Immoraliste, La Porte étroite, La Symphonie pastorale, Thésée*) and a multi-stream novel, *Les Faux-monnayeurs,* and which could only end with his death, half a century later, for he would never rest with what he or anyone else might suppose man to be, or to be capable of, but must always 'go beyond'. *Passer outre* was the watchword of a great emancipator, whose life's work was to liberate men from the constraints of self-induced, as well as socially imposed, complacency, cant and abstraction.

Paul Claudel, like Gide, discovered himself and his literary vocation in the desire to embrace what he called 'the immense octave of created things'. In contrast to Gide, however, he believed with confidence in a Divine Creator, not immanent in the world, diffusely (as in *Les Nourritures terrestres*), but transcending his creation, which he produces, as it were, like a stage-play, in which each one of his creatures has been given a part.

Thus inspired and provided, Claudel composed a volume of soaring and torrential lyric poetry such as had not been written in French since the death of Victor Hugo, and a body of thrilling poetic drama which finally disposed of the ban against mixing poetry and reality on the stage which had sterilised French drama after the decline of Romanticism. No longer would playwrights have to listen to Zola's injunction of 1881: 'You must choose between poetic fantasy and real life, one or the other.'[44]

Another writer who spoke out against the *fin-de-siècle* alternative of materialism or escapism was Romain Rolland, who celebrated the heroic vigour of the French revolutionary leaders and masses in such plays as *Le Quatorze Juillet,* and proposed a cult of great individuals: Beethoven, Tolstoy and Gandhi; and the hero of his long novel *Jean-Christophe,* who seemed to him to have a lesson of humanity for the whole world, transcending time and frontiers.

A facet of real life that writers found specially fascinating at this period, at an early phase of modern mass politics, was group psychology, which had already inspired novelists such as Zola and Barrès, and Paul Adam, author of *Le Mystère des foules* (1895), as well as two monographs by the new French school of sociology: Gustave le Bon's *La Psychologie des foules*, and Gabriel Tarde's *L'Opinion et la foule*. Now Jules Romains invented a word for the group soul, *l'unanime*, and began to write poems, plays and novels imbued with a 'unanimist' vision of humanity. He acknowledged his debt to Zola and others, but claimed that the central thesis of Unanimism – 'a collection of people brought together by chance, remaining together for however short a while, and embarking on some action together, tend to become something more than just a collection of people' – was a personal revelation of a quasi-mystical kind, rather than a scientific discovery. A similarly dynamic vision of men and women in groups is found in *Les Villes tentaculaires* and *Les Forces tumultueuses* of the Belgian poet, Émile Verhaeren.

The achievement of French Impressionist and Post-Impressionist painting was, in 1900, so 'dazzling in its glory' that 'practically every artist who was to become a leader of new movements in the new century visited Paris, and many came to stay'.[45] The new movements in art showed the same marks of emancipation, energy and sensuousness as the new literature. After the bold, arbitrary colours of the so-called 'untamed' or *fauve* paintings of Derain, Rouault, Vlaminck, Friesz and the young Matisse, the Cubists (Picasso, Braque, Léger, Gris) freed the painter more thoroughly yet from the traditional task of imitation, by abstracting simple geometrical shapes and intricately faceted surfaces from nature, and by subordinating subject-matter entirely to the picture space. Glass, metal and print writhed and glittered in the decorative *art nouveau* of Gallé, Guimard and Bonnard, while Rodin, Maillol and Camille Claudel (sculptors), the painter Matisse and the composer Ravel raised dynamic rhythm, silky texture and voluptuous line or colour to the level of fine art, in *Le Baiser* (1900), *L'Action enchaînée* (1906), *La Vague* (1905);

Bonheur de vivre and *La Danse* (1906, 1909); *Rapsodie espagnole* and *Daphnis et Chloë* (1908, 1912).

After 1908 there was an *avant-garde* vogue for the 'aggressive simplicity' of Erik Satie's music and for the childlike fantasies of le Douanier Rousseau (who painted his magnificent dream jungles between 1904 and 1910).[46] The poet Apollinaire (1880–1918), at about the same time, reopened and developed a vein of candid self-display and ironic self-pity that Verlaine and Laforgue had worked in a previous generation, and which was consciously naïve. He was also a self-conscious modernist, cultivating eccentricity and exhorting artists and writers to go forward into

vast and strange domains
Where mystery flowers for the taking.
There are new fires there colours never seen
A thousand imponderable fantasies
To be made real
We want to explore goodness the huge silent country
There is also time which can be abolished or recovered
Pity us always fighting at the frontiers
Of the infinite and the future
Pity for our errors pity for our sins.

Now the summer comes, the violent season. . . .[47]

Apollinaire and his friends were indeed, in a variety of media, breaking new ground together. Braque and Picasso were inventing their art of *collage*s (fragments of real or imitation wood, lettering, newsprint, wallpaper, dishcloths and oilcloth stuck on to painted canvas or board) at the same time as Apollinaire his new literary forms: the *poème-conversation,* the *poème-promenade,* 'simultaneous poetry' (which keeps fragments of experience in a random order, so that they can be reassembled in a single instant of consciousness) and the *idéogramme lyrique,* later called the *calligramme* (which explodes the printed words and phrases of a poem and puts them together again in the form of appropriate objects: a dove, a shower of rain, a carnation). New art-forms such as these, by stressing disparities and tensions between the artist's vision of reality and an implied real life of accidental forms and chance encounters, everyday speech or materials torn from context, uprooted fragments of matter or 'news', tended to undermine completely the already worn convention that literature and the fine arts should simply mirror external nature or eternal beauty. Meanwhile, Chagall (from Russia) and de Chirico (from Italy) had come to Paris and were painting dream scenery – *Moi et le village* (1911), *Rue italienne* (1914) – and the Cubist revolution had pushed art to the point of pure abstraction, where it could develop as 'the free association of any visual elements (whether derived from nature or constructed *a priori*)'.[48]

By 1914, very few of the cultural *clichés* of the nineteenth century were left unchallenged, and many of the fundamental discoveries and inventions by which the twentieth century still lives had already been made – in many different spheres. Among the French scientific innovators and inventors of the age were Pierre and Marie Curie, who isolated the radioactive elements of uranium; Perrin, Becquerel and Langevin, working in related fields; the mathematicians Henri Poincaré and J.-S. Hademard; the aircraft designer Levavasseur, the engineer and aviator Louis Blériot (who in 1909 was the first man to fly the English Channel); Louis and Auguste Lumière and Georges Méliès, pioneers of the mechanics and the art of cinema; Peugeot, de Dion-Bouton, Panhard, Renault, Michelin, designers of automobiles and their accessories; the architects Auguste and Gustave Perret, masters of the new medium of reinforced concrete.

This age of restless and creative exploration and emancipation, of sensuous immediacy and irrational spontaneity, reached an extreme in the Futurist manifestos of 1909–14, which exalted 'the roaring motor-car', 'war, the only health-giver' and 'a life of steel, fever, pride and headlong speed'. It had its minor prophets in Georges Sorel, who taught that society, weakened by humanitarianism and parliamentary compromise, must be regenerated through proletarian violence, to be activated by the energising myth of the general strike (*Réflexions sur la violence*, 1906), and in Colonel de Grandmaison, who taught the military tactics of 'immediate all-out attack', and the superiority of the offensive spirit 'carried to excess' (1911).[49] It had two important progressive Catholic thinkers, Maurice Blondel, and Alfred Loisy the

Modernist, who asserted, respectively, the pre-eminence of active faith over intellectual contemplation and the spirit of free inquiry against fixed dogma.[50] And it had a major philosopher, Henri Bergson (1859–1941).

Starting from a discovery that the fundamental human experience of duration (*la durée réelle*) is something quite different from abstract time (scientifically measured, and commonly conceived, as the movement in space of a clock-hand from second to second), Bergson sought to revolutionise philosophy by rejecting both scientific empiricism and Kantian idealism (the ruling schools of late nineteenth-century Europe, both operating with abstract concepts and discursive reasoning) in favour of grasping what he called 'immediate' experience: *les données immédiates de la conscience*.[51] This was to be done, he taught, by an effort of sympathetic intuition, supposed to 'install' the philosopher in the heart of living reality: organic, mobile, concrete, a homogeneous and continuous stream of interpenetrating, never-to-be-repeated events. Bergson's original intuition of the open-ended, undetermined nature of real time[52] led him eventually to somewhat oracular doctrines of 'creative evolution', 'spiritual energy', '*élan vital*', which were to be contemptuously dismissed as effete or merely poetic by younger moralists such as Julien Benda and logicians such as Bertrand Russell. But Bergson's subtle, and more sober, psychology of sleeping and waking, attention, distraction, memory, habit, intelligence, his attempt to transcend the dualism of spirit and matter in a 'philosophy of the act', his insistence on the necessity of going beneath linguistic forms and conceptual language, his theory of the comic (*Le Rire*, 1900), and his aesthetics of expression,[53] have contributed much of value to modern art, literature and philosophy.

Bergson himself was a considerable literary artist. He once defined metaphysics as 'the science which claims to dispense with symbols'. But the art of philosophical exposition was another matter. When he came to write, or to lecture (Bergson was a fascinating and fashionable *conférencier*), he would use an exceptionally fluent and suggestive variety of images in rapid succession, not to stand for fixed, particular ideas, but rather to maintain contact with the stream of experience and, 'through the convergence of their action, to direct the consciousness to the precise point where there is a certain intuition to seize on'[54] – a science without symbols expressed rather like Symbolist poetry.

But the most original synthesis of what Naturalism and Symbolism tended, theoretically at least, to keep apart was achieved when Marcel Proust, who was as yet known only as a socialite and minor *homme de lettres*, having abandoned the manuscript of an unsatisfactory autobiographical novel written between 1895 and 1900 in the conventional narrative mode,[55] succeeded round about 1906 in forging the totally original style he needed for a radically new literary enterprise. This was to be the retrospective exploration of a life (his own) that would appear superficially to have been more than ordinarily immersed and dispersed in time, flesh and society, but whose deep identity, invisible to the eye of habit, to conscious memory and to Naturalistic documentation, would eventually be discovered where the Symbolists had looked for reality: 'in some dimension outside life'.[56]

The genius of Proust is a fitting climax to an exceptionally creative period of French culture. He was also typical of this age of inheritors and explorers in the capacity he showed for grafting together the double cultural heritage of late nineteenth-century Naturalism and Symbolism (as well as the great tradition of the classical French moralists), and also for assimilating and combining a great many cultural constituents brought in from other countries, and across frontiers between the arts (and between art, science and philosophy). Ruskin, George Eliot, Bergson and the French Impressionist painters decisively influenced Proust's vision, as the Russian novel renewed Gide's, and as the ancient Greek tragedies, St Thomas Aquinas, the Japanese *No* play and Wagner's music-drama imbued Claudel's. Japanese prints, Byzantine mosaics, Persian, Gothic and Romanesque art, African carvings, as well as the paintings of Cézanne, Gauguin, Van Gogh and Toulouse-Lautrec, influenced Fauvist and Cubist art, and many of these same influences were at work in *art nouveau*, together with the example of the English Pre-Raphaelites and Morris's Arts and Crafts movement. Walt Whitman and Marinetti the Italian Futurist inspired French *avant-garde* writers and painters. Javanese and gypsy music, Russian opera and Symbolist literature inspired Debussy, the greatest French composer of the age.[57] Paul Valéry, who between 1913 and 1922 wrote some of the most musical poetry in the French language ('secretly modelled', he said, on Gluck's and Wagner's art of recitative[58]), was also an assimilative as well as a creative intelligence. Together with Proust, Debussy and Bergson, and with such painters as Braque, Matisse and Bonnard, he epitomised the richness, subtlety, stylishness and refinement of French civilisation on the eve of the Great War.

9 The Great Wars

THE FIRST WORLD WAR

DEEP-SEATED tension between the Slav minority and the Austro-Hungarian ruling-class of the Habsburg Empire breached the long European peace in the late summer of 1914, when Serbian patriots assassinated the heir to the imperial throne at Sarajevo, in the troubled Balkans, setting off a chain reaction of mobilisation and counter-mobilisation which brought the Serbs' and Austrians' protectors, Russia and Germany respectively, face to face, ready for war. France, Russia's ally against the German Reich since 1895, refused to stay neutral, and Germany declared war on her on 3 August and immediately launched the main part of its powerful Army westwards through neutral Belgium to knock out the French quickly, before turning on the cumbersome Russian 'steam-roller' in the east. The violation of Belgian neutrality provoked the British to declare war on Germany, and to send an efficient but very small Expeditionary Force of professional soldiers across the Channel to aid the French.

By the end of August, the Tsar's huge though poorly equipped Army was halted for good, and the French and British were falling back well inside France. However, the invasion of their homeland had brought the socially and politically divided French nation together. 'L'Union sacrée' was a single-hearted *élan* of patriotic determination which would keep it fighting with scarcely diminished energy and idealism for a further two years, in a war of unparalleled scale and horror, during which time France would bear the brunt of the battle for the Triple Entente.

As the Germans marched swiftly on Paris, the French Commander-in-Chief, General Joffre, built up his mass of manœuvre in front of the capital, with reinforcements brought back from the Lorraine frontier, calmly and efficiently in (striking contrast to the improvident disorder of Napoleon III's armies of 1870). This time it was the Germans who were overconfident. Carried by the momentum of pursuit, they abandoned their original plan of encircling Paris from the west and south, and instead turned eastwards before reaching it. Joffre then struck back at their exposed right flank in the Marne valley, checked the invaders decisively and forced them to retreat to the Aisne and the Oise. After another eighteen months of costly and inconclusive fighting along the continuous line of trenches which soon stretched from the Vosges to Flanders and the Channel coast, the French met and held the second great German onslaught at the historic fortress town of Verdun, in a battle lasting from February to June 1916 which killed over 400,000 French and German soldiers.[1] At the first Battle of the Marne, and again at Verdun, the armies of France bought time for their British ally to enrol and equip a large citizen army of its own, which was able to take some of the strain off the French by attacking with them on the Somme in July 1916, gaining a little ground, but at terrible cost, and failing to break through. A poorly planned French offensive the following year also failed, disappointing high hopes and depressing morale. Syndicalist pacificism revived (encouraged by news of the Russian Revolution) and spread from factories to troops on leave and eventually to the front, where some units mutinied. Order was restored thanks very largely to the efforts of two men: a new Commander-in-Chief, General Pétain, the defender of Verdun, who kept punishment and exemplary executions down to a minimum, and did a great deal to improve living conditions in the trenches, and the leave roster; and a new Prime Minister, Clemenceau, who took virtually dictatorial powers to curb the peace party in Parliament and to inspire and organise the whole nation for a fight to the finish, 'jusqu'au bout'.

In the spring of 1918 the British and French armies were knocked back some of the way towards the Channel ports and the Marne by the last German offensive, but they held the line, with very heavy losses, under the overall command of General Foch, going over to the offensive themselves in the summer and autumn, to break at last, with American help, the murderous four-year stalemate of the trenches. Acknowledging defeat, Germany signed an armistice on 11 November, and the Peace Treaty of Versailles the following year.

By the Versailles Treaty France got back the eastern provinces of Alsace and Lorraine that had been ceded to Germany in 1871, but was denied the strategic security of an autonomous Rhineland state that Poincaré, Foch and Clemenceau asked for. The British and American representatives promised instead to guarantee her frontiers, but the U.S. Senate refused to ratify this and the British Government followed suit. Germany agreed to pay substantial 'reparations', but only a part of these was eventually made over, and this was no compensation for what the war had cost France: the ruin of a rich and extensive agricultural and industrial region where the war had been fought, the loss of 1,357,000 men killed and 4,266,000 wounded.[2] Out of every ten men between twenty and forty-five years old in 1914 'two had been killed, one had to be supported by his compatriots, three had some kind of infirmity for a period, and the task of keeping the country going after the war fell on the other four'.[3]

Despite the war of ideas unleashed by the Dreyfus Affair, and the increasingly violent and vocal discontents of the urban working class, France in the first decade of the twentieth century had been a self-confident and prosperous nation – a model, and a banker, for many less happier lands. A majority of her inhabitants (60 per cent in 1901[4]) were still relatively undisturbed country folk, and her *classe politique* of new Republican notables, like the older privileged and politically conscious groups they were tending to replace (or to join), had on the whole been most strongly roused by those matters of high principle, such as justice and the social order, science and religious belief, that only a relatively successful society can afford. France in the 1920s, the acknowledged leader of the war's winning alliance, with most of her people enjoying some part of the benefits of rapid industrial reconstruction and expansion, and the buoyant national mood of pride, relief and emancipated hedonism, appeared superficially to have recovered much of the strength and *élan vital* of 1914, despite obvious counter-currents of post-war distress, revulsion and revolt. Fundamentally it was a shaken, shrunken, debtor nation, facing problems far more pressing and intractable, affecting massive and widespread vital interests far more closely, than such comparatively abstract and disinterested pre-war conflicts of political morality and religious or rationalist conscience as the Dreyfus Affair and the disestablishment of the French Church. France's greatest post-war problems were inflation and the late, rapid growth of a true industrial proletariat.

The French at war had been more generous with the lifeblood of their youth than with their earnings and savings. Over a million and a quarter Frenchmen had been killed in action, but only 15 per cent of the enormous financial expenditure of four and a quarter years of total warfare had been paid for by taxes. The rest had been borrowed. By 1920 prices were at between four and six times the level of July 1914.[5] The decline of the franc to one-fifth of its pre-war value was temporarily halted by the tonic effect on parliamentary and public opinion of Poincaré's narrow financial orthodoxy and pre-war prestige, but not until 1926, and by then Parliament was ready to grant the financial saviour powers to legislate by decree, an abdication of its constitutional obligation to take responsibility for all legislation, including the unpopular kind, which would set an enervating example to parliamentary democracy in France for many decades to come.[6]

The mass production of weapons and vehicles between 1914 and 1918 greatly accelerated the growth of France's workforce of semi-skilled and unskilled factory hands. The number of firms employing between 2,000 and 5,000 workers increased by nearly 50 per cent between 1906 and 1921, and the number of those employing more than 5,000 doubled.[7] The confrontation of anonymous proletarian mass and faceless boss, comparatively new to France, would move to the centre of the French political scene during the very next decade. As it did so, Paris, and its politically 'red' belt of industrial suburbs, the largest conurbation in France, recovered some of its old authority (in eclipse since the suppression of the Commune of 1871) as a great revolutionary city.

THE DEPRESSION

The collapse of credit in New York in 1929, and the depression which followed, affected France's economy less suddenly and catastrophically than the more highly developed industries and trade of North America, Germany and Britain.

But there were at least 273,000 French unemployed by 1932 and 433,000 by 1936.[8] Migration from farms to factories slowed down, though agriculture was also depressed. Thousands of immigrant workers from Central Europe, Poland especially, were sent home. Industrialists and farmers cut back productive reinvestment in machinery and fertilisers. The deflationary reduction of public expenditure on pensions and civil service pay by which a succession of Radical Premiers (four in the year 1933) tried to ward off any further devaluation of the 'Poincaré' franc succeeded only in spreading discontent.[9]

Early in 1934, news broke of a financial scandal involving members of the parliamentary majority: a swindler named Stavisky, after investigations into an issue of forged bonds in the name of the Bayonne municipal savings bank, was found dead in a country villa besieged by police. Had he committed suicide? – or been shot by the *gendarmerie* so as to prevent embarrassing revelations? An inquiry showed that he had enjoyed the protection of certain Radical deputies. Public hostility towards the Government spread to encompass Parliament as a whole and parliamentary government as an institution. Faced with a grave and persistent economic crisis (and, in foreign affairs, the rise of Hitler's aggressively patriotic National Socialist Party, and the last hopes of war reparations dashed), the parliamentary representatives of the French nation appeared to have been stricken with paralysis of every faculty except that of speech, and every ambition except that of surviving in the expectation of graft. Only a handful of deputies were in fact involved, but given the difficult times the French, and particularly the Parisians, were going through, this was enough to bring into action the ever-alert *meneurs* (rabble-rousers) of the revolutionary left wing and the counter-revolutionary Right. The latter especially had little difficulty in swelling the ranks of mass protest by such time-honoured anti-parliamentary slogans as 'Down with the chatterboxes.' 'Down with the crooks.' ('A bas les bavards.' 'A bas les voleurs.') Stavisky was the son of Ukrainian Jew, so that another favourite bugbear, the predatory Jewish money-lender, was available for bringing tempers to white heat.

The attack on the parliamentary régime, 'Marianne la gueuse', was led by the right-wing leagues, reinforced by the cumulative effects of inflation, slump and deflation on the *petit-bourgeois* artisans, shopkeepers and white-collar employees of Paris, and spurred on by the doctrinaire and scurrilous political journalism of Maurras and Daudet in *Action Française*, the Royalist newspaper. This was peddled in the streets by *les camelots du roi*, young Royalists who were at the front of a mounting wave of violent street politics aimed at intimidating Republicans, destroying the parliamentary system and setting up in its place an authoritarian New Order on nationalistic and corporative lines. Working independently, but on a parallel course, were the newer Fascist leagues: *Jeunesses Patriotes, Solidarité Française, Le Francisme*, and Colonel de La Rocque's ex-servicemen's movement, *Les Croix de Feu*.[10]

Socialist and Communist Party supporters, and trade unionists, with as much reason for discontent as the predominantly middle-class *ligueurs*, felt little inclined, to say the least, to defend a parliamentary system dominated by the now stagnant conservatism of a party that was Radical-Socialist in name only. On the contrary, their mood was the revolutionary one celebrated lyrically in Dabit's articles on working-class Belleville for the *Nouvelle Revue Française* in February 1933:

> A new generation of workers, massed together, with their fists clenched, are determined to break their chains. . . . The factory continues to hold them in thrall, poverty pursues them into the familiar slums; but they can hear other men calling to them from all over the world. The leaden skies that oppress them are pierced with flashes of lightning.

6 FEBRUARY 1934

On this day yet another Radical-Socialist Prime Minister, Édouard Daladier, gave Parliament his plans for dealing with the crisis.[11] But the fever of extremism in the streets had by now so infected the Chamber that he could hardly make himself heard. Deputies on the right wing howled 'Resign!' and sang the 'Marseillaise', the Communist deputies shouted 'Power to the Soviets!' and sang the 'Internationale'. Outside, and across the Seine on the Place de la Concorde, a crowd of demonstrators, called out not only by *L'Action Française* but by the conservative Press and by the Communist newspaper *L'Humanité*, had built up during the day to some forty thousand. Ten thousand of these, after much confused manœuvring, under chaotic leadership, and nearly six hours of bitter fighting against the *gendarmerie* and the Republican Foot and Horse Guards, came near to forcing the barricade across the Pont de la Concorde and taking the Chamber of Deputies by storm. They were finally halted and dispersed, but the day's tumult had forced the police to fire several times, and sixteen rioters and bystanders were killed.

Though a majority of deputies had voted their confidence in the new Cabinet, Daladier resigned the next day, and was succeeded by an elderly ex-President of the Republic, Gaston Doumergue, whose Government of national unity, pitched to the right, lasted until November, but was no more successful than preceding ones, or Flandin's or Laval's, which followed, in solving France's economic and constitutional crisis. By then, however, the success of the Italian and the German dictators and the ever more threatening posture of the Royalist and Fascist leagues in France had convinced French Radicals and Communists alike (as well as Stalin in Moscow) of the immediate necessity of joining up with the Socialists in Parliament and in the trade unions, so as to form a united 'Front Populaire contre le fascisme'.

THE POPULAR FRONT

On Bastille Day, 14 July 1935, the French left wing displayed publicly, and impressively, the strength to be found in unity. A parade of supporters, 300,000 strong, marched exultantly, along the *via sacra* of the revolutionary tradition, in the East End of Paris, from the Place de la Bastille through the Faubourg Saint-Antoine to the Cours de Vincennes, clenched fists raised, Red Flag and tricolor flying together, headed by the party chiefs of the new Communist, Socialist and Radical alliance, Thorez, Blum and Daladier, symbolically arm in arm. On the same day, the *Croix de Feu* mustered a mere 30,000 in the *bourgeois* West End, though this numerical inferiority did nothing to reduce the *ligueurs*' arrogant sense of moral and class superiority, asserted with growing violence and aggravated by racialist intolerance: Léon Blum, the leader of the Socialist Party, was himself beaten up brutally by a gang of anti-Semitic Royalists.

A healthy reaction against the leagues, and contempt for the proved incompetence of the governing middle-of-the-road parliamentary majority, helped to give the Popular Front a clear victory in the general elections of 1936, and a majority of 158 in the new Chamber of Deputies. On the positive side the Front had aroused enthusiasm throughout the left wing by promising economic recovery, improved living standards and working conditions, and peace in Europe through disarmament and collective security under the aegis of the League of Nations. But the 'New Deal' it offered was necessarily rather vague, since its three component parties represented a wide range of political opinion.

The Radical Party was the oldest in France. The reforms it had fought for at the end of the nineteenth century, namely the abolition of aristocratic privilege, the separation of Church and State, and a tax on incomes, were already achieved by the end of the First World War. It now represented satisfied, therefore conservative, Republicanism, on the defensive against both the revolutionary and the counter-revolutionary extremes of French political opinion, defining its own position negatively: 'ni révolution, ni réaction!' Though they were still attached sentimentally to the 'Immortal Principles of 1789', and though they still clung to the resounding title that their movement had adopted in 1901, *Parti radical et radical-socialiste*, and were still, in theory, devoted to the defence of the 'citizen against the powers', the Radicals were now in fact close to the very heart of power in the Republic, and determined to stay there. A large new Socialist Party, and a vigorous new Communist Party, had grown up to the left of Radicalism since 1905 and 1920 respectively, pushing the Radical Party into the centre of the parliamentary *hémicycle*. Here it held a hinge position that was vital to the formation and survival of every government coalition throughout the inter-war period. It had become the government party *par excellence*, with enough disparate and flexible opinions within its loosely organised, undoctrinaire membership to motivate alliances with moderates on either side, according to the prevailing wind of political opinion. It was a particularly happy hunting-ground for ambitious politicians requiring a base in a provincial constituency and a free hand in the Palais Bourbon, the so-called *radicaux de gestion*, or 'administration' Radicals.[12] Its supporters, meeting as small committees of provincial notables, chiefly lawyers, doctors and other professional men, shopkeepers and prosperous farmers, sought their own enlightened self-interest in being represented by a member, minister or *ministrable* at the centre of gravity of the French power system.

The Radicals joined the *Front Populaire* because they wanted to keep power, because they had wooed the Socialists for ten years with only limited success, and because they saw that their liberal Republic was really in danger of going under to the old counter-revolutionary alliance of big business, social privilege and religious obscurantism in a new, totalitarian form, as had already happened in Fascist Italy and Nazi Germany. They had little real enthusiasm for the programme of positive democratic reforms planned by their leftward allies, from whom the Popular Front got its cutting-edge, namely the two French Marxist parties: the Socialists, or *Section française de l'internationale ouvrière* (S.F.I.O.), the party of Jaurès, now led by Léon Blum, where revolutionary ardour and rhetoric were tempered (and to some extent contradicted) by attachment to parliamentary and individual liberties and by a high proportion of civil service and other white-collar members and supporters;[13] and the *Parti communiste français* (P.C.F.), which was more exclusively proletarian, and more combative, and whose disciplined militants, led by Maurice Thorez, were able to call on deep-seated French Jacobin traditions and instincts, as well as on the more recent internationalist and syndicalist ideology of the French labour movement, to boost the new party line dictated by Communist headquarters in Stalin's Russia, of patriotic resistance to Hitler's plans for German aggrandisement, coupled with revolutionary working-class solidarity against the capitalist régime in France.

The three partners of the *Front Populaire* fared very differently at the polls. The Radicals actually lost 400,000 votes and 43 seats. The number of successful Socialist candidates rose from 97 to 146, and the number of Communists from 10 to

72.[14] The S.F.I.O. was now France's largest political party, and the new Government was headed by Blum. The Communists refused to join in, preferring that their revolutionary reputation should not be tarnished by taking ministerial office in a *bourgeois* Republic, under a Premier who, however devoted he might be to proletarian interests, was himself a *grand bourgeois*. This decision showed a sure grasp of French working-class opinion. The entirely new feeling of rightful and irresistible power that the workers of Paris and other French industrial cities and ports had gained from the exciting mass meetings and parades of the election campaign, and now from their triumph in the election itself, required an immediate outlet. A week after the elections, and three weeks before Blum could take office constitutionally, they began, more or less spontaneously, both in a spirit of collective celebration, and as a timely warning to the enemies of the working class, the directors and stockholders, the bankers and speculators (who were already busy selling French francs for foreign currencies and gold), to take over the factories, mines, hotels and shops from those who still dared call themselves the masters.

A series of massive sit-in strikes (*des grèves sur le tas*) spread across the country. Within a month of the polls more than a million workers were involved:

> One o'clock in the morning: the accordeons, trombones, clarinets are silent. The dancing is over. The long hours begin to weigh heavy. Even the card schools are languishing. One workshop is still singing 'Sous les roses'. But groups of sleepers have begun to bed down in corners.
>
> Round about four we had our little incident: four hundred types, foremen and superintendents, and some *Action Française* people, tried to make a sortie. We sent them back, without taking our coats off, not a blow struck. That was all.
>
> . . . Our bodyguards explain:
>
> 'It's simple, you see: there are 26,000 men in here, and they'll hold out. We've let the women out. . . . For the rest, everyone's inside locked in. Nobody leaves!'
>
> . . . In a corner, a last accordeon and a last trombone

take up 'Tout va très bien, Madame la Marquise'; the workers repeat: 'Tout va très bien'.

All the same, there's a feeling of anxiety about in the workshops. In spite of the laughter, the games, the jokes, nerves are on edge and only just kept under control by the discipline . . . the men are worried by the absence of any apparent resistance from outside, they're on the lookout for some mysterious act of provocation, for an implacable enemy.[15]

The Communists were taken by surprise by this unplanned and dynamic demonstration of working-class solidarity, but they quickly exploited their fortunate decision not to serve in Blum's Government, and assumed instead the leadership of the strikes. This direct pressure from outside Parliament enabled the Premier to exact concessions from the *patronat* and bring in some long overdue social reforms, agreed during the night of 7–8 June, between both sides of industry, meeting, with Blum in the chair, at the Hôtel de Matignon, where the new Prime Minister had just taken up his official residence.[16]

The so-called Matignon Agreement introduced official recognition of the principle of collective bargaining between employers and workers, and the right of the latter to elect shop stewards to represent them in negotiations with management. In addition it provided for a general pay rise of between 7 and 15 per cent. Also granted were the forty-hour working week and two weeks' annual holiday with pay, together with reduced excursion fares on the railways. Before rising for the summer recess, Parliament passed further measures to reform the Bank of France and to permit the nationalisation of armament factories, and to set up a Wheat Office with a view to raising and stabilising farm prices. French railways were nationalised in 1937.[17]

During the year or so following the Matignon Agreement, much of the immediate benefit to the French working class of these sweeping reforms was worn away by rising prices, short time, and employers' reneging promises made on their behalf allegedly under duress. Industrial strife broke out again, and speculation by the moneyed class against the franc continued, keeping industry and business depressed, frustrating the effort to rearm against Hitler, and forcing Blum to devalue the currency and to announce a 'pause' in the programme of reform.

The Popular Front was subjected to great internal stress, and more aggressive pressure from its conservative opponents, when General Franco, in the same hot summer of the French sit-in strikes, raised the standard of revolt against the Popular Front Government of the Spanish Republic. The French Communists wished the Government to send substantial aid to the embattled Spanish Republicans, but Blum was afraid that such an action (bitterly opposed by the French right wing) might bring civil war to France and perhaps a general war in Europe between the democracies and the Italian and German dictators. He also resisted the right-wing counter-demand that France should aid Franco, as Italy and Germany were doing. Blum was thus unable to avoid alienating the left wing of the alliance which had carried him to power, while exacerbating further the vengeful loathing of the anti-Republican and anti-Semitic leaguers, and their fellow-travellers, for his democratic principles and his Jewish blood. In June 1937 he asked for 'full powers' to decree draconian measures against unpatriotic tax evasion and currency speculation ('la fraude fiscale et les milliards déserteurs'). In the Chamber of Deputies the Communists joined with the Socialist party to authorise *les pleins pouvoirs*, giving the Government a comfortable majority. But the conservative majority of the Senate voted against what they saw as a proposal to legalise revolution. Rather than set the Chamber against the Upper House, Blum resigned.[18] He came back to head a second Popular Front Government in the spring of 1938, but this lasted only a month.

The first Blum Government of 1936, however brief and harried, managed to accomplish a real if limited advance for social democracy in France. Its rise and fall illustrate a characteristically French style of reform by crisis: a convulsive leap forward, powered by pent-up stagnation and frustration, followed by divided counsels on the democratic side, and silent reaction on the other from all the nation's many resisting strongholds of economic, social, administrative and ideological conservatism.

LITERATURE AND ART, 1914–39

French writers responded in various ways to the First World War. Péguy, a reserve officer, was mobilised on 1 August 1914 and was killed, fittingly, in action, on the eve of the first Battle of the Marne. Barrès and Maurras devoted their talents for the duration of hostilities to propaganda for a total French victory. The ageing Anatole France kept his doubts and despairs more or less to himself. Romain Rolland, living in neutral Switzerland, tried to rise above the conflict and take an objective and humanitarian view of the war, condemning the demented belligerency of both sides equally: *Au-dessus de la mêlée* (1915). Georges Duhamel, an admirer of pre-war Unanimism, and a wartime medical officer, published *Vie des martyrs* (1917) and *Civilisation* (1918), moving chronicles of suffering and fraternity at the front. Apart from these, and Henri Barbusse's best-seller, *Le Feu* (1916), detailing the horrors and squalor of trench warfare, and celebrating the dour endurance and the revolutionary stirrings of the French infantryman, the best war books came later: Montherlant's *Le Songe* (1922), Drieu la Rochelle's *La Comédie de Charleroi* (1934) and Romain's *Verdun* (1938). The war was a richly creative period of non-committed art by such established masters as Gide, Proust, Valéry, Matisse and Picasso, and for the poet Apollinaire, who was badly wounded in 1916 and who died in the influenza epidemic of 1918.

The most interesting public event in the cultural history of France at war took place on 18 May 1917. This was the ballet *Parade*, the first named example of Surrealism, a combined demonstration of what Apollinaire called the New Spirit,[19] produced by Diaghilev (whose spectacular Russian ballets had captivated fashionable Paris in the last great festival years of the European peace), with a scenario by the young Cocteau (whom he had once challenged to 'astonish us!'), music by Satie, choreography by Massine, sets and costumes by Picasso. It caused a scandal. May 1917 was a month of industrial strikes and the most serious outbreak of French 'revolutionary defeatism' in the entire war. The metalworkers' union had proclaimed that its members would know when the time came how to 'rise and unite with our Russian and German comrades in an international action against the war and conquest'. On 20 May several regiments refused to move up into the firing-line.[20] There was no direct link between the strikes and the mutinies on the one hand and the ballet on the other, though outraged patriots denounced the latter as an assault inspired by the Boche on the integrity of French culture. But the coincidence of these events was not entirely fortuitous. In the provocative novelties of *Parade* – Cubist spectacle, Surrealist plot, ragtime and concrete music – the influence could be felt, attenuated and enlivened by freshly springing art and Parisian wit, of an all-out cultural offensive against the war launched the year before from neutral Zürich. This was the 'demolition business' known as Dada, which called for the total destruction of the whole edifice of human society: 'plus rien, *rien, rien, rien.*'[21]

Dadaism never produced a great work of art (it had no such intention), but its headstrong iconoclasm (spreading from Switzerland to Berlin, Paris, Barcelona and New York), its cult of chance associations (juxtaposed as *collages* and gibberish poems), the shock aesthetic use it made of everyday materials and objects (a urinal, the page of a telephone directory), helped to bring Surrealism to life in literature and the arts during the last two years of the war and the first decade of the short-lived Peace of Versailles.

When peace of a kind returned to Europe in 1918, art and literature in victorious France at once flourished vigorously, but did not at first show any great originality. The 1920s got their character from the liberation of forces engendered in the pre-war and war years, rather than from any cultural revolution of their own making. Culturally speaking, post-war France lived for a decade off her pre-war and wartime *avant-garde,* though more adventurously and with more enduring effect than the simultaneous effort being made by French Governments to live off the dilapidated financial resources of the *belle époque.* Where pre-war art-forms had been opulent and intricate, the characteristic new styles of painting, sculpture, design and fashion, in the work, for example, of Arp, Brancusi, Ozenfant, Le Corbusier and Chanel, looked indeed as if they had been stripped for adventure. The new literary styles were similarly spare, simple and agile: the constraints of logic (rendered suspect by Freud's theory of the unconscious), amplification, ornament and the rhetoric of high principles (devalued by exploitation in wartime propaganda: *le bourrage de crâne*) were all cut back. Adventure was also a major theme of French literature after the war. Popular stories of adventures in foreign parts prolonged the pre-war vogue of cosmopolitan travellers' tales, essays and poems by Barrès, Cendrars, Valery Larbaud and others, and provided escapist reading for the war-weary. Two strong new writers, Henry de Montherlant and André Malraux, gave the French their own version of a universal twentieth-century hero, the self-conscious adventurer who seeks a hard and dangerous life in order to forge and test 'to the limit' his own, and by implication mankind's, powers of invention, endurance, self-reliance and self-knowledge. The Surrealists, for their part, by adventuring across the frontiers of convention and reason, took possession of that 'vast and strange domain, where mystery flowers for the taking' which Apollinaire had claimed for the pre-war *avant-garde*, in 'La Jolie Rousse'.[22]

The subject matter of Surrealist literature and painting was drawn from dreams, hallucination, childlike apperception and fantasy, irrational desire, spontaneous volition. Many of these sources of inspiration had been reconnoitred by such culture heroes of the previous generation as Rimbaud, Jarry (the author of *Ubu Roi* and *Le Surmâle*) and Gide, whose satirical novel, *Les Caves du Vatican*, published in 1914, appealed particularly to the post-war *avant-garde* because of its attractive presentation of total spontaneity in young Lafcadio, hero of *l'acte gratuit*, the unpredictable, entirely disinterested action: 'born of itself . . . purposeless . . . owning no master'.[23] Now, thanks to techniques in part derived from Freud's new science of psychoanalysis – free association, automatic writing, day-dreaming, hypnosis – the dark continent of the surreal lay open to more systematic exploration, close at hand. Thus de Chirico, by painting landscapes and interiors with geometrical precision, and familiar objects out of context (for example furniture on a seashore, trees in a bedroom), hoped to reveal 'mysteries lying all the time within our reach and which we cannot see because we are too short-sighted'. In Aragon's early poetic novels also – *Anicet* (1921), *Le Paysan de Paris* (1926) – imagination is a 'secret staircase' leading straight off the familiar streets of the French capital into such 'everyday marvels as the fantastic, the beyond, the dream-world, survival after death, paradise, hell, poetry – all 'signifying concrete reality'.[24] Nor did André Breton have to travel far from the Boulevard Bonne-Nouvelle ('one of the great strategic points of disorder I am looking for, and which I persist in regarding as obscure landmarks') to get his chance revelation of the 'convulsive beauty' of love and revolution.[25]

The philosophy of 'perpetual revolution' that the French Surrealists inherited from Dadaism aimed at subverting all established forms of society, even the new proletarian Soviet one: 'There is no such thing as revolutionary order,' wrote Éluard in 1925, 'there is only disorder and madness.'[26] 'Western world, you are condemned to die,' Aragon told a meeting of Madrid students in the same year:

> We are the defeatists of Europe. Let the East you fear at last answer our cry. Everywhere we shall engender confusion and unease. We are the agitators of the mind. Every barricade is good, every shackle on your happiness is accursed. . . . Arise, O world! Do you not see how this earth is dry tinder for every conflagration?[27]

Such visions of indiscriminate destruction inspired and have continued to inspire the Surrealist ethic in its purest form. The 'simplest Surrealist act', wrote André Breton, in a famous piece of provocation published in his *Second Surrealist Manifesto* (1930), 'consists in going down into the street with a revolver and firing at random into the crowd, for as long as one can'. But the same manifesto also singled out for special attention those particular left-wing abominations: 'family, fatherland and religion'. Indeed the triumphant *bourgeois* and imperialist France of Poincaré and Marshal Lyautey lent itself readily to even more narrowly defined political and partisan targeting. At a Parisian Left Bank literary supper held in honour of the poet Saint-Pol-Roux le Magnifique, a colourful survivor of the age of Rimbaud, three shouted slogans in particular were to be heard above the riot with which the evening ended: 'Long live Germany!' (the 'hereditary enemy' of official France); 'Long live China!' (then in the midst of its first revolutionary upheaval); 'Long live the Riff!' (where Abd el-Krim, the Moroccan warrior chief, was making his last stand against the imperial 'protection' of France and Spain).

It was natural that disciples of Rimbaud, who had written 'Let life be changed', should be drawn towards the followers of Marx, who had summoned the proletariat to 'change the world'. It was equally natural, given the bureaucratic discipline of the young French Communist Party, and given its official doctrine of historical materialism, that when, after eighteen months of active fellow-travelling, five leading Surrealists, including Breton, Aragon and Éluard, applied for membership of the P.C.F., the incorporation of such converts would arouse rather less excitement in the party than in themselves and their literary circle. Suspected, understandably, of anarchism and idealism, they were given a rough initiation. Breton, for instance, was told to draw up a statistical report on the production of steel in Italy![28]

The alliance of the French Surrealist movement and the French Communist Party was uneasy and short-lived. After a pilgrimage to Moscow in 1930, Aragon repudiated his Surrealist past and became the P.C.F.'s leading, entirely orthodox, man of letters. Breton tried to avoid a clear-cut choice, but was dismissed from the party in 1933 (with Éluard) for refusing to conform to the official Stalinist line of puritan morals and servile art. Éluard rejoined the party in the war against Hitler, and was an active Resistance writer. Meanwhile, independently, the Surrealists continued to proclaim their enthusiasm for the liberation of the masses, as promised in particular by the French Popular Front of 1934–7, Republican Spain, the exiled Russian Bolshevik Leo Trotsky – and the 'May Revolution' of 1968, when the walls of the university quarter of Paris burgeoned with anarcho-surrealist slogans such as 'La beauté sera convulsive ou ne sera pas', 'La société est une fleur carnivore', 'On travaille mieux en dormant, formez des comités de rêves' and 'L'imagination au pouvoir'.

Revulsion against capitalist law and order, and sympathy for the way of life, the moral values and the political outlook of the common people under capitalism, marked much besides Surrealism that was vigorous and original in French thought, art and letters between the wars. The best-selling multi-volume family novels of Roger Martin du Gard and

Georges Duhamel were, no doubt, as Professor Thody observes, only superficially anti-*bourgeois*.[29] In the twenty-seven volumes of *Les Hommes de bonne volonté*, Jules Romains portrayed the unanimistic 'group soul' of whole streets, armies and cities quite impartially. But a more definite 'populist' slant appeared in the proletarian and peasant novels of Eugène Dabit and Jean Giono, two writers who inspired some of the best film-making of the thirties,[30] for example Marcel Carné's *Hôtel du Nord*, set in a grey working-class suburb of Paris, and based on a novel by Dabit, and Marcel Pagnol's *Regain* and *La Femme du boulanger*, about village life in the Mediterranean and Alpine Midi, from stories by his Provençal compatriot, Giono. Jacques Prévert brought the idiom and climate of working-class Paris to the screen in brilliant scenarios for Carné's *Quai des brumes* (based on a story by Pierre MacOrlan) and *Le Jour se lève*, and Autant-Lara's *Fric-Frac*. In such literary influences, and in the master hands of the anarchist director Jean Vigo (*Zéro de Conduite*, *L'Atalante*), of René Clair (*Sous les toits de Paris*, *A nous la liberté*, *Quatorze Juillet*) and of Jean Renoir (*Boudu sauvé des eaux*, *Une Partie de campagne*, *La Grande Illusion*, *La Règle du jeu*), the French pre-war cinema found its characteristic and very influential style, combining the poetry of life at its most drab and humble with ever blacker satire against established principles, prejudices and powers.

Jacques Prévert (who besides his film scenarios wrote several volumes of satirical and sentimental verse: *Paroles*, *Histoires*, *Spectacle*, *Le Pluie et le beau temps*) and Céline (the author of two notoriously iconoclastic, nightmare novels of alienation and degradation under capitalism: *Voyage au bout de la nuit* and *Mort à crédit*), assaulted the literary as well as the moral conventions of the ruling middle class they hated, and used an imitation of unrefined speech, laced with aggressive working-class slang and the burlesqued *clichés* of middle-class respectability, for their sardonic denunciations and parodies of the established order. In contrast to this colloquial idiom (which the poet and novelist Raymond Queneau also used, not so coarsely and with less obvious social preoccupations) and also to the characteristically anti-heroic tone of Prévert and Céline (which also pervades the films of Carné and Renoir), the playwright Jean Giraudoux and the novelist André Malraux lifted up the great public terrors and antagonisms of their age to the level of true tragic or epic diction and form. With them French was still a language of heroism, though punctured with ironic wit in Giraudoux's *Judith* (1931), *La Guerre de Troie n'aura pas lieu* (1935) and *Électre* (1937); and pitted with black, private doubt in *La Condition humaine* (1933), Malraux's novel about fraternal self-sacrifice in revolutionary Shanghai in 1927, and in *L'Espoir* (1937), his anxiously observed chronicle of the just war against Fascism in Spain in 1936. For the most ambitious of his 'baroque' dramas of Christian heroism, *Le Soulier de satin* (1929), Claudel needed a stage representing the whole world, and all the resources of sound and spectacle, beside the unchecked spate of his rhythmic free verse and sublime verbal imagery. Two younger Catholic writers, François Mauriac and Georges Bernanos, raised the register of post-Proustian prose fiction in France with a succession of intensely emotional and corrosively anti-*bourgeois* stories of God and Satan in the French provinces: *Thérèse Desqueroux* (1927), *Le Nœud de vipères* (1932), *La Pharisienne* (1941); *Sous le soleil de Satan* (1926). *Le Journal d'un curé de campagne* (1936), *Monsieur Ouine* (1943).

The mounting pre-war and class-war tensions of the years between 1936 and 1939 pitched into the arena of political controversy most of the leading French writers and philosophers who had not yet taken sides for, or against, Radicalism, Socialism, Communism, Fascism, Royalism. Outstanding in this general movement towards *littérature engagée* (which Julien Benda, on the other hand, in *La Trahison des clercs* (1927) had condemned as a betrayal of what should, according to him, be the writer's 'priestly' detachment from worldly matters) were Gide's and Céline's accounts of their separate disenchantments with Soviet civilisation (*Retour de l'U.R.S.S.* and *Mea Culpa*, both published in 1936); Giono's pacifist *Refus d'obéissance* (1937); Bernanos's anti-Semitic diatribe against the alleged servility of France's middle-class Catholics (*La Grande Peur des bien-pensants*, 1931) and equally furious condemnation of the Fascist terror in Franco's Catholic Spain (*Les Grands Cimetières sous la lune*, 1938); and Montherlant's and Giraudoux's open accusations of French decadence: *L'Équinoxe de septembre* (1938), followed, after the defeat of France, by *Solstice de juin* (1941); *Pleins pouvoirs* (1939), followed by *Sans pouvoirs* (1946). Compared with the 'leonine' conduct of affairs in the new totalitarian dictatorships of Europe, wrote Montherlant, France was 'behaving like a shop-girl' (*une morale de midinette*); only the mailed fist and national humiliation could save her soul. Was France a dead star, asked Giraudoux, only seeming to shine, with a light her people no longer emitted? Paul Valéry, the poet, in *Regards sur le monde actuel* (1931), and Antoine de Saint-Exupéry, the airman and novelist, in *Terre des hommes* (1939), expressed more temperate but no less anxious views on the overall predicament and prospects of European civilisation and industrial society, now under the threat of its second 'civil' war within a generation.

As a matter of fact, France in the 1930s, so far from being culturally effete or extinct, was creating new ideas and forms which during the next three decades were to become widely influential, far beyond the physical frontiers of the hexagon. Already, before the outbreak of war, Teilhard de Chardin, Sartre, Camus, Beckett and Artaud were writing; Messiaen was composing his highly original music, and Le Corbusier, the Swiss-born architect and planner, was beginning to see his ideas take shape in French print and concrete. Picasso, Braque, Bonnard, Chagall and Rouault continued to paint masterpieces in France. Matisse, and three younger artists, Léger, Gromaire and Dufy, were putting on canvas, in their clear colours and simple, firm forms, something gay and strong that shines in the gathering gloom of French and world politics. Lurçat magnificently revived the art of French tapestry. Maillol and Giacometti produced great sculpture. Perrin, Leprince-Ringuet and Joliot-Curie made important discoveries in physics. France was still a force in Western civilisation.

THE SECOND WORLD WAR

The Radical governments led by Chautemps and Daladier were every bit as paralysed as the two Blum ministries by the admittedly terrifying spectacle of domestic and foreign affairs, as bitterness intensified between a working class cheated of its high hopes of 1936, and a *bourgeoisie* furious at its loss of control and face (and of its Mediterranean beaches, invaded by proletarian crowds on their newly granted holidays with pay: *les congés payés*), and as Stalin, Franco and Hitler rose to their zenith. The black comedy of Renoir's film *La Règle du jeu*, and the irony of a popular song, 'Tout va très bien, Madame la Marquise', seemed to express perfectly the prevailing public mood of cynical resignation.

When Hitler, in the spring of 1936, marched his soldiers into the demilitarised German Rhineland, and began to fortify it, in breach of the Versailles and Locarno Treaties of 1919 and 1926, Britain was reluctant to join France in a military counter-move, and this gave cause, or pretext, for a French foreign policy, over the next three years, of almost total resignation to German aggression and British appeasement. The French system of European security was in ruins. Her military strategy, influenced by the appalling bloodshed of the First World War, and by the military thinking of the still influential Marshal Pétain, was purely defensive. Trained to man the continuous fortifications of the Maginot Line (solid enough but unfortunately stopping short of the classic invasion route through Belgium), her armies, psychologically at least, were incapable of offensive warfare. Yet France, in order to try and contain the resurgent power of Germany, a nation getting on for twice her own size, and more heavily and efficiently industrialised, had bound herself by pacts of mutual defence to Poland, Czechoslovakia and Roumania, allies now locked to the east of the new Siegfried Line that she was allowing Hitler to fortify along the Rhine. The offensive that the French Army would have to undertake if she were to combine effectively with her friends in *Mitteleuropa* looked less credible than ever. Thereafter, French governments could only watch passively with the British while the German dictator subdued Austria and Czechoslovakia.[31]

In the vacuum of power at the heart of the French Republic, Fascism and Communism both grew strong, at the expense of the Radical and Socialist parliamentary majority. On the eve of the Second World War, France was more deeply strained by the centrifugal force of political extremism than at any time since the Commune of 1871, and divided to such a degree that both extremes were driven to look beyond the nation's frontiers for support against their political and social adversaries at home.

On the one hand, the victory of the left wing in the parliamentary elections of 1936, and especially the demonstration of proletarian power that followed the elections, locking out the employers from their 'own' factories and 'dictating' the Matignon reforms, caused the moneyed classes – *patrons, possédants, rentiers* and *propriétaires* – to wish for a stronger defensive barrage against revolution in France than the loosely disciplined, moderate, parliamentary coalition of right-wing Radicals, 'Independents' and farmers' deputies could provide, and to dream of an anti-Bolshevik alliance with the tough, belligerent dictatorships of Rome and Berlin: 'Better Hitler than Blum!' French distrust of the British Foreign Office (ever close to the surface), and a pervasive mood of defeatism which had been gathering since the reoccupation of the Rhineland, the Austrian *coup* and the sacrifice of Czechoslovakia at Munich, further prepared the way for the subservience of Pétain's Vichy Government in Hitler's Europe.

On the other hand, the failure of the Blum ministries to break down the 'wall of money' (*le mur d'argent*) in France, or to stand up for the Republicans in Spain, led more and more French working-class wage-earners and middle-class sympathisers to conclude that Socialist reform through the French parliamentary system was a snare and a delusion, and that only revolutionary Communism, triumphant in Moscow, and represented in France by the P.C.F. and the C.G.T. (where since 1936 the Communists dominated the much enlarged industrial membership), was really capable of achieving the reign of justice and equality. Even Léon Blum, ever steadfast against totalitarian dictatorships of whatever political colour, would be driven to admit, while in German captivity after 1940, that the French 'representative or parliamentary system of government' might be basically unsuited to French society, and to remind himself, and his readers, that 'parliamentary government is not the unique, exclusive and necessary form of democracy'.[32]

The signing of a pact of non-aggression by Hitler and Stalin, at the end of August 1939, completed the confusion of French opinion. The middle classes could no longer look to German National Socialism as a bulwark against Soviet Communism. The French Communists, on the other hand, would be asked by their leaders to turn about face, as the Soviet Union had done, and add voices for peace at all costs to the defeatist propaganda of the pro-German right wing, which was publicly questioning the need for any single Frenchman to 'die for Danzig'. The required *volte-face* was too much to ask for all at once, however, and when at last the French Government prepared to declare war on Hitler, six hours after the United Kingdom, as Poland went under, the Communist deputies signified their assent with the rest of Parliament by voting the necessary military supplies.

Any hope of challenging Hitler with the 'sacred' unanimity and the dynamic energy that confronted the German invaders of 1914 was quickly dissipated. The French Communist Party, as a supporter of Hitler's new Soviet ally, was suppressed by the French Government. Most of its leaders dispersed into hiding, their neutrality towards this private quarrel of rival imperialist gangs confirmed. The sham *drôle de guerre* followed: seven months of inactivity in the Maginot Line, leading Frenchmen of every political persuasion to hope that Hitler would not attack in the West, that he would leave France alone, that everything would be all right, and so tending to undermine what fighting spirit the Army had left after the sudden reversal of loyalties brought about by the Nazi–Soviet Pact. When the Germans did strike through Belgium and the Ardennes with lightning speed, in the early summer of 1940, they soon broke the defences of a nation that was both politically disunited and, like the Belgian and British allied forces in the same battle, militarily outclassed.

The defeat of the Allied armies on the Continent brought the Germans in five weeks to the Loire, and the French Parliament to its final act of abdication to forces and factions beyond its control. On 16 June the Prime Minister, Paul Reynaud, who had done his best to rally support for continuing the war from French North Africa, was ousted in favour of the defeatist Marshal Pétain. The octogenarian hero of Verdun (he was eighty-four in 1940) immediately sought an armistice. Hitler's terms included: the retention in captivity of the million and a half French prisoners-of-war; the German occupation and military government of northern France and the entire Atlantic coast, three-fifths of French territory; the fleet to be laid up in French home ports and demobilised under German and Italian supervision; anti-Nazi German refugees in France to be handed over.[33] Three weeks later, at Vichy, where the French Government had set up its capital, in the southern, unoccupied zone, Parliament voted Pétain 'full powers to promulgate a new constitution for the French state'.

All those 'integral nationalists' who had for so long questioned the Republican institutions of 1875 now had the chance of launching a so-called 'National Revolution', which would cast aside the Republican creed of Liberty, Equality, Fraternity, by which they alleged France to have been fatally weakened, and put in its place the supposedly sounder traditionalistic and authoritarian ideals expressed in the motto of the Vichy state: 'Work, Family, Country'. Trade unions were dissolved and labour relations were reorganised through corporative guilds dominated by the employers. Church schools were given state aid and an attempt was made to 're-Christianise' primary education.[34] Rustic simplicity, the outdoor life, physical training, sport, scouting, the independent artisan and craftsman, respect for tradition and natural superiors, were all encouraged. Liberal and Socialist forms of democracy were proscribed. The adulation of the Marshal was organised on a quasi-mystical basis. He was in fact at first almost universally admired. Many shared his belief that, by staying in France at the head of his stricken people, the prestigious and compassionate victor of Verdun was at least shielding them from the worst effects of 'polandisation' – direct rule by Nazi Gauleiters. Until 1943, indeed, Hitler was anxious not to bear too harshly on the French, in the hope of winning them over to his side. Pétain also kept in touch secretly with the Western Allies, and many of his countrymen, suspecting this, hoped that France might gain more substantial advantages than the Marshal's wavering double game was able in fact to secure. Right until the end he could still draw out affectionate crowds. He was, in any case, like Maurras, honestly, if blindly, for 'France alone'.

Although, generally speaking, the French respected Marshal Pétain, few were taken in by his reactionary National Revolution, which never struck deep, in spite of the fact that the reputation of parliamentary democracy in France was, naturally, at a low ebb. Most Frenchmen recognised that some preferably minimal degree of collaboration with the occupying power was for the moment inevitable, but few would whole-heartedly commit themselves to Hitler's New European Order. They were disposed rather to wait and see, and survive – a philosophy known as *attentisme*.

Pierre Laval, who became 'Vice-President of the Council' in July 1940, and who returned to head the Government from 1942 to the fall of the Vichy state in 1944, and Admiral François Darlan, who replaced him for a time in 1941, were both more active collaborators. They were sure, at first, that Hitler had won the war, and both tried to get what practical benefits for France they could from this event. Neither, however, went far enough for such convinced French Nazis as Marcel Déat, author of the notorious pre-war editorial 'Why Die for Danzig?', and Jacques Doriot, former Communist sheet-metal worker, Mayor of Saint-Denis, in the Paris 'Red Belt', and founder, in 1936, of the Fascist *Parti populaire français* (P.P.F.). These accused the French authorites in Vichy of compromising the rightful place of France in the New Europe by favouring *attentisme* and clinging to outdated forms of *bourgeois* privilege and narrow patriotism: what they wanted was an anti-Bolshevik crusade and thoroughgoing 'proletarian' National Socialism. A third French Fascist leader, Joseph Darnand, formed a small group of young militant 'Legionaries' of the National Revolution, sworn to fight 'democracy, the Gaullist Resistance and the Jewish contagion', which was the nucleus of a brutal 'anti-Communist' auxiliary police force called *la milice* (militia) founded, in January 1943, to help the Germans to seek out and destroy the Resistance networks operating inside France. None of these men had a genuinely popular following.

Before the armistice had yet been signed, General Charles de Gaulle, a recently appointed member of Reynaud's Government, had taken the decision to fight on. France had 'lost a battle', she had not 'lost the war'. From voluntary exile in London he broadcast a first appeal for continued French resistance on 18 June. A fortnight later, the British Government, fearing that the Germans might seize France's fine fleet and use it against the island's vital supply-lines, requested all French ships in the Mediterranean to proceed to British or neutral ports out of Hitler's reach. When the commander of the squadron in harbour at Mers-el-Kébir refused, the Royal Navy was ordered to shell and sink it. A thousand French sailors were killed and a wave of anti-British feeling, already beginning after the evacuation of a large part of the British Expeditionary Force from Dunkirk, swept over France. But this was only the first of many trials that de Gaulle had to get through before his triumphant return four years later to a liberated France as the unquestionable chief of the Resistance. He began with little more than his high purpose, his inflexible determination, and Churchill's immediate, bristly admiration (which he reciprocated): 'I understood and admired, while I resented, his arrogant demeanour ... he seemed to express the personality of France – a great nation with all its pride, authority and ambition';[35] 'la Grande-Bretagne, conduite par un pareil lutteur, ne fléchirait certainement pas'.[36]

French Equatorial Africa and scattered French territories in the Pacific rallied to de Gaulle almost at once, and volunteers escaped from France to join the small Free French forces in London. But a seaborne Franco-British expedition to Dakar was repulsed by the Governor, loyal to Vichy, and Syria was taken, by a mixed force of British and Free French troops, only after a month's stiff fighting. The General's call in fact posed a painful conflict of loyalties to many patriotic Frenchmen, forced to choose between the waiting game in obedience to an illustrious and respected Head of State (who was supported, at first, by the overwhelming majority of the French Parliament and people), and adventurous active service with an almost unknown 'dissident' aged forty-nine, who had the support of a recent ally, but old rival, of France, and whom it was only too easy to caricature as the tool of the British Foreign Office.[37] But de Gaulle was quite clear-headed and determined about his official relations with his British hosts:

> Go on with the war? Yes, certainly! But to what end and within what limits? Many, even among those who approved of the undertaking, wanted it to be no more than aid given by a handful of Frenchmen to the British Empire, still standing and in the fight. I did not look at the enterprise in that way for a moment. For me what

> had to be served and saved was the nation and the State. . . . What was the good of supplying with auxiliaries the forces of another Power? No! For the effort to be worth while, it was essential to bring back into the war not merely some Frenchmen, but France.[38]

De Gaulle's long-term political aim explains his hypersensitive reaction whenever he sensed pressure or patronising from the immensely stronger Allies with whom he must work. He was too 'destitute' of material resources and too vulnerable to criticism from his countrymen in the captive homeland to make concessions on foreign soil to the foreign powers who protected and supplied his perilous enterprise: 'Limited and alone though I was, and precisely because I was so, I had to climb to the heights and never then to come down.'[39]

A year after the fall of France, the Free French forces in Britain, the Middle East and French Equatorial Africa were some 70,000 men, 50 naval vessels, a merchant navy of 170 ships and a growing company of pilots flying with the Royal Air Force.[40] In 1942 a First Free French Light Brigade of 5,000 men was fighting with distinction alongside the British against Rommel's *Afrika Korps* in the Libyan desert. By 1944, more than a quarter of a million French and French colonial soldiers, equipped by America, constituted a fine modern army. Its crack troops were in the vanguard of the Allied forces who broke through the Germans' mountain line in central Italy, to take Rome, in May of that year. In August, beside a smaller American army, it was put on to the French Mediterranean coast, and after swiftly liberating eastern France from Provence to Burgundy, it took the Belfort Gap and Strasbourg in November.[41]

Inside the French homeland, small isolated groups of resisters had begun to muster as early as the summer of 1940, both in the southern, unoccupied zone of Vichy France, and in the more dangerous northern and western areas, under German military government. A cadre of French regular officers held themselves in readiness to re-enter the war at an opportune moment. The Navy had secret orders to blow up the fleet at Toulon (which it carried out when the Germans marched south in 1942 to occupy the whole of France, as a riposte to the Anglo-American landing in French North

Africa). Civilian officials successfully infiltrated the information services of government ministries. But it was not until the summer of 1941 that the serious shooting started, bringing, in retaliation, the execution of civilian hostages, many of them Communists already in custody, in twos and threes at first, and later fifty at a time. Hitler had by now broken his non-aggression pact with Stalin and invaded the Soviet Union. This brought the whole P.C.F. enthusiastically over to the side of the few communist militants who had begun to resist earlier, as individuals, and of the non-communists already active in such groups as the *Comité National de Salut Public*, founded in 1940, at the Paris *Musée de l'Homme* and decimated by arrests and executions in 1941–2. *L'Organisation civile et militaire* (mainly officers, civil servants and professional men), *Libération-Nord* (mainly trade unionists), *Ceux de la Résistance, Ceux de la Libération, Libération-Sud, Combat, Franc-Tireur, Témoignage Chrétien*. The shock-troops of the Communist Resistance took the name of *Francs-Tireurs et Partisans* (F.T.P.), and their leaders held key positions in one of the largest and most ambitious groups, *Front National*. For the next three years the second front of Fighting France, in the mother-country itself, burned fiercely.[42]

The active Resistance in France was not numerically large (until early in the year of France's liberation, when the French Forces of the Interior – F.F.I. – passed the 100,000 mark), but the variety, scale and co-ordination of their operations had been growing steadily since 1941: collecting and passing information, and men, to London, and back; hiding and guiding to safety escaped prisoners, comrades on the run or Allied pilots who had been shot down over France; cutting railway lines and telephone lines, sabotaging power supplies and industrial production, publishing clandestine news-sheets (by the million); executing collaborators, shooting Germans. All of this demanded very great courage and total dedication and concentration. During the first great action fought by the Free French forces, the defence of Bir Hakeim in the Libyan desert by the First Light Brigade in June 1942, the Germans announced by radio that de Gaulle's men would be treated as irregular *francs-tireurs* (in accordance with Article 10 of the armistice agreement signed two years before by the Vichy Government[43]), and that any prisoners taken would be shot.

De Gaulle immediately broadcast a promise to do likewise to Germans captured by the French, and the threat was withdrawn. But the Resistance inside France was never recognised as a regular force, and the men and women who joined it could expect no quarter. The slightest slip meant capture, torture, and execution or deportation to a concentration camp. At least 20,000 resisters were shot, and 115,000 were deported, of whom only 40,000 survived. Moreover, the F.F.I. were not only engaged in the violence and counter-violence of a patriotic guerrilla, they were also committed to the special anguish of a civil war. They were hunted by the Special Brigades of the French *Préfecture de Police*, and by Darnand's militia, as well as by the Germans. And even after the Allied counter-offensives in North Africa, Italy and Russia had rekindled the hopes of most patriotic Frenchmen, and driven the Germans to bear more harshly than before on the population of conquered France, they were a minority movement, confidently denounced, by such men as Philippe Henriot on the Paris Radio, and Charles Maurras in the Vichy Press, as factious terrorists thirsting for the blood of good Frenchmen.[44]

Recruitment to the F.F.I. was boosted by the Nazis' increasingly desperate shortage of industrial man power. To escape deportation and forced labour in German arms factories, many youths went into hiding in the wilder parts of France, where they swelled the ranks of the guerrilla companies armed by parachute drops from England and North Africa (though not so well or so early as they had wished). This part of the F.F.I. was called the *maquis* (from the name of the high Mediterranean scrub and forest that was the traditional refuge of Corsican bandits). By the summer of 1944, when the United States and the British Commonwealth launched their combined armada across the English Channel and broke into Hitler's continental fortress, the French *maquis* was operating on a very large scale, particularly in the Massif Central, the Alps (where 3,500 *maquisards* engaged in one battle a force of 20,000 regular German troops, just before the Allied landings) and Brittany (the homeland of the famous Chouan guerrillas against the French Revolutionary Government of 1793), where 80,000 partisans operated very effectively on the flank of the advancing armies of liberation. These and many other groups of armed *résistants* succeeded in causing widespread dislocation of rail and road traffic conveying German reinforcements to the main Normandy front: 'Without their help,' wrote the Allied Commander-in-Chief, General Eisenhower, 'the liberation of France would have consumed a much longer time.'[45]

The British and the Americans had planned their invasion of French North Africa, in November 1942, without de Gaulle. The American Government in particular was suspicious of his influence, looking on him at first as both a potential dictator and a friend of the Communists. Having invaded Algeria and Morocco and negotiated their surrender, after much tortuous intrigue and some expedient bargaining with Vichy's Admiral Darlan, who was assassinated in Algiers six weeks after the Allied landing, the Americans brought forward their own candidate for the leadership of Free France. This was General Giraud, a distinguished but politically naïve professional soldier who had just escaped from a German prisoner-of-war camp, and to whom it was supposed that the military and civilian establishments of French North Africa, hitherto mainly loyal to Marshal Pétain and hostile to de Gaulle, would readily rally. But the Free French leader edged Giraud out, and having set up an all-party French Committee of National Liberation, which was to be the nucleus of a Provisional Government of the Republic, finally convinced even the United States authorities that he was the best man to unite the French for the liberation of their country. But he was still excluded from the high planning and direction of the 'Anglo-Saxon' Operation Overlord against *Festung Europa*, and not until he had visited the Normandy battle zone, and had been welcomed with emotion by its inhabitants, and his nominees had begun their well-prepared takeover of the liberated sub-prefectures and prefectures, a week after the beach-heads had been secured, was the idea of a provisional Allied Military Government for France dropped.

De Gaulle was not able to persuade even those men and women of his own nation who had chosen to stay in the fight, or to rejoin it, after the defeat of 1940, all to accept his leadership willingly. He had particular difficulty in preventing the Communist partisan chiefs from taking independent action.

In 1942, Jean Moulin, a former Prefect, who had already resisted the German exactions and suffered for it, before escaping to England, was parachuted back into France to try to persuade all the underground groups operating inside France to unite in a single organisation, which de Gaulle could control. Moulin succeeded in founding the *Conseil National de la Résistance*, of which he was the first president. But he was shortly afterwards betrayed, caught and tortured to death. His place at the head of the C.N.R. was taken by a former schoolmaster, Georges Bidault. The British also made independent liaison with the French Resistance, and provided training and arms through the Special Operations Executive (S.O.E.).[46] The supreme authority that de Gaulle claimed to exercise over the F.F.I. in the name of his Provisional Government was not universally recognised until his exile was ended, but it proved real enough, when the test came, if not to prevent, at least to check the spread of disorder and violence, and the hopes of sudden revolution, which would spring up in the French homeland, as they did elsewhere in liberated Europe, from the bloody tracks of the retreating Nazis.

As the Germans began to pull out of Paris, with the Allied armies still some distance away, the F.F.I. in the capital rose so that 'Paris should liberate herself'. The Communists and the Paris police were the most active (and politically rival) heads of the insurrection, which cost the lives of about a thousand partisans and six hundred civilians.[47] On the fifth day of the insurrection, the armoured division of General Leclerc, who with his veterans had set out from Lake Chad twenty months before to march across the Sahara and join up with the British Army in North Africa, entered Paris.

The part played by French forces in the liberation of their country, and in the subsequent invasion of Germany, was secondary to and heavily dependent upon the Anglo-American effort. Nevertheless, out of crushing defeat, and through the storm and stress of a war of giants, de Gaulle's vision, diplomacy and resolution, and the work and courage of thousands of less exceptional French men and women, brought France into post-war Europe as one of the Third Reich's conquerors (albeit a minor one), with a military zone in occupied Germany, a place (though not a very influential one) at the London Conference of the victors' Foreign Ministers and a permanent seat with the other great powers on the Security Council of the United Nations.

In March 1944 the *Conseil National de la Résistance* had drafted a confident double programme for the punishment of traitors and the political, social and economic renovation of France, what Bidault would later call a revolution within the law.[48] The French people, consulted in three national referenda on the Constitution, chose not to go back to the political régime by which France had been governed before the war but on to something they believed would be new. Elections to two Constituent Assemblies and the first National Assembly of the Fourth Republic resulted in a large parliamentary majority for the three major political movements of the Resistance, all three claiming to stand for radical change: the P.C.F., which won the support of from 20 to nearly 22 per cent of the electorate in 1945–6; the Socialist S.F.I.O., for which support declined from 18 to less than 14 per cent during the same period; and the *Mouvement républicain populaire* (M.R.P.), a new progressive Catholic party, which reached a peak of 22·6 per cent of the votes cast in June 1946, declining to just under 20 per cent five months later. The philosophy of the M.R.P. was Christian democracy; its social doctrine, in contrast with both the individualistic Radical tendency and the collectivist Marxist tendency into which the French left wing had been hitherto divided, was corporativist, envisaging ideally a 'plural' society, in which each individual person might discover his duties and his rights as a member of natural groups (family, town, region, profession, factory, age, sex, etc.), or active teams (*équipes*) of workers, peasants, managers and so on. Among the five and a half million votes it received in the second summer after the war there was undoubtedly much temporary support from old-fashioned Catholic conservatives whose former political representatives were for the moment in disgrace for their support of Vichy. The strongholds of the movement were in Catholic Brittany and Alsace, where it attracted all classes. Elsewhere, even when its crypto-Pétainists had left, most of its supporters were middle-class, and more conservative than the idealistic *avant-garde* of party workers. So, in general, was the parliamentary leadership.

De Gaulle brought the Communist, Socialist and M.R.P.

parties together in the first post-war Government, and their leaders continued to serve in three more so-called tripartite administrations, under Gouin (Socialist), Bidault (M.R.P.) and Ramadier (Socialist), for a further eighteen months after his resignation, in January 1946. During this period several important reforms proposed in the 'Charter of the Resistance' were implemented, but the 'hard and clean' reforming zeal of the moment of liberation ('La République pure et dure') lost much of its original driving force, and the tripartite unity of the Left was broken.

10 Post-War France

L'ÉPURATION

AMID the inevitable anger and disorder of France's violent liberation, many pro-Nazi or Vichy administrators, propagandists and militiamen, black-market and other profiteers of the German occupation were shot with little ceremony. Some private vendettas were also settled by the guns of the *maquis*, and a political purge of unknown dimensions was carried out, under cover of patriotic vengeance, by the Communist *Francs-Tireurs et Partisans* and the *Milices Patriotiques*. The total number of summary executions was wildly exaggerated by the ex-Vichy right wing after the war, the official figure of 10,000 being raised to 60,000, 100,000 and even 120,000.[1]

De Gaulle was determined that all members of the F.F.I. should as soon as possible be disarmed or drafted into the Army under the central authority of a Republic which, he claimed, had 'never ceased to exist', having been legitimately embodied, without a break, in the 1940 London Committee of the Free French, in Fighting France from Bir Hakeim to the Seine, in the Algiers 'Committee of National Liberation' and in the Provisional Government he now headed in the liberated capital of the mother-country (though this Government was not recognised officially by the Anglo-Saxons until October). This was done, but not all at once. In some parts of central and south-western France, away from the main advance of the Allied armies, the rule of the *maquis* in its triumph (with some help from a mob of last-minute hangers-on) and the rough justice of the patriotic militias continued unchecked for some weeks.

At the most important trials of the official purge, in the regular courts, Laval was condemned to death, Pétain and Maurras to life imprisonment. Intellectuals were generally treated more harshly than 'economic collaborators', a back-handed compliment to the power of the word in the French scale of values. Over 2,800 persons were condemned to death, but only 767 death sentences were carried out. There were 39,000 prison sentences and some 40,000 people were sentenced to some kind of official 'indignity' and loss of civil rights.[2]

SOCIAL AND ECONOMIC REFORMS

The 'Charter of the Resistance' included 'the setting-up of a true economic and social democracy, entailing the eviction of the great economic and financial feudalities', the 'return to the nation of the great monopolies in the means of production, the sources of energy, mineral wealth, insurance companies and large banks', the 'participation of the workers in the direction of economic life'; it also guaranteed wage levels, social security and the restoration of independent and more effective trade unions.[3] The Popular Front was on the move again, and this time the French Communist Party was ready to assume governmental responsibilities. Its leaders in the clandestine struggle against Nazi oppression and Vichy collaboration may perhaps have planned to use the patriotic enthusiasms and organisations of the Resistance in a revolutionary seizure of power at the moment of national liberation. In the light of day, when the Liberation came, they realised not only that de Gaulle's position was unshakeable, but that the immense popular prestige that the Communists had acquired in the Resistance was enough to give them a place of power in the post-war state, and ways of infiltrating its administration and perhaps eventually of dominating it, without revolutionary violence. In any case, Stalin was against immediate revolution in the West. So it was decided not to exploit the cruelly earned and carefully publicised reputation of French Communism as *le parti des fusillés*, the martyrs' party, against the parliamentary régime, at least not before co-operation with the parliamentary left wing, within the framework of traditional Republican institutions, had been seriously attempted, under the Premiership of de Gaulle in 1944 and 1945, and under Socialist and Christian Democrat (M.R.P.) Prime Ministers for a further eighteen months of 1946 and 1947.

During these three years some of the reforms called for in the 'Charter of the Resistance' passed into law: a comprehensive social security scheme, for instance, and the nationalisation of the coal, gas and electricity industries, together with civil aviation, Renault Motors, the Bank of France, the four largest deposit banks and several big insurance companies. Equally important was the creation by de Gaulle's Government of a single postgraduate training school for civil servants of the administrative grade (*L'École Nationale d'Administration* – E.N.A.) and a new central research and development organisation, *Le Commissariat Général du Plan*, from both of which the influential post-war French 'Keynesian' style of dynamic and flexible economic planning began to radiate throughout the managerial levels of state and industry. At production level, workers' 'participation' remained more or less a dead letter. To have a part in the reforms (which for them, of course, were minimal), and to help, from positions of power within the state, to get France's shattered and semi-paralysed economy going again, after the destruction of a thousand bridges, fourteen thousand locomotives, half a million houses, and the drastic reduction of coal and electricity supplies, the P.C.F. and the C.G.T. were prepared to work with the Socialists and the M.R.P., urging their own rank-and-file in the factories and the mines to ever greater feats of production, holding back wage demands, and accepting useful but secondary Ministries like Labour and Social Affairs and Reconstruction when they were refused any of the key ones – Defence, Interior and Foreign Affairs – that they had asked for.

Between 1945 and 1947, however, France was pulled sharply away from the exceptionally co-operative and constructive mood of the Liberation, and drawn in two opposite directions, forwards towards new problems posed by a deteriorating international situation, and backwards towards traditional politics at home.[4]

THE FOURTH REPUBLIC

The new régime was founded in October 1946 without de Gaulle, and indeed against him. After it had become plain to him, at the beginning of that year, that, with the country out of immediate danger, the parliamentary parties were in a mood and a position to demand the restoration of what they regarded as their 'normal' right – unrestricted power to make and break governments within the closed sanctum of Parliament for a secure term of five years – the leader of Free France brusquely announced his resignation. The office of Prime Minister was proving, against both his personal inclination and his considered political philosophy, quite as vulnerable as in the disastrous thirties to what he would recall, with undiminished contempt, in the last volume of his *Memoirs*, as 'all the old claims, ambitions, and outbidding . . . which had just cost our people unparalleled misfortunes'.[5] Six months after his resignation he opened the first campaign of a long war against the 'régime of the parties', with a speech at Bayeux, in Normandy, on the second anniversary of his return to France, denouncing the tripartite coalition's proposals for the new Assembly-based Constitution as being, in his view, certain to perpetuate the pre-war preponderance of omnicompetent and irresponsible Parliaments over weak and unstable governments, and making proposals of his own for a presidential system. When the constitutional referendum went against him, in October 1946, de Gaulle founded a Rally of the French People, *Le Rassemblement du Peuple Français* (R.P.F.), dedicated to national union above the parties.

Disruptive forces at home and abroad were beginning to work on the tripartite coalition itself. The first outbreak of anti-French violence by Arab nationalists in Algeria, and its excessively severe repression, had occurred at Sétif in May 1945.[6] In 1946 fighting broke out between Ho Chi Minh's nationalists in Indo-China and troops sent to restore the pre-war French protectorate. In 1947 a rebellion in Madagascar was put down quickly and harshly. Meanwhile the Soviet and American power blocs were shaping up against each other across an 'iron curtain' dividing Western from Eastern Europe. In France itself, the reforming impetus of the Resistance movement was beginning to peter out and a general feeling of reaction against the high hopes and tensions of the Liberation period was spreading. There was cynicism at the continuing shortages and renewed inflation of the currency (which the French people were only too ready to attribute to a relapse into 'normal' official bungling: *la pagaille*), and there was also a readiness among the moderates and the moderately well off to settle for easy-going compromise. The Communists were beginning to feel ill at ease in a coalition using mere repression to deal with colonial unrest and showing increasing hostility towards Soviet Russia. They were also uneasy at the prospect of a new 'pause' in the programme of social and economic reforms at a time when the *laissez-faire* black market was thriving more than ever on the inadequacies of official supply-lines and the inefficiency of official rationing. Prices were rising at an unprecedented and increasing rate (four times between 1938 and 1945, sixteen times between 1938 and 1949). Town workers were having to spend nearly three-quarters of their wages on food.[7] To the Catholic Democrats and the Socialists, the alliance with Communism was also becoming an embarrassment: France needed American aid too badly, they believed, for her not to turn to the West.

When, in May 1947, from justifiable fear of becoming unpopular with the working class and being outflanked on the left by the Catholic trade unions, the Communist Ministers went so far as to support a strike at the Renault motor works against the Government's wage-freeze (the current price-freeze as usual having failed), the Socialist Prime Minister, Paul Ramadier, dismissed them, and the P.C.F. went back to its accustomed place of isolated and self-righteous opposition to the *bourgeois* Republican establishment, in a politically sterile wilderness from which it has not yet re-emerged. In the month following Ramadier's 'firing of the Reds', General Marshall announced the U.S. Government's plan to help Europe recover from the war by sending material and financial aid on a vast scale across the Atlantic. This was welcomed by most of the French, but suspicion of the political strings that might be attached to the much-needed dollars, wheat and machine-tools put the left wing in a quandary. Thorez, for the Communists, described the Marshall Plan as a 'Western trap'.[8] In November, as economic conditions worsened and the gulf between Communism and anti-Communism within the French labour movement and across the world scene widened, two million French workers were called out by the Communist leaders of the C.G.T. in a nationwide series of aggressive strikes, which were vociferously supported in Parliament by all 183 Communist deputies.

In these dramatic circumstances, amid the widespread fear of a Communist uprising supported by Soviet Russian armed force, de Gaulle's Rally of the French People, founded six months earlier, and theatrically stage-managed by André Malraux, soared to corresponding heights of messianic counter-revolutionary fervour. The R.P.F., the first organised version of Gaullism as a specifically political force, grew from the permanent nucleus of the General's philosophy of action, that is, from a call to all Frenchmen, and Frenchwomen, to follow his lead beyond party-political dissensions to the higher level of the national interest. On the other hand, the new, and passing, style of massed leader-worship employed at meetings of the Rally, and the strong-arm tactics of its stewards and brawlers, partly to be explained by the overheated political climate of 1947, and partly by de Gaulle's relative political immaturity, seemed to justify the charge laid against it of reviving Fascist violence in France. Even at this early stage, however, Gaullism was not the simple cult of personal power. The Constitution of the Republic was to be overhauled and radically altered to reflect the presidential principles outlined at Bayeux, and with the immediate purpose of resisting Communist subversion; but it was not intended that Republican institutions should be swept away and France submerged under a totalitarian mass movement of the true Fascist or Nazi variety.

In the municipal elections of October 1947, the R.P.F. polled more votes than the M.R.P. and the Socialists together. But when, two months later, the strikes were broken, by dissension within the labour movement and by vigorously repressive counter-measures ordered by a Socialist Minister of the Interior, Jules Moch, who brought out the troops to break the strikes (like Clemenceau, Briand and Daladier, left-wingers turned strike-breakers before him), then the first high tide of Gaullism began to ebb. The revolutionary, and so the counter-revolutionary, potential of the French people in 1947 proved to be less than either of the anti-constitutional extremes had counted on. As a result both extremes lost support, and the moderate parliamentarians, having been frightened into an effectively united fighting position of Republican defence, reconstituted under a new name that governing Centre of the French political spectrum which, for nearly a hundred years, has shown its will and capacity to survive.[9] Where Opportunism and Radicalism had successively ruled the

Third Republic, there now came to govern the Fourth a centre coalition of Socialists, M.R.P. and the leftward margin of the Radicals and the Independent conservatives (rapidly recovering from their discomfitures in the war and Liberation): a middle-of-the-road coalition that was firmly constitutionalist and was aptly named *La Troisème Force*.

THE THIRD FORCE

Having weathered the storm of 1947, *La Troisième Force* consolidated its position under the unusually long Ministry of the Radical Premier Henri Queuille, which lasted thirteen months (September 1948 to October 1949), during which time prices stopped rising, a successful government loan was floated, and the French people recovered from their fear of a Red invasion or preventive 'Black *maquis*', and recoiled from the brink of civil war. Moderate conservative opinion began to leave the temporary shelter of the R.P.F. (and of the M.R.P.) and vote in the open again for Radicals and Independent or Peasant representatives. In the parliamentary elections of June 1951 the R.P.F. was still able to collect four million votes (16·5 per cent of the electorate) as against the Communists' five million 20·6 per cent). But not many of the 120 Gaullists elected to the Assembly (whom de Gaulle wished to remain a united and intransigent opposition group) were prepared for long to obey the General's whip. Some voted for the popular conservative Premier, Antoine Pinay, yet another French champion of financial orthodoxy and 'the little man', while others, a few months later, gave their support to the Radical, René Mayer. De Gaulle realised that his Rally of the French People had failed to shake the system of Assembly régime, and he withdrew to the edge of the political arena, in watchful retirement at his home in the east of France, Colombey-les-Deux-Églises, there to compose his *War Memoirs*, and to bide his time.

The French Republic after 1947, like the Third before 1940, would be ruled from the Centre by coalition governments leaning leftward or rightward with prevailing pressures: under Premiers Schuman and Bidault veering towards Christian democracy (while the M.R.P. party simultaneously lost half its strength and moved in from the Left to the

Centre); under Pinay and Laniel towards orthodox finance and free-enterprise conservatism; and under Mollet towards a kind of Socialism. Radical leaders all the way from the near-Socialist Mendès France to the near-conservative René Mayer provided the linking positions, and themselves came to preside at the Hôtel de Matignon roughly twice every two years: Marie and Queuille in 1948, Queuille and Faure between 1950 and 1952. Mayer in 1953, Mendès France in 1954. Faure, Bourgès-Maunoury and Gaillard between 1955 and 1958. The Radical Party recovered its pre-war influence at the centre of gravity of French politics to the extent of providing the country with seven Prime Ministers between 1948 and 1958,[10] and also with a President of the National Assembly (Édouard Herriot), and a President of the Senate (Gaston Monnerville) who would survive in that office for the first ten years of the Fifth Republic.

United to keep out both anti-constitutional extremes, the moderate *ministrables* at the centre of the *hémicycle* were divided against each other on many other issues, and divided differently on each particular issue. Thus, whereas in 1949 all the *Troisième Force* parties, together with the Gaullists, were in favour of the Atlantic Pact, against only the Communists, in 1954 half the Socialists were against the formation of a supranational Army for Western Europe, which the M.R.P. supported *en bloc,* and some Socialists and nearly all the M.R.P. voted against the separate rearmament of Western Germany within NATO. In 1956, on the question of financing pensions, the Socialists and more than half the Radicals were aligned (on the same side as the Communists) against the conservatives, with the M.R.P. abstaining. A year later, the Socialists and the M.R.P. were solidly united in favour of the creation of a European Common Market, against both the Communists and the extreme right wing. Such cross-currents were further complicated by the persisting historic problem of clericalism versus anti-clericalism in France, particularly as it affected education. State subsidies for Catholic education received support from all the conservatives and the M.R.P. and a few Radicals (with all the Gaullists), against the united opposition of most of the Radicals and all the Socialists (together with all the P.C.F.).[11]

Party leaders of the Fourth Republic thus had plenty of

opportunity for tactical manœuvres but little scope for long-term strategy. Strong, decisive government, particularly if directed against some well-established right or privilege (*droit acquis, situation acquise*), was always likely to propel some part of the coalition towards one or other of the extreme opposition parties, and was therefore avoided. The result was known as *immobilisme*. There were some notable exceptions to it, however,

Firstly, in economic growth, which (largely because its promoters at the *Commissariat Général du Plan* kept clear of party politics, and, generally, were left alone by Parliament) achieved a rate, volume and impact unknown since the great retooling and expansion of French industry and communications during the Second Empire a century earlier. Secondly, the Ministry of Foreign Affairs was kept off the party roundabout until 1954, when Mendès France finally took it away from the M.R.P. The Catholic Democrats had held it continuously for nearly ten years, during which time, under Bidault and Schuman, the Coal and Steel Community and other foundations of a united Europe were firmly laid by French initiative. Thirdly, there was the whole episode of Pierre Mendès France at the Hôtel de Matignon. From June 1954 to early February 1955, the 'system' admitted a man whose motto, 'To govern is to choose', was a direct challenge to the Third Force. But Mendès France was allowed to hold the premiership only long enough to put his exemplary decisiveness and speed of action to work on the necessary but nationally undignified task of winding up the long, costly and inglorious business of colonial war against Ho Chi Minh's nationalist uprising against the French protectorate in Indo-China, a war which the immense majority of the French people at home were thoroughly tired of and which was ending in disaster after the fall of the fortress of Dien Bien Phu. Mendès France also confronted the Assembly with its responsibility of at last deciding whether or not France should join in forming a single European Army, with the Germans but without the British. He received a negative answer. Finally, he warded off an outbreak of nationalist violence in Tunisia by opening negotiations for ending the French protectorate there. But he was not given time to develop a similarly liberal riposte to the opening shots of the Arab rebellion in neighbouring Algeria, for when he signalled his intention of tackling overdue economic reforms in the home country, by going for the most powerful and anti-social of French *situations acquises,* namely the alcohol lobby, the system threw him out.[12] The attempt that 'P.M.F.' made subsequently to modernise and galvanise the Radical Party with a shot of its ancient zeal for genuinely radical solutions to real contemporary problems was a failure, apparently splitting French Radicalism beyond repair, though a new attempt to use it as an instrument of dynamic reform was being made in the early 1970s by Jean-Jacques Servan-Schreiber.

Mendès France's successors kept up the momentum of his liberally conceived imperial policy. In 1956 the independence of Morocco was recognised, and friendly relations based on 'interdependence' and French aid were negotiated. In the same year a general 'framework law' gave parliamentary approval for the rapid advance of French territories in West and Equatorial Africa towards self-government, and formed the basis of a peaceful transition to complete political independence four years later. This beginning of independence for French colonial Africa, completed by the Fifth Republic, must be counted among the successes of the Fourth, although a belated one. The moderates at the centre of the *hémicycle* between 1947 and 1958 also succeeded in carrying through the original Third Force policy of 'Republican defence'. By allaying the threat of Communist revolution, and by absorbing the counter-revolutionary force of de Gaulle's Rally of the French People and, later, of Poujadism, they preserved the traditional forms of French parliamentary democracy for more than a decade. But faced with the extraordinarily difficult situation of a colonial war on what was officially the French 'home' territory of Algeria, the leaders of the parliamentary Centre had finally to appeal for help outside their ranks, from a man of decision whom they would not get rid of so easily as Mendès France, a man who would stay, to change the 'system' radically.

THE ALGERIAN WAR

For more than a century French colonial policy in Algeria had been as strongly assimilative as anywhere in the Empire (in 1964 renamed 'French Union'). Unlike the Tunisian, Moroccan and Indo-Chinese protectorates (renamed Associated States after the Second World War), but like the colonies of Black Africa and Madagascar (renamed Overseas Territories), Algeria was treated as an integral part of the Republic. It was divided into *départements* administered by Prefects, and its population was represented by deputies and Senators in the French Parliament in Paris. There was, it is true, a Governor-General of Algeria (later called the Resident Minister) who was responsible to the French Minister of the Interior for the administration of all the services except defence, justice and education, and there were local consultative assemblies. These represented both European and Arab communities but were electorally weighted in favour of the former (additionally so through electoral fraud). Such institutions signified some degree of Algerian separateness within the French Republic. But the long-term concept of a French 'presence' in Algeria was essentially Roman – centralised and assimilative. It was envisaged in theory that the Berber and Arab native peoples would gradually accede to full French citizenship by being educated to conform to the moral and intellectual patterns of metropolitan France and by limited political and administrative responsibilities. But in practice only a tiny middle-class fraction was so assimilated, and many, though by no means all, of these almost immediately rebelled against the process. Only about a quarter of all Arab-speaking children went to school, and poverty, unemployment and ignorance continued to abound in a population with one of the highest rates of annual increase in the world: 8,500,000, increasing by nearly a quarter of a million per year. On the other hand, several generations of mixed marriage had produced a large, intermingled 'Mediterranean' population in the big prosperous cities of the coast. The influence of French civilisation, brought by Catholic missionaries and state servants in schools, law-courts and public health departments, was strong throughout most of Algeria.

Resentment against persistent European domination and privilege, and nationalist revulsion against the idea of being assimilated into an alien European system of values, both increased sharply towards the end of the Second World War. On 1 May 1945 there was a brief explosion of Arab terrorism in the hill town of Sétif; about a hundred Europeans were murdered and, in the disproportionately ferocious repression that followed, several thousand Arabs were shot down. The next eight or nine years were superficially quiet. Then on 1 November 1954, while negotiations between the Government of Mendès France and the representatives of the Tunisian and Moroccan nationalists were being successfully pushed towards independence (which came in March 1956), an armed revolt, carefully prepared since Sétif by a small group of young Arab nationalists (*L'Organisation secrète*), and hailed by Cairo Radio as a 'holy war' for 'freedom, Arabism and Islam', was launched from the Aurès mountains. The rebels struck simultaneously at seventy different places all over Algeria and took the French authorities by surprise. Over the next three years, during which time France had five different Prime Ministers, *Le Front de libération nationale* (F.L.N.) built up a force of some 15,000 nationalist fighters and terrorists capable of defying a French army of pacification reinforced to 350,000 men. Large areas of rural Algeria were under the control of rebel administrators, tax-collectors and judges, and supplies of arms were coming in across the Tunisian border where F.L.N. units could also withdraw to rest, train and reform. Hundreds of European settlers, and thousands of Moslems suspected of collaboration with the French authorities or who were reluctant to support the rebels with food and money, were killed and mutilated.

The first two rebels sentenced to death for bearing arms against France were executed in March 1956. After this the rebellion became a mass movement; terrorism, and counter-terrorism by Europeans, entered the cities. Attacks by the F.L.N. on civilians and the explosion of bombs planted indiscriminately in cafés, tramcars, sports stadia, etc., were more or less completely stamped out by General Massu's 10th Parachute Division, which was sent into the city of Algiers in January 1957. But the use that *les paras* were to make of intimidation and torture in order to create the atmosphere and extract the information that enabled them to win the 'Battle of Algiers' had begun to stir consciences and provoke well-publicised protests from a body of scrupulous and thinking men and women in France.

Mendès France had proposed simultaneously the restoration of order and a liberal offer of fairer elections, land reform, immediate relief for the 'starvation areas' and negotiations with 'Algerian representatives'. Later French governments, however, came under heavy pressure from the Army and the settlers to refuse all negotiations until the country had been 'pacified' and to reaffirm that Algeria would remain in any case an integral part of France. Jacques Soustelle, whom Mendès France sent to Algiers as a liberal Governor-General in January 1955, was converted to the idea that reform must come by way of the faster and more genuine integration of the Arab population within the indivisible French Republic: a generous, expensive and finally impracticable version of the traditional French imperial philosophy of assimilation. Guy Mollet (Prime Minister in 1956) had had his Socialist ideas on the future of Algeria changed for him during his first visit to the country by a volley of tomatoes, cabbages and verbal abuse hurled by an excited mob of young Europeans.

Apart from their revulsion from the idea of French troops torturing suspects, most of the metropolitan population of France was sympathetic to the cause of *Algérie Française*. There was particular sympathy for the hundreds and thousands of modest European settlers who had no other home, and knew no other livelihood than the one they made in shops, offices, garages, restaurants, trades and minor government service in Algiers, Oran, Constantine, Bône, Bougie, Orléansville. Big business interests were also involved, on both sides of the Mediterranean. The intransigence of the French was strengthened by pride in the modern civilisation that their colonists and administrators had brought to a medieval country, by the belief that French power and status depended on the survival of a French Algeria, and by faith in its special destiny, going back four generations and rooted far more deeply in the history and culture of this part of North Africa (once Roman) than any other part of France's Empire overseas. The French attitude was further hardened by the rebels' calculated policy of indiscriminate terrorism.

The conversion of Soustelle and the capitulation of Mollet encouraged the European *colons* and the professional Army officers (who, besides waging a war of pacification, were deeply involved in the local administration of justice, health, education, housing, rations and employment in Arab and Berber villages brought under French control) to believe that Paris would always follow where they led firmly. In particular, it seemed that 'there was nothing that street violence could not achieve'.[13] They took more and more into their own hands, and the initiative and authority for what was being done in Algeria passed from Paris to Algeria. Eventually, there was a junta of colonels and generals and civilian officials who were convinced that it was their duty and destiny to reform root and branch the entire French Republic (which had betrayed and abandoned them in Indo-China and was planning to do the same in North Africa). They began to plot a French counter-revolution in the name of order, Western civilisation and the 'mobilisation of the masses' against Bolshevism, materialism, atheism and other alleged kinds of modern degeneracy.

The decision to divert to Algiers airport the plane conveying four Algerian Arab nationalist leaders between the former French protectorates of Morocco and Tunisia, and to kidnap its important passengers at the very time when King Mohammed and President Bourguiba were trying with the F.L.N. to work out proposals for ending the Algerian war on the basis of a compromise, was taken by subordinate intelligence officers in Algiers, and only subsequently covered by Lacoste (a second Resident Minister to espouse the cause of *Algérie Française*) and by the Prime Minister in Paris, Guy Mollet. The onus of counter-terror and torture in Algiers was taken by the military after Lacoste had handed over police and security responsibilities to General Massu.[14] Finally, it was a local Army commander who ordered the bombing of the border town of Sakhiet in Tunisia, where F.L.N. troops were accustomed to take refuge from harassment by the French army of pacification, and from whence they brought back arms and fresh troops. This was the incident that, in February 1958, through complaints by Tunis to the Security Council and counter-complaints by France, and the eventual acceptance by the Government in Paris of Anglo-American 'good offices' for the settlement of the dispute, started the train of anxiety and anger which would lead white Algeria to open rebellion against Paris on its own account three months later.

13 MAY 1958

Suspicion of Anglo-American pressure against the French position in Algeria, the execution of three French soldiers by the F.L.N. as a reprisal for the execution of three of their own men, the absence of the Resident French Minister and the imminent formation, after an exceptionally long crisis of indecision, of a new Government in Paris, suspected of planning to abandon Algeria by some sort of 'diplomatic Dien Bien Phu', all heightened the tension in Algiers. On 13 May 1958 a small group of students stormed Government House on the Place du Forum with the connivance and sympathy of the Army, thus giving the many different conspiracies already afoot (including a Gaullist one) the chance to combine in a military and civilian 'Committee of Public Safety', greeted with delirious enthusiasm by the European population.

The Commander-in-Chief of the French forces in Algeria, General Salan, declared that the Army had 'provisionally taken over responsibility for the destinies of French Algeria'. The insurgency spread quickly among the settlers throughout Algeria and was supported by a few 'assimilated' Moslems. It called for the 'renaissance of France and the restoration of her greatness' and demanded the formation in Paris of a 'Government of Public Safety' under the leadership of General de Gaulle. He must free France from the 'régime of the parties' and devote his unique authority to the reconciliation of Europeans and Arabs in Algeria and to the 'maintenance of Algeria as an integral part of France'.

De Gaulle broke his long political silence to announce that he was indeed 'ready to assume the powers of the Republic' but that 'he belonged to nobody and everybody', denying in particular that he intended, if recalled to power, to attack public liberties. The rapid disintegration of governmental authority which followed led directly to such a recall, within just over a fortnight of the Algiers *coup*. Mass demonstrations continued almost without a break in Algiers and Oran, there were smaller sympathetic outbursts and some counter-demonstration in the French capital. There were defections in the French armed services and the police. Power was seized in Corsica by a Committee of Public Safety and there were rumours of an attack by the Army on Paris itself. Finally, after the parliamentary majority had failed either to rouse and organise French public opinion against the Algiers insurgents and their sympathisers, or to form a Government strong enough to discipline them or curb their ambitions by executive action, the President of the Republic, René Coty, in a message to Parliament proposed de Gaulle for the office of Prime Minister. The alternative, he said, was his own resignation and the formation of a Popular Front including the Communists, with consequent grave danger of civil war.

On 1 June, de Gaulle, having assured Parliament that he wished to restore and not overthrow the State and the Republic, was invested as Prime Minister with a Cabinet of new men joined by parliamentary leaders of all parties except the Communists and Poujadists. On 2 June the new Government obtained a big majority in the National Assembly to promote a Bill reforming the Constitution according to the long-accepted Republican principles of power proceeding from universal suffrage and government answerable to Parliament, and a controversially new Gaullist one insisting on the separation of the executive and the legislative powers. The draft Constitution would be submitted to the country in a referendum. Without specifying the exact political position of Algeria within a reformed French Union, de Gaulle promised equality of rights and duties to all the ten million French citizens in Algeria – Arab, Berber and European alike – also an amnesty to the rebel nationalists and immediate financial aid for the relief of poverty and the extension of education and industry.

On 28 September all the adult citizens of the Republic were invited to show their attitude to the new Constitution in a single referendum; overseas territories producing an adverse majority were to be regarded as wishing to secede from the proposed new French 'Community', and given their independence. 85 per cent of the electorate of metropolitan France went to the polls, of whom 79 per cent voted for the Constitution. An even higher percentage of affirmative votes was reported, officially, from Algeria, where the Moslem electorate included women for the first time. All the overseas territories except French Guinea, in West Africa, which produced an adverse majority, approved the new Constitution by large majorities.

ALGERIAN INDEPENDENCE

Once firmly in power, it took de Gaulle another three and a half years of continued war, repeatedly unsuccessful peace offers and negotiations, and diplomatic pressure on all the parties and factions concerned, before he was able to reconcile the majority of the French people, the Army (or most of it) and, no doubt, himself, to the idea of Algerian independence. In September 1959 he took the decisive step of proclaiming the Algerian people's right to self-determination, though he still demanded that this be 'expressed legitimately' by 'universal suffrage', not forced on the country by the 'knives and machine-guns' of a group of nationalist 'agitators'.[15] Not until March 1962, however, was the Algerian war brought to an end, and then only after full Algerian independence had been recognised in an agreement, signed at Évian, by President de Gaulle for the French Republic, and the leaders of the rebel National Liberation Front for the 'Provisional Government of Algeria', whose military and terrorist organisation the French Army had succeeded in containing but had not defeated.

De Gaulle's tortuous approach to the recognition of Algerian independence turned many of his former supporters who had hoped for quite a different outcome into enemies who felt bitterly that he had betrayed them. Three desperate rearguard actions against the surrender of French Algeria to Arab control disturbed the early years of the Fifth Republic. The first, in January 1960, was the so-called 'Week of the Barricades'.

This was a rising in Algiers led by civilians but gaining considerable passive support from units of the 10th Parachute Division stationed in the city. Thousands of armed civilians occupied the centre of Algiers and were allowed by the friendly paratroops to set up a sort of citadel there and to supply it continuously with water, food and arms for a further five days, defying the Government in Paris in quite the old manner. De Gaulle, however, was not to be bullied like his predecessors. Government H.Q. in Algeria was withdrawn from Algiers (a move ominously like Thiers's withdrawal to Versailles between the outbreak and the grim repression of the Paris Commune) and de Gaulle appeared on television in uniform to condemn the 'accommodating uncertainty of various military elements', elements who might be 'tempted to think that this is their war, not France's war'. He reaffirmed that his policy was self-determination for Algeria, and ordered every soldier to dissociate himself immediately from the insurgents:

> What would the French Army become but an anarchic and absurd conglomeration of military feudalisms, if it should happen that certain elements made their loyalty conditional? As you know, I have the supreme responsibility. It is I who bear the country's destiny. I must therefore be obeyed by every French soldier. I believe that I shall be obeyed, because I know you, because I have a high regard for you, because I feel affection for you, because I have confidence in General Challe whom I have placed at your head, soldiers of Algeria, and finally, because I have need of you for France.[16]

De Gaulle's remarkable speech, combining perfectly the Republican tradition of anti-feudal indivisibility, the monarchical principle identifying state and personal ruler ('I have . . . I must . . . I believe') and the eternally charmed circle of great captain, picked men, beloved country, was totally effective. The rebellion collapsed at once.

In January 1961 de Gaulle was given a strong vote of confidence, by means of a national referendum, for his policy of self-determination for Algeria. Yet before agreement with the F.L.N. could be reached, another attempt was made in the name of French Algeria to obstruct the process of what de Gaulle now called 'necessary decolonisation'. This *coup* was plotted by Army officers. Its public directorate consisted of four retired generals, including Salan and Challe, who covered a secret organisation led by younger men (*L'Organisation de l'Armée Secrète* – O.A.S.) which had laid meticulous plans to take over the whole of Algeria. In the event, the Parachutists and Foreign Legionaries who were its principal instruments met firm resistance from the rest of the Army, Navy and Air Force in Algeria, and no support for the rebels was forthcoming from the French Army stationed in Germany. The myth of French military unity against the new régime was exploded, and the leaders of the rebellion resigned themselves to defeat rather than risk a clash of arms.

Once again, de Gaulle's persuasive eloquence was effective in arousing loyalty and building resistance to rebellion, especially among the conscript troops in Algeria (who listened to him on their transistors).[17] De Gaulle also reinforced his personal authority by claiming the presidential emergency powers allowed in the new Constitution. All the main parties and trade unions were for the time being on his side. Rumours (unfounded as it turned out) of an imminent airborne attack on the capital had brought thousands of volunteers for its defence, clamouring for arms (which were not, in fact, distributed), in a Paris bristling all night with tanks, guns and buses used as road-blocks. On the third day of the insurrection, ten million people came out in a token general strike, of unprecedented size. The great majority of the French were by now thoroughly, and confidently, hostile towards the French Algerian *ultras*. The Communist party, true to form and the mood of the hour, complained bitterly that the Government had not made use of 'popular forces', or armed the workers.

Though the generals' *coup* failed, the O.A.S. remained in being and the following year took a sort of revenge. French Algeria was to go down in the next fourteen months in a lurid twilight of blood and fire. Both the F.L.N. and the O.A.S. increased their terrorist activities after the opening of negotiations between the French Government and the F.L.N. Clashes also occurred, not only between Moslems and Europeans but between Moslems and Jews. A peak of the killing was reached in the first quarter of 1962: hundreds, of all races, were cut down, by machine-gunning, knifing, clubbing, bomb-throwing in cafés and on crowded beaches, and by lynching mobs as many as a thousand strong. Once the cease-fire had been agreed, the F.L.N., for its part, stopped, but the O.A.S., inspired by the theories of subversive warfare that many French officers, back from Indo-China, had learned in the handbook of Mao Tse-tung, sought systematically to break down all law and order and, in particular, to provoke the Moslems into breaking the truce. On 2 May over a hundred people were murdered in Algiers. The F.L.N. told the Arab community to resist provocation calmly, and obtained a remarkably disciplined response. Nearly all the casualties were now Arabs, though there were, understandably, some reprisals.

In a last wave of despairing violence, the O.A.S. (fought now by the Government's own counter-counter-terrorists, the *barbouzes*) launched a 'scorched earth' campaign to reduce Algiers by arson and 'plastic' explosives to its undeveloped condition of 1830, when the French had first taken it from its Arab rulers. They failed, but there was a mass exodus of Jews and Europeans from Algeria, in spite of O.A.S. orders against it and attempts to sabotage it. Bomb outrages in Algeria and France ceased, though attempts on the life of President de Gaulle continued in 1963.

FRANCE UNDER DE GAULLE

The speed with which the French nation recovers from catastrophe and multiple injuries has been admired many times. Our great-grandfathers marvelled at its rapid recuperation after the *année terrible* of Sedan and the Commune. Now the din of battle for Algeria, the alarums of military *Diktat* and civil war vanished as suddenly, leaving the country at peace for the first time for sixteen years (for nearly a quarter of a century, if the short interval between the end of the Second World War and the beginning of the war in Indo-China is discounted). Freed from the barbed imperial entanglements of post-war Asia and Africa, with a new, and what was for her really a first true industrial revolution quickening and prospering at home, with trade, travel and ideas flowing more freely than for a hundred years across the fading frontiers of Western Europe, and within a Greater Europe, from the Atlantic to the Urals, as de Gaulle put it, in which even the stubborn East–West tensions of the Cold War seemed to be relaxing at last, France in 1962 appeared once again to have recovered from a terrible national crisis almost instantaneously. The majority of the French people showed their belief in the achievement and their approval of the means employed by voting 'yes' in two government referenda seeking popular support for de Gaulle's agreement with the Arab leaders to end French rule in Algeria, and for his proposed constitutional reform introducing presidential elections by direct universal suffrage; also by electing him to a second term as President, albeit with a slightly reduced majority.

Despite de Gaulle's rough 'presidential' reaction against the eighty-year trend of French parliamentary democracy towards government by 'assembly', the resolution of the Algerian crisis was followed, true to Third and Fourth Republican form, by the rise of a new government party of the Centre, in the tradition of Opportunism, Radicalism and the Third Force. This was a new managerial and technocratic variety of Gaullism, backed by the 'new notables' of mid-twentieth-century France (*cadres*, planners, engineers) and by the mass consumers of its rising production and revenue, and more pragmatic and moderate in outlook than the original 'epic' varieties engendered by the crises of 1940, 1947 and 1958. For ten years, through three general elections. *L'Union pour la nouvelle république* (U.N.R.) and the more left-wing *Union démocratique du travail* (U.D.T.), which combined as one group, *L'Union des démocrates pour la république* (U.D.R.), in 1968, held the confidence of the largest single group of French voters and, with the qualified support of a small group of conservatives, led by Valéry Giscard d'Estaing, who called themselves Independent Republicans, gave what was for France quite exceptionally united Parliamentary support to four Gaullist Prime Ministers: Debré, Pompidou, Couve de Murville and Chaban-Delmas.[18]

It was easy to overrate the depth and speed of France's post-imperial and new-European 'mutations' (a biological metaphor much favoured by Gaullists), and to underestimate the degree of strain that such changes of pace and direction would impose on considerable sections of the French people. Intense bitterness against de Gaulle ('the broadcasting General'), doubly traitor to the France of Marshal Pétain and to the Algeria of the 13 May, persisted in a small right-wing faction of the French *classe politique*. At the other end of the spectrum, a large and generally younger politically conscious group which opposed not only *Algérie Française* but also the paternalistic and patronising style of de Gaulle's 'personal rule', and the irritatingly complacent ascendency of the Gaullist party that the agony of French Algeria had imposed on France, endured some years of depression.[19] By the mid-1960s, however, anti-Gaullist feeling among the masses and post-Gaullist expectations in political circles were increasing, as a result of rising prices and unemployment, a failing social security budget, and the Government's authoritarian countermeasures; also the President's age and his alarmingly high-handed and somewhat incoherently nationalistic interpretation of France's new 'freedom of action' in foreign affairs 'such as no other nation enjoys' (Germany courted, Russia wooed, Poland encouraged, Communist China recognised, Mexico and South America toured, Israel condemned, the freedom of Quebec Province proclaimed against Ottawa, the 'universality' of gold asserted against the dollar, the *force de frappe*, France's nuclear strike force of planes, missiles and submarines, made ready, 'tous azimuts', against all comers).[20]

In the new climate, de Gaulle's democratic and internationalist opponents recovered some of their confidence and drive, and a measure of tactical political unity, which enabled them to reduce the parliamentary majority of the Gaullist party and its Independent Republican allies, in the general election of March 1967, almost to vanishing-point.[21] But a year later the French left wing as a whole came under the reactionary backlash provoked by a spectacular student revolt in Paris and other university cities in which young Trotskyists, Maoists and anarchists took a leading part, and which eventually triggered off a general strike and occupation of factories by between nine and ten million workers, organised by the three main trade union confederations. A snap parliamentary election held immediately after the so-called 'May Revolution' restored and indeed strongly reinforced the Gaullist majority.[22]

The following year, however, it was de Gaulle who overplayed his hand, by trying to turn yet another national referendum (this time on his proposal to give the country a new system of large-scale local government based on elected regional councils representing both territorial and socio-professional interests, and to amalgamate the Senate with the Economic Council in a new, partially corporative and purely consultative second House of Parliament) into a personal plebiscite, for or against his continuing in office as President of the Republic. Instead of the affirmative majority he called for, the result was twelve million 'noes' and not quite eleven million 'ayes'. De Gaulle resigned immediately and retired from politics. He died suddenly at Colombey-les-Deux-Églises in November 1970, aged seventy-nine.

'De Gaulle's Republic' stood, however, and the transfer of power to its next President followed smoothly the constitutional procedure introduced by its founder seven years before. The successful candidate was a former Gaullist Prime Minister, Georges Pompidou, and the Premier that the new President appointed to lead the Government, Jacques Chaban-Delmas, who had been a general in the Gaullist wartime Resistance, leader of the Gaullists in the Parliament of 1951–5, a U.N.R. deputy from 1958, and President of the National Assembly, was the very model of both the epic past and the managerial present of Gaullism. He was also a declared champion of de Gaulle's fundamental doctrine of presidential preponderance within the Executive.

The French left wing was a house still deeply divided against itself, while the sacrifices that France's dynamic mid-century mutations were demanding of agricultural smallholders, unskilled workers and employees, craftsmen, clerks and executives whose skills or experience had been made redundant by technical progress and international trade across lowered tariff barriers, and of poorly housed families in fast-growing cities and mass-taught students in swollen universities, continued to demonstrate the crying need of a large, politically effective left-wing opposition party – in the absence of which, pressures seemed likely to build up for yet another French outbreak of extremism and possibly violence. This is the most difficult long-term problem of de Gaulle's successors. The General left them with a password from the twenty-five-year-old 'Charter of the Resistance': *participation*. But participatory democracy, of workers in the management of industry, of students and teachers in the running of universities, of private citizens and corporations in regional administration, is little more as yet than a pious but powerless incantation against the dangers of economic, educational and provincial alienation, and narrowly sectarian opposition politics – dangers recognised but not remedied.

On the other hand there are some notable achievements in the balance-sheet of Gaullist France. Some of these are entirely its own: the settlement of the Algerian crisis, the reassertion of the civil power over a rebellious Army, the popularly elected Presidency, and the improved efficiency of the legislative process in Parliament. Others tend to reveal continuity between the Fourth and the Fifth Republics, and reflect credit on the French and their leaders both before and after 1958: economic co-operation and a lavish French aid programme within the franc zone of French-speaking Africa, peacefully decolonised; reconciliation with Germany, and commitment to the European Common Market and to some kind of further European unification, though which kind remains for the time being vague – Gaullists tend to favour what their leader once called 'l'Europe des États', as against supranational federation, and a 'European Europe', against an 'Atlantic' Euro-American system; widespread, accelerating, though still patchy modernisation and expansion of both agricultural and industrial production, which raised France's gross domestic product per capita by nearly 50 per cent between 1958 and 1965;[23] the preservation, through a severe crisis of confidence, of the basically liberal society that both the Fourth and the Fifth Republics inherited from pre-war France, and which is protected by a Parliament with reduced but real, and potentially decisive, powers, by the traditional Republican freedoms of assembly, parties and Press, and by the more tardily unmuzzled mass media of radio and television.[24]

LITERATURE, ART AND THOUGHT SINCE 1940

The trials of defeat, foreign occupation and resistance seemed to develop a new sobriety and forthrightness in French prose, from the thoughtful chronicles of the agonising present by Saint-Exupéry and Vercors (*Pilote de guerre* and *Le Silence de la mer*) to the classic economy of Montherlant's historical dramas, *La Reine morte* and *Le Maître de Santiago*, and André Gide's concisely, quietly persuasive last *récit*: *Thésée*. There was also a spate of passionate, plain-spoken verse, inspired by the patriotic courage and the revolutionary ardour of the Resistance (and much of it published by the underground Press). Some of this new, committed verse touched greatness, for example Aragon's 'La Rose et le Réséda' and Éluard's 'Liberté'. But only a little of it seems likely to endure, and the most original poetry of the period continued for the greater part to be written, by such as Jouve, Char, Saint-John-Perse and Michaux, in the more inward, complex vein of Symbolism and Surrealism.

The most profound revolution in French thought and letters between the Popular Front and the Liberation was announced unknowingly by Antoine de Saint-Exupéry in the headline of a newspaper article written at the time of the Munich surrender (and later incorporated in *Terre des hommes*): 'Il faut donner un sens à la vie des hommes' – 'Mankind must be *given* a reason for living'. That man's life is an idiot's tale signifying nothing is an old theme of literature. But it has been given a new edge in the present century, by a double loss of faith in God and in science, by two great wars and innumerable small colonial and civil ones, and by mounting frustration at the apparently ineradicable injustices and violence of human society. In France, well before the Second World War, there had been writers such as Barrès and Malraux who had consciously fought off the paralysing belief that the human predicament is an inherently absurd one by engaging in romantically nationalist or revolutionary politics. To others, like the philosopher and novelist Paul Nizan, and the poet Éluard, joining the disciplined Communist Party seemed the only chance of making sense out of history and of giving some purpose to their own existence.[25] For others again, such as Claudel, Mauriac and the sociologist, Simone Weil, the Christian faith alone cancelled out nihilism. Then, under the advancing shadow of the war, three new writers emerged: Jean-Paul Sartre, Albert Camus and Samuel Beckett, working independently of each other but subject to the same French climate of ideas (in which Dostoevsky, Nietzsche, Kafka, Joyce and Faulkner were important foreign influences). Between 1938 and 1951 they produced the first of the novels and dramas that were to put the anguished consciousness of the Absurd at the very centre of wartime and post war literature in Europe and America: *La Nausée* (1938), *Le Mur* (1939), *Les Mouches* (1943), *Huis-Clos* (1944), by Sartre; *L'Étranger* (written 1939–40, published 1942), *Le Malentendu* (1944), *Caligula* (1945), *La Peste* (1947), by Camus; *Murphy* (in English 1938, in French 1947), *Molloy* (1951), by Beckett.

Sartre, Camus and Beckett all wrote from the standpoint of

an intensely felt personal experience of the seeming absurdity of human existence, and each would develop an authentically personal way of rendering this experience in the form of prose fiction, stage plays, exemplary lives or autobiography. Sartre,[26] who was trained as a professional philosopher at the *École Normale Supérieure* (and won second place in the philosophy *agrégation* of 1929), was also the leading exponent of French Existentialism. This philosophy, like Sartre's imaginative literature, is based on the primacy of lived experience over abstract, theoretical system. Taught by experience, observation, and his masters Kirkegaard and Husserl, Sartre assumes that Existence precedes Essence, in other words that there is no given 'essential' truth supposedly transcending the particular conditions, perspectives, reflections and projects of individuals 'existing' in real, personal and historical situations. There is no given order, hierarchy or authority which we must or should accept. There is no given 'human nature' to command men's thoughts and actions. There is not even a pre-ordained essential 'self'. Each man is *free* to choose how to act in the context in which he finds himself. Being free, each of us is always responsible for what we make or fail to make of our own lives. Men are 'condemned to be free'. To abdicate the responsibility that goes with freedom is to abdicate our humanity, to sink abjectly, comfortably and usually hypocritically to the level of a passive *object*. This affirmative doctrine of freedom and responsibility, and what it implies that we should do together with others, as much as by and for ourselves as individuals ('Il s'agit de faire l'homme' – 'We must *make* mankind'), led Sartre to claim, justifiably, that 'Existentialism is a form of humanism'.[27] It has also fired his vigorous campaigning for the cause of proletarian and colonial emancipation, as a formidable *écrivain engagé*: analyst, publicist, pamphleteer, and the editor of an important, unorthodox, left-wing monthly review founded in 1946, *Les Temps modernes*.

For Sartre, the Absurd was the crawling, viscous, literally nauseating irrationality of the given universe of objects which man, as subject, is free to make his own sense of (*La Nausée, Les Mouches*). Camus experienced the sensation of the Absurd rather differently, as a scandalous 'divorce' between the mind of man and the inexplicable universe which is the scene of our little life, and in which he feels an 'outsider' (*L'Étranger*). But during the years of resistance and liberation, Camus moved onward from metaphysical scandal to humanist defiance and reached a political position close to Sartre, having learned, like the hero of Sartre's first play, *Les Mouches*, that 'man's life begins on the other side of despair' – in active, fraternal rebellion against oppression and injustice. The two writers differed sharply on the question of how to reconcile the means and the ends of revolution, however, when Camus, in a long, critical study of the rebel in history, *L'Homme révolté* (1951), asserted his deep-seated liberal scruples against unchecked 'abstract' revolutionary violence – scruples which could only bring comfort, thought Sartre, to the already self-satisfied, inactive (or openly reactionary) *salauds* of the ruling French middle class.[28]

In Beckett's black country of the Absurd there is no compensating, forward-looking faith in revolutionary action of either the liberal or the radical variety: only the seemingly irremediable derision of human existence confronted with the purely literary ambition to find its difficult, exact expression, in the struggling narrative precision of *Molloy* (1951), *L'Innommable* (1953), *Comment c'est* (1961), his enigmatic novels, and in the haunting word-music and dumb-show of his tragic farces: *En attendant Godot* (1953), *Fin de partie* (1957), *La Dernière Bande* (1960), *Oh! Les Beaux Jours* (1963). The pathos and humour of Beckett's derelict specimens of humanity, caught in an eternal present of loneliness and longing to be together, of impotence perpetually frustrating the perpetual hope of significant action (and portrayed without the traditional reference of French humanist drama to either current affairs, colourful history or ancient mythology), made their creator famous some years after his contemporary, Sartre, and his junior, Camus. Beckett's comparatively late success as a playwright, and the even more popular contemporary success of Ionesco's farcically self-multiplying, terrifyingly violent world of people, things, words and monsters that have got out of control[29] (in *La Leçon, Les Chaises, Amédée, Tueur sans gages, Rhinocéros,* etc.), signified some disenchantment with the belief, held by Surrealists, Marxists and Existentialists alike since the 1930s, in the writers' mission to 'change' the world.[30]

The rise of the so-called 'new novel' in these same years of Beckett's and Ionesco's new theatre (that is, the mid-1950s, ten years after the Liberation) marked an even more radical rejection of publicly committed literature in favour of private aesthetic experience and experiment. The techniques of objective description, repetition, infinitesimal variation, simultaneity and discontinuity that are used in Alain Robbe-Grillet's novels and films (*Le Voyeur, La Jalousie, L'Année dernière à Marienbad*) and Michel Butor's *L'Emploi du temps, La Modification, Mobile,* etc., give the reader freedom to discover for *himself* the overall significance of the rudimentary plots and sketchy characters, the profusion of indicative or allusive words, the simply given gestures, shapes, things, events (and non-events) which crowd the page or fill the cinema screen.

It seems unlikely, however, that the French nation will soon lose its literary and philosophical clerisy or that the French intelligentsia will cease to operate as a source of universal generalisations, public instruction and political proselytising. Ionesco and the new novelists, like the majority of French writers since the seventeenth century, explained themselves painstakingly in prefaces and manifestos. Genet, Arrabal and Georges Michel used the methods of the new theatre (and Godard the freedom of 'new wave' film-making) to shock and belabour established conventions. Sartre was going on with his attempted synthesis of Existentialism and Marxism.[31] His contemporary at *Normale,* Raymond Aron, continued to try, as Simone Weil and Albert Camus had tried, to reduce the abstraction and violence of political conflict in France by confronting the myths of the Left and the Right (revolution, proletariat, equality, authority, property, materialism, grandeur and so on) with reality and common sense (*L'Opium des intellectuels, Espoir et peur du siècle*). In a busy sacred grove of philosopher-kings, Claude Lévi-Strauss, the structural anthropologist, Michel Foucault, the founder of philosophical structuralism, and Louis Althusser, the Marxist fundamentalist, competed for the succession of Jean-Paul Sartre.

Meanwhile the most illustrious, and in many ways the most exemplary, French writer of the last fifty years – the years since Verdun, the October Revolution and the awakening of

Asia – André Malraux, in the last stage of his sensational career as archaeologist, adventurer, novelist, airman, soldier, partisan, art historian, orator and government minister, was gathering a lifetime's significant recollections, obsessions and symbols for his *Antimémoires,* composed in the humanist mainstream of his (and his country's) literature, calling on universal history and contemporary events, personal experience and the creative imagination, leaders of nations (Nehru, de Gaulle, Mao), and ordinary men and women observed in action, under stress, individually and in the mass, to bear witness equally, at the continuing grand inquiry of French civilisation, to the nature and stature of mankind: 'Ce qui m'intéresse dans un homme quelconque, c'est la condition humaine.'[32]

Notes

CHAPTER 1

1. Unless stated otherwise, figures are taken from the *Annuaires statistiques* of the *Institut national de la statistique et des études économiques* (I.N.S.E.E.) or the *Statesman's Year Book.*

2. e.g. J.-M. Sourdillat, *Géographie agricole de la France* (Paris, 1964) pp. 18–19, 75, 83–4, 89, 91.

3. See, e.g., below, Chapter 5, n. 8.

4. I am greatly indebted to my colleague Dr K. M. MacIver, Head of the Geography Department of the University of St Andrews, for the geological explanation of migration routes and centres of culture that is used in this paragraph, and for the map she has drawn to illustrate it on p. 8.

5. F. R. Alleman, 'The Alsatians', *Encounter,* XXIII 5 (November 1964) 45–54; I. B. Thompson, *Modern France: A Social and Economic Geography* (London, 1970) pp. 277–88.

6. Chamber of Commerce and Industry of Marseille.

7. Such Spanish themes are found in, for example, Corneille's *Le Cid* (1636), Molière's *Dom Juan* (1665), Hugo's *Ruy Blas* (1838), Mérimée's *Carmen* (1845), Heredia's *Les Trophées* (1893), Claudel's *Le Soulier de satin* (1929), Montherlant's *Le Maître de Santiago* (1947). For *douce France,* see *La Chanson de Roland,* lines 109, 115, 360, 573, 706, 1054, etc.

8. W. S. Churchill, quoted by C. de Gaulle in *War Memoirs,* trans. J. Griffin (London, 1955) II 227.

9. So called after the ruling revolutionary party of 1792–4, which led the nation in arms ('le peuple libre' – Danton) against conservative, monarchist, Europe. See pp. 99–100, 156–7.

10. A. Prost, 'L'Immigration en France depuis cent ans', *L'Esprit* (Apr 1966) pp. 532–45.

11. See pp. 155–7, 189–91, 211, 231–41.

12. C. Delmas, *L'Aménagement du territoire* (Paris, 1962) p. 118. The Cévennes mountains, which form the south-eastern escarpment of the Massif Central, have lost nearly three-quarters of their population since 1900 (J. Beaujeu-Garnier, *Geography of Population,* trans. S. H. Beaver (London, 1966) p. 196).

13. See pp. 143–5.

14. Thompson, *Modern France.* Also J.-F. Gravier, *L'Aménagement du territoire et l'avenir des régions françaises* (Paris, 1964); J. Bastié, *Paris en l'an 2000* (Paris, 1964); P. George, P. Randet and J. Bastié, *La*

Région parisienne (Paris, 1964); and J. J. Branigan, *Europe excluding the British Isles and the USSR* (London, 1965).

15. *La Région parisienne* p. 54; P. Avril, *Politics in France* trans. J. Ross (London, 1969) p. 227.

16. *La Région parisienne,* p. 106.

17. The wheat crop of this area is as great as the whole of West Germany's and bigger than Britain's: 'On 15 per cent of the area and with 19 per cent of the population of France [it] produces: 41 per cent of its wheat, 43 per cent of its oats, 92 per cent of its sugar-beet, ... (Sourdillat, *Géographie agricole,* p. 61).

18. After Strasbourg. Paris, the largest French river port, handles a slightly bigger tonnage than Dunkirk, France's third seaport (after Marseille and Le Havre). Paris to Rouen by road is only 84 miles.

19. Beaujeu-Garnier, *Geography of Population,* pp. 195–6, and *La Population française* (Paris, 1969) pp. 137–9; Thompson, *Modern France,* p. 440; J.-F. Gravier, *Paris et le désert français* (Paris, 1947) pp. 38–49; A. Blanc, E. Julliard *et al., Les Régions de l'Est* (Paris, 1960) pp. 10–12.

20. See also Branigan, *Europe,* pp. 235–7.

21. J. Ardagh, *The New France* (London, 1970) pp. 205–19.

22. See pp. 129–30.

23. Ardagh, *New France* pp. 195–220.

24. Ibid., p. 180; Avril, *Politics in France,* pp. 227–8, Thompson, *Modern France,* p. 51.

25. See pp. 101–2 and Beaujeu-Garnier, *La Population française* pp. 10–17.

26. Ibid., pp. 24–5.

27. P. Massé, quoted in J. Hackett and A.-M. Hackett, *Economic Planning in France* (London, 1963) p. 396.

28. A. Sauvy, *Mythologie de notre temps* (Paris, 1966) p. 188.

29. 31·6 per cent of accommodation was overcrowded in 1968 (40 per cent in Paris).

30. J. A. Lesourd and C. Gérard, *Histoire économique, XIXe et XXe siècles* (Paris, 1963) I 228. The summary history of recent immigration that follows is based on the article by Prost, 'L'Immigration en France depuis cent ans', quoted above, n. 10.

31. Beaujeu-Garnier, *La Population française,* pp. 84–5.

32. M. Guibert, 'Présentation des étrangers en France', *L'Esprit* (Apr 1966) pp. 550–1. More refugees came to France in the 1960s than to any other European country, according to the U.S. Committee for Refugees, quoted by W. Petersen, *Population* (New York, 1969) p. 285.

CHAPTER 2

1. Simone de Beauvoir, *Memoirs of a Dutiful Daughter,* trans. J. Kirkup (London, 1963) pp. 76–7, 255.

2. French farmers also *sold* food to the cities at the inflated prices of the black market.

3. See below, Chapter 6, 'The Civil Service and Local Government'.

4. The social composition of a holiday Club Méditerranée in the 1960s is given as 20 per cent workers, 30 per cent employees, 20 per cent technicians, 30 per cent liberal professions (E. Marc, 'Populations et groupes sociaux', *Tendances* (June 1965) p. 298).

5. Approximately 1,160,000 in 1968, as against 447,500 in 1954 and a predicted 3,000,000 in 1980.

6. E. Dabit, 'Parisiens de Belleville', *La Nouvelle Revue Française* (Feb 1933).

7. Thompson, *Modern France*, pp. 49–67.

8. Paris, 1955; trans. P. Wiles as *The Sovereigns* (London, 1960).

9. S. Mallet, *La Nouvelle Classe ouvrière* (Paris, 1963).

10. See Chapter 3, n. 14.

11. *Boules*, also called *la pétanque*, played with metal bowls on hard ground in public squares and gardens.

12. *Salaire minimum interprofessionnel de croissance* (S.M.I.C.).

13. 22 per cent of basic monthly wage for two dependent children and 33 per cent for the third and each subsequent child, with certain supplements and a maternity grant.

14. See above, Chapter 1, n. 29, and *Le Monde*, 9 and 25 Nov 1966. Also P. Chombart de Lauwe, *La Vie quotidienne des familles ouvrières* (Paris, 1956), and Ardagh, *New France*, pp. 302–15.

15. Slang for cheap wine.

16. G. Navel, *Travaux* (Paris, 1945), pp. 216–22.

17. See p. 60.

18. E. Beau de Loménie, *Les Responsabilités des dynasties bourgeoises* (Paris, 1943–54).

19. S. Mallet, *Les Paysans contre le passé* (Paris, 1962) pp. 162.

20. J. Lacouture, *De Gaulle* (Paris, 1965) pp. 5–6.

21. 622,800 in 1968.

22. This term covers trade in all kinds of drinks.

23. Marc, *Tendances* (June 1965) p. 293. See Philip Williams, *Crisis and Compromise* (London, 1964) pp. 162–9.

24. 'Le labourage et le pastourage, voilà les deux mamelles dont la France est alimentée, les vraies mines et trésors du Pérou' (Duc de Sully (1559–1641), minister and friend of Henry IV of France).

25. Branigan, *Europe*; F. J. Monkhouse, *The Countries of North-western Europe* (London, 1965); R. Lacour-Gayet, *La France au XXe siècle* (Paris, 1954); M. Tracy, *Agriculture in Western Europe* (London, 1964); Lesourd and Gérard, *Histoire économique*.

26. The average size of French farms increased between 1955 and 1967 from 35 to 47 acres. Nevertheless only 7 per cent were bigger than 125 acres in 1967. Nearly half the holdings officially listed as *exploitations* are smaller than 25 acres, but many of these are plots or gardens cultivated part-time by agricultural labourers or industrial workers (*paysans-ouvriers*) or tradesmen, and altogether they make up only one-tenth of the total land area under cultivation. 'The essence of French

farming is contained in the size category of 10–50 hectares' [25–125 acres] accounting for 46 per cent of the total holdings and 56 per cent of the agricultural land area' (Thompson, *Modern France*, p. 143).

27. G. Wright, *Rural Revolution in France* (Stanford, 1964) p. 6; Monkhouse, *North-western Europe*, p. 415.

28. In 1968, 2,459,800 and 588,200 respectively. Tenant farmers work about half the farmland and half the number of holdings, but in only a fifth of these holdings does the tenant rent the entire farm (Thompson, *Modern France*, pp. 140–1; L. Gachon, *La Vie rurale* (Paris, 1967) p. 120).

29. J. Giono, *The Dominici Affair*, trans. P. de Mendelssohn (London, 1956) p. 79.

30. Ibid., pp. 81–6.

31. P. Oyler, *The Generous Earth* (London, 1950) pp. 65–6, 74–7.

32. A. Dauzat, *Le Village et le paysan de France* (Paris, 1941) p. 9.

33. Lacour-Gayet, *La France au XXe siècle*, p. 282.

34. J.-M. Jeanneney, *Forces et faiblesses de l'économie française, 1945–1959*, 2nd ed. (Paris, 1959) p. 65.

35. P. Pellegrin, quoted by J.-D. Reynaud, in *Tendances et volontés de la société française* (Paris, 1966) p. 95.

36. Wright, *Rural Revolution in France*, pp. 1–2.

37. Ibid., p. 1.

38. G. Dupeux, *La Société française, 1789–1960* (Paris, 1964) pp. 245–6.

39. Open-field cultivation (*champagne, plaine*) is customary north of a line joining Lake Geneva and the mouth of the Seine, and also in southern France from the Rhône valley westwards to the Garonne region, Poitou and Berry. Settlement is in fairly large, compact villages, or big courtyard-farmsteads, surrounded by ploughlands and grazing, divided into long strips or irregular plots only by ditches, or a line of stones, or an unploughed furrow, or temporary fences. Vistas are wide, and the countryside is comparatively treeless. Enclosed fields are found in Provence, and throughout the Midi the older villages are often perched high on hilltops, for defensive reasons. Normandy south of the Seine, Brittany and Vendée have typical *bocage* cultivation and settlement: a patchwork of small fields surrounded by hedges, bushes and trees, or low dry-stone walls, with only small villages and hamlets, and many isolated farmhouses standing each in its own land, which is, for the most part, permanently enclosed. Sociability and the collective spirit are all, naturally, stronger in open-field regions, while rugged, and wary, habits of independence are traditional in *bocage* country (M. Bloch, *French Rural History*, trans. J. Sondheimer (London, 1966) pp. 56–9; Branigan, *Europe*, pp. 213, 241, 248).

40. Beaujeu-Garnier, *La Population française*, p. 205.

41. *Cercles de jeunes agriculteurs* (C.J.A.), *Centres d'étude technique agricole* (C.E.T.A.), *Coopératives d'utilisation de matériel agricole* (C.U.M.A.). 'We are accused of being too individualistic. *My* generation isn't', a young farmer told André Maurois in 1954 (A. Maurois, *Portrait de la France* (Paris, 1955) p. 72).

42. L. Wylie, 'Social Change at Grass Roots', in S. Hoffmann *et al.*, *France: Change and Tradition* (London, 1963) pp. 159–234.

CHAPTER 3

1. German, Dutch, British and U.S. figures for 1968 also.
2. M. Faure, *Les Paysans dans la société française* (Paris, 1966) pp. 56–60; J. Fourastié and H. Montet, *L'Économie française dans le monde* (Paris, 1950) pp. 104–10.
3. Thompson, *Modern France*, p. 140, Faure, *Paysans*, p. 104.
4. J.-M. Jeanneney, *Forces et faiblesses de l'économie française, 1945–1959* (Paris, 1959) p. 70.
5. American aid, amounting in all to $4,600 million, ceased between 1956 and 1960 (J. Guyard, *Le Miracle français* (Paris, 1965) p. 20).
6. I.N.S.E.E. See Guyard, *Le Miracle français*, and Avril, *Politics in France*, pp. 222–4.
7. Thompson, *Modern France*, p. 97.
8. Monkhouse, *North-western Europe*, p. 441.
9. 73·4 per cent of the total value of French exports in 1965 (Thompson, *Modern France*, p. 155).
10. Ibid., p. 156. These figures are for 1964.
11. Jeanneney, *Forces et faiblesses de l'économie française, 1945–1959*, pp. 259–60.
12. J.-J. Servan-Schreiber, *Le Défi américain* (1967). See also C. Layton, 'European Pygmies, American Giant', *Encounter* (Apr 1967).
13. In 1968 France still had about 700,000 self-employed shopkeepers (as against 1,300,000 in 1954).
14. The composition of taxes in 1968, including social security contributions, as a percentage of total taxes was as follows:

	Taxes on income			*Social security contributions*	
	Households	*Corporations*	*Taxes on expenditure*	*Total*	*of which paid by employers*
France	12·8	5·0	42·9	39·3	28·1
U.K.	30·9	7·2	47·2	14·7	7·5
U.S.A.	36·2	15·6	30·4	17·8	9·2
Canada	28·2	12·5	48·4	10·9	6·0

15. R. Clozier, *Géographie de la France* (Paris, 1967) p. 87; A. Shonfield, *Modern Capitalism* (London, 1965) pp. 86–7; Avril, *Politics in France*, pp. 161–3, 170–3. Corsica became the twenty-second Region in 1970.
16. See pp. 212–13 and W. S. Shirer, *The Collapse of the Third Republic* (New York, 1969) pp. 236–8.
17. Hackett, *Economic Planning in France*.
18. Ibid., p. 28.

19. 'The Government's Directives ... for the Elaboration of the Fourth Plan', quoted ibid., pp. 372–3.

CHAPTER 4

1. From Le Chapelier's preamble to the introduction of his Bill in the National Assembly, 14 June 1791.

2. W. O. Henderson, *The Industrial Revolution on the Continent* (London, 1967); G. Lefranc, *Le Syndicalisme in France* (Paris, 1966).

3. Report of the Finance Committee of the Chamber of Deputies, July 1936, quoted in D. Thomson, *Democracy in France since 1870* (Oxford, 1964) pp. 70–1.

4. Ibid.; also A. Werth, *The Destiny of France* (London, 1937) p. 343, and Philip Williams, *Crisis and Compromise* (London, 1964) p. 384 n.

5. Williams, *Crisis*, p. 379 and P. Williams and M. Harrison, *Politics and Society in De Gaulle's Republic* (London, 1971) pp. 144–8.

6. Wright, *Rural Revolution*, pp. 18–22; Faure, *Les Paysans*, pp. 30–6.

7. Wright, *Rural Revolution*, pp. 21–2.

8. See pp. 91–4 and 193–4; also E. Weber, *Action Française* (Stanford, 1962), A. Cobban, *A History of Modern France*, vol. III: *1871–1962* (London, 1965) pp. 137–46, Shirer, *The Collapse of the Third Republic*, pp. 201–4.

9. Faure, *Les Paysans*, pp. 60–4; Wright, *Rural Revolution in France*, pp. 49–54.

10. Wright, *Rural Revolution in France*, pp. 75–113; Faure, *Les Paysans*, pp. 69–72, 79–85.

11. Wright, *Rural Revolution in France*, pp. 24–5, 37–9.

12. Faure, *Les Paysans*, pp. 75–6.

13. Ibid., pp. 118–23.

14. Wright, *Rural Revolution in France*, pp. 148–62. A pseudo-agricultural French pressure group which has had a particularly successful, and anti-social, history is the alcohol lobby. It secured state support, in a country with an outstandingly high level of chronic peasant and working-class alcoholism, for the production of a large surplus of alcoholic spirits from two main sources: sugar-beet (grown by rich, mass-producing, powerfully organised northern farmers – *les betteraviers*) and fruit-trees (owned by great numbers of modest *bouilleurs de cru*, small orchard proprietors – half the adult male population of twenty, mainly western, *départements*, and a quarter of another forty – who have the right to distil alcohol for their own use, but in fact market it. Not all are even genuine farmers: there are travelling distillers, and 10,000 *bouilleurs* living in Paris). The use of surplus alcohol in motor fuel was stopped in 1953. Mendès France attacked the lobby head-on in 1954, but it took another ten years, and a change of Republics, before it was forced to begin to yield up its privilege, by a vote of special powers to the Debré Government of 1960, against a parliamentary rearguard action which collapsed only in 1965 (Williams, *Crisis*, pp. 355–9, and *The French Parliament, 1958–1967* (London, 1968) pp. 85–9).

15. G. Lichtheim, *Marxism in Modern France* (New York and London, 1966) p. 34. F. F. Ridley, *Revolutionary Syndicalism in France* (Cambridge, 1970).

16. Cobban, *Modern France,* III 128–34; J. Chastenet, *Histoire de la IIIe République* (Paris, 1952–63) v 68.

17. J.-D. Reynaud, *Les Syndicats en France* (Paris, 1963) pp. 66–71.

18. L. Jouhaux, quoted ibid., p. 73.

19. Ibid., pp. 72–5.

20. Lefranc, *Le Syndicalisme en France,* pp. 75–7.

21. See pp. 198–9.

22. In 1936 only nine *départements* had more than 185 trade union members per thousand workers (including government employees). In 1938, eleven *départements* had more than 710 per thousand (*Atlas historique de la France contemporaine, 1800–1965* (Paris, 1966) p. 132). Membership of French trade unions is generally smaller than in Britain and the United States. It fluctuates widely in response to short-term prospects: 1895, 400,000; 1914, 1,000,000; 1920, 2,000,000; 1930, 600,000; 1936, 5,000,000; 1939, 1,250,000; 1945–6, 6,000,000. Since the Second World War it has declined to between 3,750,000 and 2,750,000 (J. Blondel and E. Drexel Godfrey, Jr, *The Government of France* (London, 1968) p. 154; see also Reynaud, *Les Syndicats,* pp. 126–8, Avril, *Politics in France,* pp. 245–8, Williams and Harrison, *Politics and Society,* p. 150.

23. François Mauriac, André Malraux, Edward Mortimer; George Lichtheim, in *Marxism in Modern France,* p. 70.

24. See pp. 225–6.

25. See pp. 220–1.

26. Preamble to the statutes of C.F.D.T. quoted in Lefranc, *Le Syndicalisme,* p. 118. The newest confederation claims 750,000 members, as against approximately 2,000,000 by C.G.T. and 600,000 by *Force Ouvrière.* F.E.N. has about 400,000 and C.G.C. about 200,000 (Avril, *Politics in France,* p. 247).

27. *Jeunesse communiste révolutionnaire* (J.C.R.), *Fédération des étudiants révolutionnaires* (F.E.R.) *Union des jeunesses communistes marxistes-léninistes* (U.J.C.M.-L.), *Comité Vietnam National* (C.V.N.), *Syndicat national de l'enseignement supérieur* (S.N.E. Sup.), *Comité d'action lycéen,* etc. See P. Seale and M. McConville, *French Revolution 1968* (London, 1968).

28. See p. 172.

29. See pp. 139–40.

30. A. Dansette, *Religious History of Modern France,* trans. J. Dingle (London, 1961) II 9–15.

31. S. R. Schram, *Protestantism and Politics in France* (Alençon, 1954) pp. 127–36.

32. A. Thibaudet, quoted ibid., p. 74.

33. See pp. 73–4.

34. E. Poulat, *Naissance des prêtres-ouvriers* (Paris, 1965) p. 384. See A. Dansette, *Destin du catholicisme français, 1926–1956* (Paris, 1957).

35. There were 4,000 priests in captivity from 1940 to 1945 (Poulat, *Prêtres-ouvriers,* p. 209).

36. Ibid., pp. 207–8.

37. Anonymous worker-priest quoted in Dansette, *Destin*, pp. 243–4.

38. *The Worker-Priests: A Collective Documentation*, translated from the French by J. Petrie (London, 1956).

39. See pp. 90–3. Pope Pius XI's decree consigning *Action Française* in the Index in 1926 was rescinded, however, by the next Pope, Pius XII, just before the outbreak of the Second World War.

40. W. Bosworth, *Catholicism and Crisis in Modern France* (Princeton, 1962) p. 93.

41. See p. 172.

42. Law of 7 December 1904, quoted by B. Mégrine, *La Question scolaire en France* (Paris, 1963) pp. 44–5.

43. 'Around 1875, out of 6,000 missionary priests, 4,500 or 75 per cent were French' (Dansette, *Religious History*, II 432). In 1960, by which time many more countries, and especially Italy and Germany, had joined the French, one-fifth of all Roman Catholic missionaries were still French, putting France at the head of forty missionary nations (L. Dollot, *La France dans le monde actuel* (Paris, 1964) p. 10).

44. Dansette, *Religious History*, II 432.

45. See the trilogy of novels by J. Lartéguy: *Les Mercenaires, Les Centurions, Les Prétoriens* (Paris, 1960–1).

46. See pp. 230–41.

47. P. Déroulède, President of the League, quoted by H. Tint, *The Decline of French Patriotism, 1870–1940* (London, 1964) p. 41.

48. See pp. 168–75.

49. See pp. 99–102.

50. Reproduced from Tint, *Decline of French Patriotism*, p. 151.

51. Weber, *Action Française*; S. M. Osgood, *French Royalism under the Third and Fourth Republics* (The Hague, 1960).

52. Osgood, *French Royalism*, pp. 182–213.

53. Shirer, *The Collapse of the Third Republic*, pp. 201–4, 226–8. Neo-Fascist movements of the last two decades are *Jeune Nation, Occident* and *Ordre Nouveau*.

54. G. Vedel, *La Dépolitisation: mythe ou réalité?* (Paris, 1962).

55. See pp. 168–75, 231–41.

56. See pp. 124–32.

CHAPTER 5

1. See Thomson, *Democracy in France*, 'The Revolutionary Tradition'.

2. Preamble to the Constitution of 1791, in J. M. Thompson, *French Revolution: Documents* (Oxford, 1948) p. 111, and J. H. Stewart, *A Documentary Survey of the French Revolution* (New York, 1951) p. 231. The *parlements* of pre-revolutionary France were the supreme judiciary authorities of Paris and certain provinces, which had the duty of registering new legislation, and the right of remonstrating against it. This right of 'remonstrance' was the source of a claim to control and check the King's Government. But *parlements* were never representative bodies in the English sense of the word 'parliament'. All

offices of the magistracy were purchasable and heritable, moreover, though this did not necessarily preclude the equitable discharge of justice.

3. M. Barrès, *Leurs figures* (Paris, 1932) p. 239.

4. See pp. 91–3.

5. 'The aim of every political association is the preservation of the natural and inalienable rights of man; these rights are liberty, property, security and resistance against oppression' ('Declaration of the Rights of Man and of the Citizen', in Thompson, *French Revolution: Documents*, p. 109).

6. C. B. McPherson, *The Political Theory of Possessive Individualism: Hobbes to Locke* (Oxford, 1962) p. 261.

7. P. Mendès-France, *La Republique moderne* (Paris, 1962) p. 109.

8. 'France is *par excellence* a champion of co-operation ... by virtue of her nature, which is to be sociable towards all men, and by virtue of her historical reputation, which allows her a kind of latent credit balance in all matters touching the universal' (Charles de Gaulle, quoted in *Le Monde*, Sep 1965).

9. This is the title of one of Alain's most celebrated collections of political essays, published in 1926, and it gives a good idea of the Radical doctrine in France in the period between the world wars, when the party was at the peak of its influence. See also his *Éléments d'une doctrine radicale* (Paris, 1925).

10. Mendès-France, *La République moderne*, pp. 44–5.

11. The terms 'Assembly régime' (or government by assembly) and 'presidential régime' (or presidential government) are used by the French to denote opposite constitutional extremes. Between 1875 and 1946 the trend was towards the subordination of the Cabinet to Parliament and the unrestricted legislative power and budgetary control of the National Assembly, but the Presidency of the Republic was never abolished, while a second Assembly of Parliament and a Council of Ministers that was constitutionally distinct from Parliament, with prescribed responsibilities of its own, were retained until the end. Similarly the present régime differs from the strictly presidential system of the United States, with which it is sometimes loosely compared, in that (*a*) the Government is appointed by the President of the Republic and – except in a national emergency, when the President decides alone – 'all policy decisions are taken ... only after agreement between the President and the Prime Minister' (Georges Pompidou, in a speech to the National Assembly, 24 April 1964, quoted, in this translation, in W. G. Andrews, *European Political Institutions*, 2nd ed. (Princeton, 1966) pp. 498–9), but is responsible to the National Assembly, 'on which the Prime Minister's existence depends at any moment' (ibid.); (*b*) the President has the right, in certain circumstances, to dissolve the National Assembly (ibid. pp. 43–63, 495–506; F. Goguel and A. Grosser, *La Politique en France* (Paris, 1964) p. 207).

12. The texts of these constitutions may be found in J. M. Thompson, *French Revolution: Documents, 1789–94* (Oxford, 1948); J. H. Stewart, *A Documentary Survey of the French Revolution* (New York, 1951); J. J. Chevallier, *Histoire des institutions politiques de la France*

de 1789 à nos jours (Paris, 1952); D. Thomson, *France: Empire and Republic, 1850–1940* (London, 1968) and *Democracy in France since 1870* (Oxford, 1964); P. Williams, *Politics in Post-War France* (London, 1954) and *Crisis and Compromise* (London, 1964); J. Blondel and E. Drexel Godfrey, Jr, *The Government of France* (London, 1968); G. Dupeux, *La France de 1945 à 1965* (Paris, 1969); D. Pickles, *The Fifth French Republic*, 2nd ed. (London, 1962).

13. Williams, *Crisis*, pp. 307–20.

14. Goguel and Grosser, *La Politique en France*, pp. 241–3.

15. Extracts from Articles 2 and 3. The translation of these and subsequent passages from the Constitution of the Fifth Republic is taken from Blondel and Drexel Godfrey, Jr, *The Government of France*.

16. Georges Pompidou, speech to the National Assembly, 24 April 1964 (*Journal officiel, Débats parlementaires, Assemblée nationale*, 25 Apr 1964, pp. 941–58). An English translation, from which this and further extracts on pp. 111, 112 and 114 are taken, appears in W. G. Andrews, *European Political Institutions*, 2nd ed. (Princeton, 1966) pp. 495–501.

17. Blondel and Drexel Godfrey, Jr, *The Government of France*, pp. 52–4. See also below, pp. 113–15.

18. Pickles, *Fifth Republic*, p. 135.

19. See pp. 239–40,

20. See p. 243.

21. Williams, *Crisis*, pp. 33, 203–7, 422–7 and Appendix III.

22. P. Pflimlin, *Discours d'investiture*, 13 May 1958 (*Journal officiel, Débats parlementaires, Assemblée nationale*, 14 May 1958, pp. 2253–5). C. de Gaulle, *Discours de Bayeux*, 16 June 1946 (quoted in Goguel and Grosser, *La Politique en France*, pp. 228–9).

23. Blondel and Drexel Godfrey, Jr, *Government*, pp. 63–72; P. Williams and M. Harrison, *De Gaulle's Republic* (London, 1960) pp. 138–40.

24. Pickles, *Fifth Republic*, p. 95, Williams, *Crisis*, pp. 220, 242–56, and *Parliament*, pp. 42–51, 61–9.

25. 'Interpellations' were regularly followed by a division in the Third and Fourth Republics. The Fifth introduced 'Questions without voting'. Williams, *Crisis*, pp. 223–4, and *Parliament*, pp. 46–51.

26. Williams, *Crisis*, pp. 236–41.

27. Between January 1946 and June 1958, there were twenty-five changes of leadership; between June 1958 and January 1972, there were four. See pp. 241–2, Chapter 10, n. 18, and Fig. 2.

28. See the speech to the Commons by Prime Minister Churchill on 28 October 1943: 'There are two main characteristics of the House of Commons which will command the approval and the support of reflective and experienced Members. They will, I have no doubt, sound odd to foreign ears. The first is that its shape should be oblong and not semicircular. Here is a very potent factor in our political life. The semicircular assembly, which appeals to political theorists, enables every individual or every group to move round the centre, adopting various shades of pink according as the weather changes. I am a convinced sup-

porter of the party system in preference to the group system. I have seen many earnest and ardent Parliaments destroyed by the group system. The party system is much favoured by the oblong form of the Chamber. It is easy for an individual to move through those insensible gradations from Left to Right but the act of crossing the floor is one which requires serious consideration' (quoted in Andrews, *European Political Institutions*, 2nd ed. (Princeton, 1966) pp. 327–8).

29. Williams, *Crisis*, p. 255.

30. S. Hoffmann *et al.*, *France: Change and Tradition* (London, 1963) pp. 8–11, 16–17, 71–105, 115–17.

31. Ibid., and Williams, *Crisis*, pp. 10–11, 422–7. See also Goguel and Grosser, *La Politique en France*, p. 252.

32. Williams, *Parliament*, pp. 37–40.

33. e.g. Pickles, *Fifth Republic*, pp. 108–27; Williams, *Parliament*, pp. 35–40, 50–5, 97, 114–24; Blondel and Drexel Godfrey, Jr, *Government*, pp. 72–5; J. Chapsal, *La Vie politique en France depuis 1940* (Paris, 1966) p. 403, P. Mendès-France, *La République moderne*, chaps II–V; P. Avril, *Politics in France* (London, 1969) pp. 219–95.

CHAPTER 6

1. There are also four *départements d'outre-mer*, the oldest and most effectively assimilated countries of the French Community: Guadeloupe, Martinique, French Guiana (in the West Indies and South America) and Réunion (an island in the Indian Ocean between Madagascar and Mauritius – both formerly French overseas possessions).

2. D. Pickles, *France: The Fourth Republic* (London, 1955) pp. 98–9; H. Finer, *The Major Governments of Modern Europe* (London, 1960) pp. 343–4.

3. Goguel and Grosser, *La Politique en France*, pp. 216–18; Pickles, *Fourth Republic*, p. 100; Avril, *Politics in France*, pp. 138–40.

4. The *École Polytechnique*, founded in 1794, continues to produce scientists and engineers for the specialist branches of the military and civil services.

5. See pp. 143–5.

6. Reynaud, *Tendances et volontés de la société française*, pp. 248–67; Goguel and Grosser, *La Politique en France*, p. 141; Avril, *Politics in France*, pp. 142–5, 148–9; A. Sampson, *The New Europeans* (London, 1968) pp. 335–46.

7. B. Chapman, *Introduction to French Local Government* (London, 1953) p. 32.

8. Pickles, *Fourth Republic*, pp. 105–10; Finer, *Major Governments*, pp. 369–72; M. Duverger, *Les Institutions françaises* (Paris, 1962) pp. 237–78.

9. J. Barthélemy, *Le Gouvernement de la France*, quoted by Pickles, *Fourth Republic*, p. 109; Finer, *Major Governments*, p. 372: 'This Court answers affirmatively the question ... whether an administrative court can be relied upon to be just to the individual against the state.'

10. This body supervises and audits public accounts and the social security balance sheet.

11. Disputes between the administrative and the ordinary courts over the correct attribution of borderline cases are settled by a *Tribunal des conflits* (representing both the Council of State and the Judiciary).

12. Sampson, *The New Europeans*, pp. 340–2.

13. See Ardagh, *The New France*, pp. 233–48.

14. Forerunners of Napoleon's Prefects were the revolutionary deputies 'on mission' in provincial France, and the earlier *Intendants*, first appointed by Cardinal Richelieu in the seventeenth century, to govern the French provinces against the local feudal authorities, as part of the policy of strong administrative centralisation upon which the modern French nation-state was founded.

15. F. Ridley and J. Blondel, *Public Administration in France* (London, 1964) p. 160.

16. Ibid., pp. 92–4, 160–64; Chapman, *French Local Government*, pp. 96–147, and *The Prefects and Provincial France* (London, 1955).

17. This is recruited and organised by the Ministry of Defence, however.

18. Chapman, *French Local Government*, p. 83.

19. For terms of six years. In the totally centralised state conceived by Napoleon I after the French Revolution, mayors and municipal councillors, like Prefects, were appointed by the Government in Paris. Local liberties were gradually restored through the nineteenth century: municipal councillors were elected after 1831, mayors after 1882, and their powers extended to, broadly speaking, their present scope in 1884.

20. Chapman, *French Local Government*, pp. 19–20, 56–63, 179–80; Blondel and Drexel Godfrey, Jr, *Government*, pp. 130–1.

21. Chapman, *French Local Government*, pp. 63–78.

22. Such as 9 military regions (including Paris), 17 postal and telecommunications regions, 23 Academies, 28 Courts of Appeal.

23. Chapman, *French Local Government*, pp. 25–7, 120–3.

24. E. Garcin, Communist deputy, in the National Assembly debate of May 1964.

CHAPTER 7

1. A. Prost, *L'Enseignement en France, 1800–1967* (Paris, 1968) pp. 32–95.

2. Sauvy, *Mythologie de notre temps*, p. 188.

3. In spite of recent rapid improvement. In 1939 only 1·6 per cent of French university students came from working-class homes, as against 5·5 per cent in 1957 and 8·3 per cent in 1965 (Minister of Education). See Ardagh, *The New France*, p. 452, who estimates 12 per cent in 1970.

4. B. Cacérès, *Histoire de l'éducation populaire* (Paris, 1964).

5. There are also a few Protestant, Jewish and experimental schools.

6. i.e. the state primary school teacher (as distinct from the secondary-school *professeur de lycée*).

7. Bosworth, *Catholicism*, pp. 279–308; A. Coutrot and F. Dreyfus,

Les Forces religieuses dans le société française (Paris, 1965) pp. 227–36.

8. M. Glatigny, *Histoire de l'enseignement* (Paris, 1949), pp. 114–15, 122–3; Prost, *L'Enseignement en France*, pp. 450–4.

9. Ardagh, *The New France*, pp. 448–75.

10. J. G. Weightman, 'The Sorbonne', *Encounter* (June 1961) pp. 28–42.

11. To attempt to cope with an unprecedented increase since 1951 in the numbers of French children attending secondary schools, the total number of secondary-school teachers has been more than doubled. But of these only one in six is today an *agrégé*. The majority are now recruited by different, and less academically rigorous ways: *licence, maîtrise*, and C.A.P.E.S. (*Certificat d'aptitude au professorat de l'enseignement secondaire*) (Prost, *L'Enseignement en France*, pp. 450–1).

12. *Philo* and *math*(*ématiques*) *élém* (*entaires*) are slang names for the classes that prepare candidates for the traditional arts and science *baccalauréat* examinations. *Hypokhâgne* and *khâgne, hypotaupe* and *taupe* are the last two, post-*baccalauréat*, years at the *lycée*, in arts and science respectively, where pupils prepare for the competitive entrance examinations for the *grandes écoles* (see pp. 143–5).

13. Weightman, *Encounter* (June 1961) pp. 28–42.

14. Moch: Minister of the Interior from 1947 to 1950; Giscard d'Estaing: leader of the Independent Republican Party and Presidential candidate in 1965; Servan-Schreiber: anti-Gaullist Radical, former editor of *L'Express* and author of *Le défi américain* (1967). See Sampson, *The New Europeans*, pp. 331–5; Ardagh, *The New France*, pp. 37–8, 496–505.

15. Heads of the *Commissariat Général du Plan* from 1959 to 1965 and 1967 to date, respectively.

16. The linear accelerator of the Orsay research centre comes under *Normale*, and most of the great French mathematicians are *normaliens*, including the famous Bourbaki team; so are two recent Nobel Prize winners, the physicists A. Kastler (1966) and L. Néel (1970).

17. *Normaliens* can live out if they wish. There is also a women's *École normale supérieure*, and two others not requiring Greek or Latin, at Saint-Cloud (men) and Fontenay-aux-Roses (women).

18. Institut Pédagogique National, *Cahiers de documentation*, no. 1 C.D.: 'L'organisation de l'enseignement en France (1966–67)'.

19. *Le Monde*, 29 Sep 1968.

20. See above, p. 128.

21. Though the principle of irremovability does not apply to them (or to the judges of the Administrative Courts).

22. Replacing the *juges de paix* since 1958.

23. Judgement is given in these special courts not by professional magistrates but by elected representatives of the trades and industries concerned.

24. There are a further six in the *départements d'outre-mer*.

25. There are three more in the *départements d'outre-mer*.

26. M. Duverger, *Les Institutions françaises* (Paris, 1962) pp. 167–8.

27. Finer, *Major Governments*, p. 369; Ridley and Blondel, *Public Administration*, pp. 141–3; Williams and Harrison, *Politics and Society*, pp. 260–78.

28. See pp. 239–40 and Williams, *Parliament*, pp. 73–4.

CHAPTER 8

1. M. Howard, *The Franco-Prussian War* (London, 1961) p. 231.
2. Bismarck to the French at Sedan, quoted ibid., pp. 220–1.
3. Favre, quoted ibid., pp. 231–3.
4. Ibid., p. 233.
5. The indemnity was paid off in two and a half years, through loans oversubscribed by the mass of modestly prosperous savers that had grown up in France since the Revolution.
6. D. Brogan, *The Development of Modern France (1870–1939)* (London, 1940) pp. 55–74; A. Cobban, *A History of Modern France* (London, 1961) II 196–210; G. Chapman, *The Third Republic of France: The First Phase, 1871–1894* (London, 1965) pp. 11–13, A. Horne, *The Fall of Paris* (London, 1965) pp. 411–18.
7. G. Lefranc, *Le Syndicalisme en France* (Paris, 1966) pp. 13–14.
8. Brogan, *Development*, p. 110; Thomson, *Democracy in France*, chapter III, 'The Democratic Instrument'.
9. Chapman, *Third Republic*, pp. 160–87; Brogan, *Development*, pp. 127–43.
10. Brogan, *Development*, Book III; D. Halévy, *La République des ducs* (Paris, 1937).
11. The 'Belleville Manifesto' (1869), translated into English, in Thomson, *Democracy in France*, pp. 315–16; *France: Empire and Republic, 1850–1940* (London, 1968) by the same author, pp. 82–4.
12. J. Chastenet, *Histoire de la Troisième République* (Paris, 1952–63) II 208–9; Chapman, *Third Republic*, pp. 265–87.
13. Chapman, *Third Republic*, pp. 321–6; Chastenet, *Histoire de la Troisième République*, III 325; Brogan, *Development*, p. 285.
14. 'About 1880 ... the word "Jew" was synonymous with usurer and banker' (Weber, *Action française*, p. 90).
15. M. Barrès, *Un Homme libre* (Paris, 1922) pp. i–ii.
16. *Essai sur les données immédiates de la conscience*, by Henri Bergson, was first published in 1889.
17. Chapman, *Third Republic*, p. 368.
18. Good histories of the Dreyfus Affair are to be found in G. Chapman, *The Dreyfus Case* (London, 1955); A. Cobban, *A History of Modern France* (London, 1965) vol. III; and Brogan, *The Development of Modern France*.
19. Weber, *Action Française*, pp. 63–4.
20. One of the earliest features in *La Libre Parole* had been a series of articles called 'Les Juifs dans l'armée' (Cobban, *Modern France*, III 50).
21. Chapman, *Dreyfus Case*, pp. 66, 357–8.
22. Brogan, *Development*, pp. 356–87.
23. Ibid., p. 341.
24. See pp. 91–3.

25. Notes for *Justice* quoted by G. Robert, *Émile Zola* (Paris, 1952) p. 165.

26. C. Péguy, *Notre Jeunesse*, in *Oeuvres en prose, 1909–1914* (Paris, 1957) pp. 644–7).

27. M. Barrès, *Le Culte du Moi: examen* (Paris, 1892).

28. *La Nouvelle Revue Française.* This literary monthly, founded in 1909 by Gide and others, soon established its own publishing house, directed by G. Gallimard. Both were successful and influential in the 1920s and 1930s.

29. E. Tersen, *Histoire de la colonisation française* (Paris, 1950); X. Yacano, *Histoire de la colonisation française* (Paris, 1969); Chapman, *Third Republic*, pp. 252–9.

30. Tersen, *Colonisation*, p. 65.

31. Ministers of Louis XIII, XIV and XV respectively. Law was an expatriate Scots financier.

32. Tersen, *Colonisation*, p. 70.

33. Grouped together as *Afrique Occidentale Française* (A.O.F.) between 1895 and 1899. All are now independent republics. So is Madagascar.

34. Grouped together as *Afrique Équatoriale Française* (A.E.F.) in 1910 (now independent republics). A few islands in the Indian and Pacific Oceans – the Comoro Archipelago, New Caledonia, Wallis and Futuna, French Polynesia (capital Papeete, on the island of Tahiti) – and the French Territory of the Afars and the Issas (formally French Somaliland) remain 'overseas territories'.

35. Syria and Lebanon became independent Republics in 1941–6.

36. Outside France itself, in Switzerland, Belgium and the French-speaking areas of Africa, the Pacific Ocean and Canada, there are about twenty million people whose mother tongue is French (L. Dollot, *La France dans le monde actuel* (Paris, 1964) p. 31).

37. Brogan, *Development*, pp. 322–6.

38. C. Péguy, *Notre Patrie* (1905); C. Maurras, *Kiel et Tanger* (1910).

39. Chapman, *Third Republic*, p. 354.

40. Maurice Barrès, who had preached the cult of 'national energy' since the 1890s, was asked by *L'Auto* (*Journal sportif de Paris*) to do a series of articles of 1906 and 1907 on such stirring subjects as 'A Dangerous Post', 'The Sense of Danger', 'The Samourai', 'Endurance', where military and other perilous callings were presented as exhilarating sport. In 1906, Georges Sorel celebrated the coming of a 'new civilisation' forged by proletarian syndicalist violence, in the general strike and the class war (*Réflexions sur la violence*, and 'Apologie de la violence', *Le Matin*, 18 May 1908).

41. See pp. 75–7 and Lefranc, *Syndicalisme*, p. 33.

42. J. Julliard, *Clemenceau, briseur de grèves* (Paris, 1965) p. 104.

43. A. Gide, *Si le grain ne meurt*, in *Œuvres complètes*, vol. x (Paris, 1936) p. 321.

44. *Le Naturalisme au théâtre* (Paris, 1881) p. 360.

45. H. Read, *A Concise History of Modern Painting* (London, 1959) pp. 32–3.

46. R. H. Wilenski, *Modern French Painters* (London, 1954); M. Rheims, *The Age of Art Nouveau*, translated from the French by P. Evans (London, 1966); M. Cooper, *French Music from the Death of Berlioz to the Death of Fauré* (Oxford, 1961).

47. 'La Jolie Rousse', from *Calligrammes*.

48. Read, *Modern Painting*, pp. 91–6.

49. Staff lecture by Colonel de Grandmaison, 1911, quoted by J. Feller in *Le Dossier de l'armée française* (Paris, 1966) pp. 77–8.

50. M. Blondel, *L'Action* (1893); A. Loisy, *Études évangéliques* (1902).

51. I. W. Alexander, *Bergson, Philosopher of reflection* (London, 1957) pp. 8–9.

52. 'Time is invention, or it is nothing' (*L'Évolution créatrice*, chap. IV).

53. Alexander, *Bergson*.

54. *Introduction à la métaphysique*, in *La pensée et le mouvant*, 47th ed. (Paris, 1962) p. 185, quoted by Alexander, *Bergson*, pp. 17–18.

55. *Jean Santeuil*, published posthumously in 1952.

56. J. M. Cocking, *Proust* (London, 1955) p. 30.

57. Cooper, *French Music*, pp. 88–93.

58. R. Gibson, *Modern French Poets on Poetry* (Cambridge, 1961) p. 188–9.

CHAPTER 9

1. Including the bitter fighting before and after the main battle, over the same blood-soaked ground, the figure has been put as high as 420,000 dead and 800,000 gassed and wounded. The French suffered marginally more casualties than the Germans. One of the direct results of the battle was that from July 1916 'the main burden of the Western Front devolved upon Britain' (A. Horne, *The Price of Glory* (London, 1962) pp. 327–31).

2. Shirer, *The Collapse of the Third Republic*, p. 133.

3. Dupeux, *La Société française*, pp. 222–9.

4. Thompson, *Modern France*, p. 50.

5. A. Sauvy, *Histoire économique de la France entre les deux guerres* (Paris, 1965–7) I 19–23, 377–8, 495–9.

6. The Right was against raising direct taxation (of incomes), the Left was against raising indirect taxes (on goods and services). The Cartel des Gauches (the leftish coalition Government of Édouard Herriot, in power 1924–5) had raised neither kind (Cobban, *Modern France*, III 133–4). See Chastenet, *Troisième République*, V 154.

7. Dupeux, *La Société française*, p. 226. The rapid growth of a ring of proletarian manufacturing suburbs continued after the war when, in particular, Renault and Citroën made Paris the centre of the French automobile industry.

8. Sauvy, *Histoire économique*, II 554. According to Lefranc (*Syndicalisme*, p. 69), the 'real number' of jobless in 1935 was nearly 1,100,000.

9. Sauvy, *Histoire économique*, II 126–37.

10. See pp. 91–4 and Weber, *Action Française*, Brogan, *Development*,

pp. 651–61; also Shirer, *The Collapse of the Third Republic*, pp. 201–4. Popular organs of the right-wing political gutter Press were *Je suis partout*, *Gringoire* and *Candide*, which had three times the circulation of its most successful left-wing competitor, *Marianne*.

11. Shirer, *The Collapse of the Third Republic*, pp. 199–230. See also Brogan, *Development*, pp. 659–61, and M. Beloff, *The Intellectual in Politics* (London, 1970) pp. 143–71.

12. F. de Tarr, *The French Radical Party from Herriot to Mendès-France* (Oxford, 1961) pp. 156–7; P. J. Larmour, *The French Radical Party in the 1930s* (Stanford, 1964) p. 164.

13. In the industrial north the S.F.I.O. was more truly proletarian.

14. G. and E. Bonnefous, *Histoire politique de la IIIe République* (Paris, 1960–8), v 419.

15. Emmanuel d'Astier de la Vigerie visits the Renault works at Billancourt in the Paris Red Belt (*Vu*, quoted in Lefranc, *Juin, 1936* (Paris, 1966) pp. 182–3.

16. Shirer, *The Collapse of the Third Republic*, pp. 285–96.

17. Ibid., and Thomson, *France: Empire and Republic*, pp. 177–9.

18. Bonnefous, *Histoire politique*, VI 149–59.

19. R. Shattuck, *The Banquet Years* (London, 1959) pp. 118–20, 228.

20. Chastenet, *Troisième République*, IV 287–95; Bonnefous, *Histoire politique*, II 262.

21. 'Manifeste du Mouvement Dada', quoted in A. Balakian, *Literary Origins of Surrealism* (London and New York, 1967) p. 133.

22. See above, p. 184.

23. *Le Prométhée mal enchaîné* (1899) and *Les Caves du Vatican* (1914).

24. *Le Paysan de Paris* (Paris, 1926) pp. 245, 250.

25. *Nadja* (1928); new ed. (Paris, 1964) pp. 177, 187; *Manifestes du Surréalisme* (Paris, 1963).

26. Quoted in M. Nadeau, *Histoire du Surréalisme* (Paris, 1947) I 115–16. There is an English translation of this book by R. Howard, *The History of Surrealism* (London, 1968).

27. Quoted by Nadeau, *Histoire du Surréalisme*, p. 115.

28. 'Transformer le monde', a dit Marx, 'changer la vie', a dit Rimbaud, ces deux mots d'ordre pour nous ne font qu'un' (A. Breton). See Nadeau, *Histoire du Surréalisme*, and F. Alquié, *The Philosophy of Surrealism*, trans. B. Waldrop (Ann Arbor, 1965). Also R. S. Short, 'The Politics of Surrealism, 1920–1936', *Journal of Contemporary History* I (2) (1965) 3–25; D. Caute, *Communism and the French Intellectuals* (London, 1964).

29. R. Martin du Gard, *Les Thibault* (11 vols, 1922–40) and G. Duhamel, *Chronique des Pasquier* (10 vols, 1933–41). P. Thody, 'Politics of the Family Novel: Is Conservatism Inevitable?' *Mosaic* (Manitoba), fall 1969.

30. G. Sadoul, *French Film* (London, 1953).

31. Shirer, *The Collapse of the Third Republic*, pp. 251–413.

32. L. Blum, *A l'échelle humaine*, in *L'œuvre de Léon Blum 1940–1945* (Paris, 1955) pp. 429–30.

33. Shirer, *The Collapse of the Third Republic*, pp. 879–82. The prisoners and several hundred thousand civilians deported as forced labour were kept in Germany until the end of the war; 43,000 died there (A. Crawley, *De Gaulle* (London, 1969) p. 251; J. Chastenet, *De Pétain à de Gaulle* (Paris, 1970) pp. 107–9).

34. The anti-clerical society of French Freemasons was declared illegal. Increasingly oppressive restrictions were imposed on citizens of foreign birth and, especially, on French Jews. Following the armistice agreement to hand German refugees back to the Nazis, the Vichy Government hunted out known political opponents of Hitler's régime who had sought asylum in France and connived at the mass deportation to his extermination camps of more than 150,000 foreign, mostly German, Jewish men, women and children. Less than 5,000 of these survived. Many Jewish children on the other hand were hidden and saved by French Christian families, and in this way the ordinary people of France made some amends for the behaviour of the puppet Government at Vichy (Shirer, *The Collapse of the Third Republic*, p. 881; Chastenet, *De Pétain à de Gaulle*, pp. 74–5; A. Werth, *France, 1940–1955* (London, 1956) pp. 61–5; S. Levenberg, *European Jewry Today* (Leeds, 1967) p. 14).

35. W. S. Churchill, *The Second World War* (London, 1948–54) IV 611.

36. C. de Gaulle, *War Memoirs*, trans. J. Griffin (London, 1955) I 63: 'Great Britain, led by such a fighter, would certainly not flinch.'

37. The Vichy authorities condemned de Gaulle to death. For the French Communist Party, until Hitler invaded the Soviet Union, he and his followers were simply 'the mercenaries of the City of London' (Williams, *Crisis*, p. 73).

38. De Gaulle, *War Memoirs*, I 87.

39. Ibid., pp. 88–9.

40. A. Werth, *De Gaulle* (London, 1965) pp. 133–41. The 'Normandie' fighter squadron went to fly against the Germans in Russia at the end of 1942. See also H. Michel, *Histoire de la France Libre* (Paris, 1963).

41. R. Aron, *De Gaulle Triumphant* (London, 1964) pp. 109–83.

42. R. Aron, *Histoire de Vichy* (Paris, 1954), *Histoire de la Libération de la France* (Paris, 1959), *Histoire de l'épuration* (Paris, 1967) I 433–73; H. Noguères, *Histoire de la Résistance en France* (Paris, 1967–); E. Jäckel, *La France dans l'Europe de Hitler*, translated into French from the German by D. Meunier (Paris, 1968); H. Michel, *Histoire de la Résistance*, 5th ed. (Paris, 1969); Werth, *France: 1940–1955*.

43. Shirer, *The Collapse of the Third Republic*, p. 881.

44. Michel, *Histoire de la Résistance*, pp. 119–24. Henriot's last broadcast the day before his assassination in June 1944 contained the following words, addressed to the Resistance as a whole. They give some idea of the bitter divisions in France at that time: 'Now you say that you are sure your allies will win. You declare that Germany is exhausted and beaten. And, in spite of that, you must have more blood, the blood of poor devils who are simply Frenchman carrying out their daily task: a stationmaster, a pensioner, a postman ... you say ... they are

traitors. Be serious ... they are political opponents of yesterday, and nothing more. Those you are busy executing are former members of political parties that the Communists and the Freemasons have long ago condemned ...' (quoted by R. Aron, *Histoire de l'épuration*, I 360–1).

45. D. W. Eisenhower, *Crusade in Europe* (London, 1948) p. 325. Details in Michel, *Résistance*, Noguères, *Résistance en France*, Cobban, *Modern France*, vol. III, Chastenet, *De Pétain à de Gaulle*, and Werth, *De Gaulle*.

46. M. R. D. Foot, *SOE in France* (London, 1968).

47. R. Aron, *Histoire de la libération de la France* and *De Gaulle Triumphant* (London, 1964).

48. An English translation of the 'Charter of the Resistance' is given in Thomson, *Democracy in France*, pp. 322–4.

CHAPTER 10

1. R. Aron, *Histoire de l'épuraton*, I 433 ff.; Cobban, *Modern France*, III 200; Werth, *France, 1940–1955*, pp. 284–90.

2. Werth, *France, 1940–1955*, pp. 286–8.

3. Thomson, *Democracy in France*, pp. 322–4.

4. Werth, *France, 1940–1955*, pp. 220–5, 293–386.

5. C. de Gaulle, *Mémoires d'espoir* (Paris, 1970) p. 9.

6. E. Behr, *The Algerian Problem* (London, 1961) pp. 49–53.

7. Werth, *France, 1940–1955*, pp. 358–9; Williams, *Crisis*, p. 26; G. Depeux, *La France de 1945 à 1965* (Paris, 1969) p. 32.

8. Werth, *France, 1940–1955*, p. 360; A. Grosser, *La IVe République et sa politique extérieure*, 2nd ed. (Paris, 1967).

9. J. Lacouture, *De Gaulle* (Paris, 1965) pp. 146–51; Werth, *De Gaulle*, pp. 192–225; Williams, *Crisis*, pp. 32, 132–47.

10. Williams, *Crisis*, Appendix III.

11. Ibid., pp. 43, 53 and Appendix IV.

12. See above, Chapter 4 n. 14, and Werth, *France, 1940–1955*, pp. 710–26.

13. Behr, *The Algerian Problem*, p. 90.

14. Ibid., p. 113.

15. Radio and TV broadcast, 16 Sep 1959 (C. de Gaulle, *Discours et messages*, III (Paris, 1970) 117–23, translated in Behr, *The Algerian Problem*, pp. 155–8).

16. Radio and TV broadcast, 29 Jan 1960 (de Gaulle, *Discours et messages*, III 162–6, translated in Behr, *The Algerian Problem*, pp. 247–51).

17. Radio and TV broadcast, 23 Apr 1961 (de Gaulle, *Discours et Messages*, III 306–8).

18. 'No Prime Minister since 1875 lasted continuously in office so long as Pompidou' (Blondel and Drexel Godfrey, Jr, *Government*, p. 50). The results of elections to the National Assembly since 1962 are given in the table below (in millions of votes). These figures are for the first only of the two ballots held in most constituencies under the present electoral

law (see above, pp. 120–1). Figures in brackets show the numbers of deputies elected in each group (P. Williams, *French Politicians and Elections 1951–69* (Cambridge 1970).

	1962	*1967*	*1968*
Communists	4·00 (41)	5·04 (73)	4·43 (34)
Socialists	2·30 (66)	4·22 (120) [b]	3·65 (57) [b]
Radicals	1·43 (39) [a]		
Gaullists	5·85 (233) [c]	8·45 (200) [d]	9·66 (294) [e]
Independent Republicans	1·09 (35)	(44)	0·92 (64) [f]
M.R.P.	1·66 (55) [g]		
Conservatives	1·40 [i]	2·83 (42) [h]	2·29 (27) [h]

[a] *Rassemblement démocratique.*

[b] *Fédération de la gauche démocrate et socialiste* (F.G.D.S.) (Socialists, left-wing Radicals, *Convention des institutions républicaines* – see above, p. 94) and 4 P.S.U. (*Parti socialiste unifié*) in 1967.

[c] *Union pour la nouvelle république–Union démocratique du travail* (U.N.R.–U.D.R.).

[d] *Union des démocrates pour la cinquième république* (U.D.V^{e}.R.).

[e] *Union des démocrates pour la république* (U.D.R.).

[f] Non-U.D.R. Independent Republicans.

[g] *Centre démocratique.*

[h] (*Centre démocratique*)–*Progrès et démocratie moderne* (P.D.M.).

[i] *Centre national des indépendants et paysans* (C.N.I.P.).

19. See, for example, the third volume of Simone de Beauvoir's autobiography, *Force of Circumstance*, trans. R. Howard (London, 1968) pp. 299, 428–61, 592, 624, 658.

20. Sampson, *The New Europeans*, pp. 18–19, 196.

21. See n. 18 above and Fig. 2, p. 108.

22. See n. 18 above and Fig. 2, p. 109.

23. France's gross national product per capita at market prices (in dollars at current exchange rates) grew by an estimated 92 per cent between 1960 and 1968 (W. Germany: 72 per cent; U.S.A.: 55 per cent; Canada: 43 per cent; U.K. 34 per cent).

24. The daily newspaper *Le Monde*, sober, detailed and intellectually demanding, is one of the finest in the world, and, in spite of its relatively small circulation (407,000), is very influential in political, professional, business and academic circles. Other politically sophisticated national dailies are *Le Figaro* (conservative, 515,000). *L'Aurore* (right-wing, 424,000), *L'Humanité* (193,000) and *L'Humanité-Dimanche* (510,000), both Communist. *Combat*, a progressive ex-Resistance newspaper, *La Nation* (Gaullist) and *Le Populaire* (S.F.I.O.) are all relatively small concerns. *Le Parisien-Libéré* (831,000) and *France-Soir* (1,238,000) are the most successful organs of the politically neutral or superficial popular Press. All the above are published in Paris and, except for *Le Monde* (only half of whose readers live in the Paris area), are read mostly by Parisians. The great majority of provincials read only provincial

newspapers, such as *La Dépêche du Midi* (leftish, 324,000), *Le Provençal* (Socialist, 230,000), *Le Progrès* (published in Lyon, 541,000), *L'Est Républicain* (Nancy, 274,000), *La Voix du Nord* (Lille, 430,000), *Ouest-France* (Rennes, in Brittany, 706,000) and *Paris-Normandie* (190,000).

Because of the strong regional interests and loyalities of the French, and because in any case they are relatively small consumers of daily newsprint (27 per 100 inhabitants), there is only one daily with a circulation of over a million (*France-Soir*). More widely read than many newspapers are such national weeklies as *Paris-Match* (1,382,000) and *Elle* (630,000), both of them popular and conservative, *L'Express* (liberal-technocratic, founded by Jean-Jacques Servan-Schreiber, 400,000), *Le Nouvel Observateur* (intellectual left-wing, 145,000) *Le Canard Enchaîné* (in satirical opposition to all the powers-that-be since 1915, 329,000). The intellectual literary Press includes *Le Figaro Littéraire* (119,000), *Les Temps Modernes* (founded by Jean-Paul Sartre, 17,500), *Réforme* (Protestant, 17,000), *Esprit* (Catholic, 15,000) and *Historia,* which, in a country that is perhaps hyperconscious of the past, boasts a readership of 350,000.

The state monopoly of sound broadcasting in France has, in practice, long been countered by so-called 'peripheral' commercial stations, such as Europe No. 1, transmitting from the Saar, though largely French-owned, backed by French advertising and directed at the French listening public. Its objective current affairs and political programmes are good and widely followed, especially at critical turning-points of contemporary history (Ardagh, *New France,* pp. 245–8, 622–37; figures (for the late 1960s) from the French Embassy, London).

25. Caute, *Communism and the French Intellectuals,* pp. 95–7, 328.

26. I. Murdoch, *Sartre: Romantic Rationalist* (Cambridge, 1953); P. M. Thody, *J.-P. Sartre: A Literary and Political Study* (London, 1960).

27. *L'Existentialisme est un humanisme* (1946). Sartre's fundamental philosophical works are *L'Être et le néant: essai d'ontologie phénoménologique* (1943), *Critique de la raison dialectique* (1960) and *L'Idiot de la famille: Gustave Flaubert de 1821 à 1857* (1971–).

28. R. Pierce, *Contemporary French Political Thought* (Oxford, 1966); P. M. Thody, *Albert Camus, 1913–1960* (London, 1961).

29. J. Guicharnaud, *Modern French Theatre from Giraudoux to Beckett* (New Haven, 1961).

30. See especially André Breton, quoted in Chapter 9, n. 28, and J.-P. Sartre, 'Qu'est-ce que la littérature?', in *Situations,* II (Paris, 1948) 55–330.

31. See Pierce, *Contemporary French Political Thought,* pp. 174–7; Sartre, *Questions de méthod* (1960).

32. A. Malraux, *Antimémoires* (Paris, 1967) p. 20.

Abbreviations

A.E.F.	Afrique équatoriale française
A.O.F.	Afrique occidentale française
A.P.E.L.	Association de parents d'élèves de l'enseignement libre
C.A.P.E.S.	Certificat d'aptitude au professorat de l'enseignement du second degré
C.E.G.	Collège d'enseignement général
C.E.S.	Collège d'enseignement secondaire
C.E.T.A.	Centre d'étude technique agricole
C.F.D.T.	Confédération française démocratique du travail
C.F.T.C.	Confédération française des travailleurs chrétiens
C.G.A.	Confédération générale de l'agriculture
C.G.C.	Confédération générale des cadres
C.G.P.M.E.	Confédération générale des petites et moyennes entreprises
C.G.T.	Confédération générale du travail
C.G.T. – F.O.	Confédération générale du travail – Force ouvrière
C.G.T.U.	Confédération générale du travail unitaire
C.N.E.J.	Centre national d'études judiciaires
C.N.I.P.	Centre national des indépendants et paysans (conservative)
C.N.J.A.	Centre national des jeunes agriculteurs
C.N.P.F.	Conseil national du patronat français
C.N.R.	Conseil national de la Résistance
C.O.D.E.R.	Commission de développement économique régional
C.R.S.	Compagnies républicaines de sécurité
C.U.M.A.	Coopérative d'utilisation de matériel agricole
E.N.A.	École nationale d'administration
F.E.N.	Fédération de l'éducation nationale
F.F.I.	Forces françaises de l'intérieur
F.F.L.	Forces françaises libres

F.G.D.S.	Fédération de la gauche démocrate et socialiste
F.L.N.	Front de libération national
F.N.S.E.A.	Fédération nationale des syndicats d'exploitants agricoles
F.T.P.	Francs-tireurs et Partisans
H.L.M.	Habitation à loyer modéré
I.G.A.M.E.	Inspecteur général de l'administration en mission extraordinaire
I.N.S.E.E.	Institut national de la statistique et des études économiques
J.A.C.	Jeunesse agricole chrétienne
J.O.C.	Jeunesse ouvrière chrétienne
M.R.P.	Mouvement républicain populaire (Christian Democrats)
O.A.S.	Organisation de l'armée secrète
O.P.	Ouvrier professionnel
O.R.T.F.	Office de radiodiffusion-télévision française
O.S.	Ouvrier spécialisé
P.C.F.	Parti communiste français
P.D.M.	Progrès et démocratie moderne (Catholic Centre party)
P.O.F.	Parti ouvrier de France (Guesdist socialists)
P.P.F.	Parti populaire français (fascist)
P.S.U.	Parti socialiste unifié
R.I.	Républicains indépendants (conservative)
R.P.F.	Rassemblement du peuple français (Gaullist)
S.F.I.O.	Section française de l'Internationale ouvrière (socialist)
S.M.I.C.	Salaire minimum interprofessionnel de croissance
S.O.E.	Special Operations Executive
U.D.C.A.	Union de défense des commerçants et des artisans (Poujadist)
U.D.R.	Union des démocrates pour la République (Gaullist)
U.D.S.R.	Union démocratique et socialiste de la Résistance
U.D.T.	Union démocratique du travail (left-wing Gaullist)
U.E.R.	Unité d'enseignement et de recherche
U.N.R.	Union pour la nouvelle République (Gaullist)

Index

Index